A
VOICE
OF HER
OWN

Women and the Journal Writing Journey

Marlene A. Schiwy, Ph.D.

A Fireside Book
Published by Simon & Schuster

FIRESIDE
Rockefeller Center
1230 Avenue of the Americas
New York, NY 10020

FIRESIDE and colophon are registered trademarks
of Simon & Schuster Inc.

Designed by Nicola Ferguson
Manufactured in the United States of America

1   3   5   7   9   10   8   6   4   2

ISBN 0-684-80342-9

For Steve,
beloved flesh- and soulmate

Contents

PART THREE   Sharing the Journey

Acknowledgments

I would like to express my loving appreciation to friends, students, and workshop members who shared their journals with me. Janet Fraka Casiano, Sheila Gelbman, Linda Hatter, Hyla Kuhlman, Dolores LaFata, Karen Laszlo, Nancy Linde, Pam De Luca, Rita Miller, Sandra Miller, Shira Moir-Smith, Dorald Patsos, Gabi Rahaman, Edie Scheie, Ellen Schwimer, Sheila Byrd Smith, Rhea White, Diane Wikse, and my niece, Chelsea Brandt, all contributed journal entries to this book. Special thanks to Jarda Bailey, Mary Brady, and Robin Garber-Kabalkin, who were with me from the beginning.

I cherish the friends with whom I've shared endless inspiring discussions about journals and the writing life, especially Margery Cornwell, Marketa Goetz-Stankiewicz, Ingrid Grüninger, Nancy Linde, Katherine MacNeill, Maureen Malowany, Shira Moir-Smith, Gabi Rahaman, and Teresa Sandhu.

My deep and loving thanks go to my mother, Lilli Schiwy, and my sister, Nellie Brandt, with whom I had my earliest experience of women sharing their lives with each other.

Sarah Baker, my editor at Simon & Schuster, showed unfailing energy and enthusiasm for the book, and gave it her careful attention during every stage of its production. Thank you.

I would also like to thank my agent, Elizabeth H. Backman, and The International Women's Writing Guild along with its executive director, Hannelore Hahn, through whom I met Elizabeth.

The Explorations Program of the Canada Council awarded me a grant in the Spring and Summer of 1995 that provided time to write. I am indebted to them.

Finally, I offer my deepest gratitude to Steve Rosen, my husband, for his thoughtful, generous, and invaluable response to every chapter. His steady belief that it would all come together and his enthusiasm for the richness of my subject never failed to delight me.

Foreword

As I read *A Voice of Her Own: Women and the Journal Writing Journey*, I experience myself in a large, round room with many doors. One by one, the doors open and several of the closest companions of my life —Virginia Woolf, Katherine Mansfield, Etty Hillesum, and others— women whose most private thoughts have profoundly influenced mine, quietly enter the room. Marlene Schiwy's clarity of organization and insight have brought these great journal writers together at a timely moment in women's evolutionary process.

Many women who are finding their own personhood are, at the same time, having dreams in which their teeth are clamped shut by silver braces, or their throats are clogged, or they speak but are not heard. One archetypal image of this condition is the tongueless Philomel. These women are attempting to find their own voices, psychically and physically. Having found their own authenticity, they are determined to speak it. They know the clamps have to come off the teeth, and the throat has to be opened, and the breath of the embodied woman has to come from her belly depth.

Journal writing has been one of my avenues to finding my own voice. When I was twelve, I began writing my secret thoughts in a little blue book with gold letters proudly proclaiming *My Diary*, with a golden lock and key that deterred intruders. That journal and the many that have followed became the still point in my life. When chaos swirled within and without, I was able to find a place of patience and peace through writing, or painting, or creating collages in my journal. My journal was and is the safe and cherishing container in which I can be any part of myself that needs to voice whoever she is in whatever words. On those clear, empty pages, parts of me have been born and nurtured into maturity. My journal has been my silver mirror, my feminine reflector in which I have looked eye to eye at myself and others as nakedly as possible. As strong reflector, it has held my anger, my terror, my jealousy, my lust—all the raw instincts that had to be held and reflected upon, until I could consciously choose how I wished to bring them into the world. Journaling, I listen to my own soul and dance my life with the divine at its center.

Ms. Schiwy has thoroughly and with utmost sensitivity explored the value of the journal in finding a voice of one's own. She explores the journal as confidante, the friend with whom we are most at home; as receiver of dreams and images that not only illumine our past but guide us in the present and future, building our self-understanding and self-esteem. She understands the journal as the sacred place in which we dialogue with our own unconscious and hear the bubbling up of our own sacred springs. Here is the place of survival, of catharsis, of transition, of healing, of uncensored confession. Here is where we recognize the reality of ourselves, our woundings and our strengths in the love that is our life with others and with the planet.

Marlene Schiwy's graceful exploration of women's journals from around the world leaves us with a deeper understanding of Rilke's letter to a young poet: "Live the questions now. Perhaps you will then gradually, without noticing it, live along some distant day into the answer."*

Marion Woodman
London, Canada, 1995

* Rainer Maria Rilke, Letters to a Young Poet, trans. M. D. Herter Norton (New York: W. W. Norton, 1954), p. 35.

PART ONE

Embarking

1

The Diary Habit

*In the beginning there were no words for women, only borrowed words; now we
are making them over to suit our bodies and sensibilities; now we are writing in
our own image.*

SUSAN CREAN, in *Language in Her Eye*

Across the continent, countless women are writing diaries and journals. Their shape and content are as varied as the writers' lives themselves, but there is a common purpose at the heart of the process.
Each diarist believes that keeping a journal will provide a richer experience of her own life. Bookstores and gift shops report enormous
increases in the sale of journals in recent years. The variety of empty
bound books now available is astonishing. In a society obsessed with
high technology and driven by superficial images, the diarist's insis-
tence on asserting her own personal voice raises fascinating questions.

What role does journal writing play in the lives of women today?
What is the powerful impulse that prompts us to sit in the corner of
a café or in an airplane, in a busy office or in the seclusion of the
woods with paper and pen in hand, to write down our thoughts and
feelings, dreams and fantasies? And why do women keep journals in
greater numbers than men? These are some of the questions that have
intrigued me for years and finally prompted me to write this book.

If you currently keep a journal, you are part of an immense world-wide community. If you picked up this book to discover why and how to begin, welcome! You are about to embark on a journey that may change your life. As a woman diarist, you'll be joining a tradition that dates back at least a thousand years, to the "pillow books" kept by ladies of the Japanese court during the tenth century. And while most journals published in the past were written by men, there is reason to believe that women were writing them in equal if not greater numbers. Often denied a voice in the public realm and the possibility of publication, women have kept diaries in order to communicate with themselves, to explore the meaning of their lives, and to give form to their creative impulses.

Keeping a journal does not mean simply recording the external facts of your life from one day to the next. I'm talking about something that goes much deeper than that. Journal writing is a process of vital reflection that plunges you below the surface of your life to its psychic roots. When you are writing at that deeper level, your life itself changes. Then your life's journey and the journal writing journey interweave, enriching and intensifying each other. At some point, they may even become one, as in the famous case of Alice James, who died just hours after dictating her final diary corrections to her best friend.

This book is about the importance of journal writing in women's lives. If you have never kept a diary before, it will introduce you to the endless creative possibilities and to the excitement and fascination of the journey itself. If you already write a journal, my hope is that it will provide you with companionship and fresh inspiration along your way.

Who Writes and Why?

Why do we write journals?

Katherine begins keeping a diary in the midst of a painful and destructive marriage breakup. The journal is her confidante, the one to whom she can say everything, pour out all of her anger and confusion. It also provides, in her words, "the chance to get to know myself and to think about my own needs for the first time."

Over a period of two years during which she loses close to a hundred pounds, Eileen keeps a diary of her feelings and changing self-image. Through consistent journal writing, she is able to support her inner self at a time when her appearance is changing so rapidly that she hardly recognizes herself in the mirror.

Rita writes in her journal in order to keep her intellect alive and stimulated while caring for her four- and one-year-old sons. Keeping a diary reassures her that her artistic side has not disappeared amidst the daily demands of caring for small children.

While undergoing Jungian analysis, Amanda keeps a dream journal, which she brings to her weekly sessions. With her analyst's guidance, she explores these symbolic expressions of her psychic life.

Gina keeps a notebook of ideas and observations for a weekly human interest column published in the local newspaper. Sometimes she finds inspiration for short stories and longer articles, too, in the pages of her journal. Thus the diary has become a rich source of material for her professional life.

Many women writers and artists have kept journals that were eventually published. In fact, sometimes it was the diary's publication that established the writer's importance, as was the case for both Anaïs Nin and May Sarton. Toi Derricotte kept a journal as a way of understanding and coming to terms with her painful and ambivalent feelings as one of the first black residents in a white neighborhood in New Jersey. Looking back, she recalls, "I hoped that writing my feelings down, especially the ones which were the most disturbing, would exorcise their power over me." Another writer, Le Anne Schreiber, kept a diary during a time of transition and turmoil in her life. Soon after leaving her position as an editor at *The New York Times Book Review* in order to begin a new life in a country house in upstate New York, she learned that her mother was dying of cancer. In the introduction to her published journal she writes,

In the pages of the notebooks I recorded the beginnings of my new life and the ending of my mother's, never imagining that, placed side by side, they might come to coexist with less painful discordance. . . . The juxtapositions of beginnings and endings were shattering as I recorded them, but ultimately, it was through them that I found points of contact between my living and her dying. I also found the points of separation.

Etty Hillesum kept a journal in order to hone her writing skills and to bear witness to the suffering of the Jewish population in Holland during the Second World War. In an entry dated August 20, 1941, she exhorted herself not to lose hope or the sense of her mission.

> You must continue to take yourself seriously, you must remain your own witness, marking well everything that happens in this world, never shutting your eyes to reality. You must come to grips with these terrible times, and try to find answers to the many questions they pose. And perhaps the answers will help not only yourself but also others.

But you certainly don't have to be a professional writer to reap the benefits of keeping a journal. The examples given above illustrate the threads of common purpose shared by all diarists, regardless of profession:

- to broaden self-awareness
- to explore personal identity
- to have a trustworthy confidante
- to pour out feelings and emotions onto paper
- to create continuity in our lives
- to preserve memories of ourselves, of people, and of events
- to cope with discontinuity, change, loss, and grief
- to explore creative impulses
- to capture ideas for stories, poems, and other projects
- to record and explore dreams
- to celebrate accomplishments and successes
- to engage in a dialogue with the world around us
- to discover what is sacred in our lives

- to deepen our spiritual journeys
- to remember beloved family members and friends
- to understand the story of our lives
- to sort out thoughts and clarify ideas
- to survive traumatic circumstances
- to take stock of our lives, from time to time
- to clarify our life's purposes
- to reap the wisdom of the unconscious

There are many other purposes, as well. Helen and her six-year-old daughter keep a shared diary of their experiences with home schooling. Karen writes a journal of her running times and distances while training for a marathon. Elizabeth describes her ambivalent feelings about a controversial medical research project in which she is participating. Annette writes about her plans to begin a new life after she is released from prison. Clearly, the passion for journal writing is not limited to any particular age group or sector of the population. To the contrary, it is a great leveler. You don't have to be a gifted writer. It doesn't matter how old you are or who you are in the world's eyes. Carolina Maria de Jesus, with only two years of formal education, kept a journal on empty pages of notebooks she salvaged from the trash in the slums of Brazil. Virginia Woolf, the most literate and literary of modern writers, kept a diary of her own artistic life and that of the Bloomsbury circle. Reading these two volumes side by side, who can say which woman's diary is more moving? The only thing that really counts on this journey is your willingness to cast a candid and probing eye on your own life, with the intent of going below the surface in order to contact the rich, mysterious, troubling, always fertile subterranean layers. That is where your life energy simmers.

A twelve-year-old student is required to keep a diary for her English class; in it she describes her first sensations of romantic attraction. A young lesbian explores her fear of coming out to her judgmental religious family. A businesswoman uses the half-hour ferry ride to and from work each day to focus on her inner life before facing the day's demands. A psychotherapist keeps track of her own emotional process in brief moments between clients. An artist describes her evolving conception of a work in progress. More women are keeping diaries now than ever before. Early in the morning and last thing at night, at home and at the workplace, during coffee breaks and leisure hours, on scraps of paper and in exquisite bound books, in periods of sorrow and times of great happiness—women are writing their journals. We write in order to understand ourselves and to explore our creative impulses, to pour our emotions out onto paper and to record our ideas.

Who writes journals? Women who live deeply and reflectively, who regard their lives as modern mythic quests and spiritual journeys. Women who want to find their own voices and write their own lives.

Backgrounds and Sources

The 1970s was an important decade for journal writers. The psychologist Ira Progoff had been conducting Intensive Journal Workshops since 1966, and in 1975 his book *At a Journal Workshop* came out. But it was the appearance of volume after volume of Anaïs Nin's legendary *Diary* that had the greatest impact during those years, especially on women readers. The publication of Nin's diaries gave journal writing a new dignity and beauty, and affirmed the importance of every diarist's inner psychic journey, even if she never wrote a single page for publication. Soon thereafter, Christina Baldwin's *One to One: Self-Understanding Through Journal Writing* appeared, and the following year saw the publication of *The New Diary: How to Use a Journal for Self-Guidance and Expanded Creativity*, by Tristine Rainer, a friend and colleague of Anaïs Nin's. Journal writing—as an important channel of self-understanding and creative expression—had come into its own. In the years since, public interest in journal writing has continued to grow. Countless workshops and courses in journal writing are offered annually across the continent.

These are also the years in which the women's movement has seen its greatest achievements. Not surprisingly, as we have been rethinking

our place in the world, we have found the diary invaluable in exploring who we are and what we want in life. And, as Tristine Rainer
predicted on the last page of *The New Diary*, the journal has continued
to "evolve, change, and re-create itself" according to the changing
needs and priorities of women diarists today.

One of the lasting legacies of the modern women's movement is
that it has encouraged women to take themselves and other women
seriously in their own right, rather than as appendages of the men in
their lives. And so, even as we write our own diaries, many of us have
found ourselves searching out other women's autobiographies and
published journals that might illuminate our lives. Two other books
appeared in the mid-seventies that did just this. *Journal of a Solitude*, by
the much-loved diarist May Sarton, who died recently at the age of
eighty-three, provides an intimate glimpse of the daily life and creative
process of a writer living alone by choice in a small town in New
Hampshire. Sarton was not prepared for the response her journal
evoked in large numbers of women readers who longed for just what
she'd described: a life devoted to poetry and writing, friendship, and
the natural world. Another book of note was *Revelations: Diaries of Women*,
which has since become the classic anthology of women's diaries,
spanning the thousand years from the *Pillow Book* of Sei Shonagon,
written in tenth-century Japan, to the modern diaries of Florida Scott-
Maxwell and Charlotte Painter, one of the book's editors. That both
books continue to sell well two decades after their publication is a
sign of our ongoing interest in other women's lives and our desire for
companionship on the inner journey.

This book, too, is intended as a companion for women who write
journals. I have drawn from many sources. Literature and psychology
both provide fertile ground for exploring human motivation and
offer access to the deep psychic wellsprings that vitalize our lives.
Twentieth-century literature, in fact, has often posed the same questions that we ask in the privacy of our journals: Who am I? What
gives my life meaning? Women's writing, in particular, has focused
on our search for an identity not governed by male definitions and
desire, and on our attempt to understand our authentic place in the
world. From the autobiography of Simone de Beauvoir and the diaries
of Virginia Woolf, to the poetry of Adrienne Rich and the fiction of

Margaret Atwood, women writers are radically rewriting the scripts that have been handed down to them over centuries. Many examples cited in this book are drawn from their journals.

Psychology, for its part, has provided useful ways of thinking about psychic wholeness, with its exploration of the subconscious realms of our being. Gestalt therapy's emphasis on consciousness of the present moment and the bodily sources of emotion is highly relevant to journal writing, since both aspire to greater self-awareness and, ultimately, to making our lives whole. Carl G. Jung's concepts of masculinity and femininity and of human development are crucial to my understanding of our psychic functioning. The work of Jungian analysts and writers such as Marion Woodman, Linda Leonard, and Karen Signell has been especially valuable for the light it sheds on the feminine dimension. In their important study of women's psychological development, Women's Ways of Knowing, Mary Field Belenky and her coauthors cite journal writing as a powerful tool in the evolution of a woman's self, voice, and mind. It's not surprising, because the diary is where women think and feel their way through key concerns and issues that determine their lives. Nowhere is the true nature of our psychic development more clearly evident. In journals we see emotion and thought, intuition and experience fused into something quite different from our usual attempts to be "logical." What we write and read in diaries is a language of the heart.

The writing that we do in our journals is a more direct and immediate kind of self-expression than other kinds of writing. It isn't affected by thoughts of a projected audience. It isn't necessarily linear or logical, or even grammatically correct. It's more likely to be spontaneous, unpredictable, playful, experimental, even outrageous. It may also be self-aggrandizing and self-lacerating at times. In the diary we try things on for size; we write our emotions large; we take risks we wouldn't take anywhere else.

I have been privileged to hear and read selections from diaries written by friends, workshop members, and students over the years. Wherever possible, I bring in passages from their writing to illustrate the richly diverse practices of the "diary habit," as Virginia Woolf referred to it. No less, my own volumes reveal the gold and the dross that, without fail, exist side by side, line by line, in the journal. Where relevant, I bring them in also.

Perspective and Orientation

This book is written from a feminist perspective. Women's voices have long been suppressed and stifled within Western culture, and this has had painful repercussions—not only for women but for all life on earth. Now, the feminine voice is breaking through that silence. I write out of my experience to you, a woman reader, with the belief that journal writing can help us both: to hear ourselves and each other into speech; and to discover, to express, and to embody this voice on the individual and cultural levels.

As a woman in a patriarchal society I know that, for the most part, female experience has gone unheeded and unexplored. Keeping a diary affirms the value of our lives. It validates our day-to-day experiences of soul-searching and questioning the world around us, of nurturing and growing, of making major and minor choices for our lives. In time we begin to understand the unique shape and texture of our journey to feminine selfhood and identity.

As a literary scholar, I know that women have historically had a different relationship with literature and language than men. We have provided the admiring audience for male linguistic performance; only rarely have we possessed pen and paper of our own. Even when we have, the language hasn't fit our experience; the words have not come out right. But now, more than ever, claims the literary critic Nicole Brossard, "The question for women in playing with language is really a matter of life and death. We're not just playing for fun in a kind of game. We're finding our own voice, exploring it, and making new sense where the general sense has lost its meaning and is no longer of use." Through keeping a diary, we begin to find our own words, our own language, our own voices. We start to tell our own stories. In the workshops and classes I have taught over the years, I've seen how journal writing increases self-understanding and esteem, and furthers growth and creativity in women. Hesitant voices grow eloquent as women write about the intricacies and subtle shadings of their lives, the secret hopes and dreams that drive them on.

As a long-term journal writer myself, I know how crucial journal writing has been—still is—in my own quest for a voice that goes beyond abstract patriarchal rhetoric and argument. Throughout the years, my journal has been the place where I bring thinking and feeling together, integrate dreams and waking life, my inner realms and the world around me, the profound and the prosaic, all without fear of being found trivial or crazy by anyone, including myself. This is where I breathe most freely. As Anaïs Nin and countless other diarists have found, the diary is where I am most at home.

A Tapestry of Influences

This book was not written in a vacuum. Here I want to acknowledge my participation in the web of reciprocal relations and support that comprises the women's movement and feminist scholarship. Not for me "the anxiety of influence" that has successive generations of male poets killing off their literary fathers and denying the impact of earlier generations on their work. It took me so long to find my literary foremothers that the last thing I want to do is to declare myself an orphan! Far sooner would I acknowledge the inspiration and claim the blessing of the numberless literary mothers and sisters whose work has moved and provoked me, stymied and angered me, impassioned and emboldened me, led me into ecstasy and often into tears. But rarely, if ever, left me cold. This book is a tapestry woven of myriad ideas, thoughts, intuitions, questions, feelings, impressions, fragments, quotations, and more. All the radiant, multicolored threads borrowed from other women's lives and journals I acknowledge with loving gratitude. Ideally, then, this book would be read in dialogue, not only with your own journal writing but with other books on women's lives.

The Politics of Pronouns and Quotes

The feminine pronoun is used throughout this book. Language is not neutral, and women readers often have the jarring sense of seeing human experience framed with masculine pronouns, sometimes in the oddest of contexts. Despite ever-changing usage, the English language still can't speak of individuals without indicating gender or, worse, assuming them male. I hope that this will change in the near future. For the moment, I assume them female. Similarly, I have chosen epigraphs, quotes, and examples from women's writing wherever possible. Perhaps this is one way to break the misleading and dangerous cycle of belief that female writers are not cited because they didn't say anything worth repeating—an insidious untruth that has left aspiring women writers bereft of role models, inspiration, and evidence that a woman writing is more than a dog standing on its hind legs, to borrow Samuel Johnson's infamous formulation. I look forward to the time when all writers, women and men alike, are quoted as freely and as frequently as their work deserves.

Journal writing is the most egalitarian of writing modes. What counts is not who the writer is or what she has achieved, but rather the degree of truthfulness, candor, and perceptiveness she has brought to her writing. The quotes and examples from many diaries and journals used here demonstrate these qualities. I have drawn many examples from journal entries generously shared with me by workshop participants, students, and friends. Where they have asked to remain anonymous, I have used a pseudonym or no name at all. Their writing itself has not been altered except occasionally in matters of punctuation or spelling, in the interests of clarity. The same is true of my own journal entries reproduced here. In several instances, however, I have altered names in order to protect another person's privacy. Generally, I've left aside journals whose main focus is external events in favor of those with a more introspective tone. I wasn't interested in diaries, either, that register the engagements of well-known women, unless, as in those of Anne Morrow Lindbergh, there was also a significant reflective dimension.

My Life as a Journal Writer

For almost three decades now, I've kept a journal. When I was eleven years old, I bought a small five-year diary with lock and key from pocket money painstakingly saved. Not much later, I discovered that my mother had read the diary, so I threw it away and started over in a blank notebook. This time I made sure that no one found it. I had no idea then that this practice would become such an important part of my life.

That was a lifetime ago! Since then, I have written in many different blank books and on all kinds of paper. More than seventy volumes of all descriptions fill the two bottom shelves of my large pine bookcase. I've used ballpoint pens, fountain pens, colored felts, pencils, and other writing implements. During the years of high school and first loves, I wrote in my diary. While attending religious college in Alberta, I wrote. During a lonely year in the Yukon Territories, at university, on a six-month trip through Europe and Israel, throughout moves to four countries, I filled volume after volume with my thoughts and reflections, my ever-fluctuating emotional states, dreams, ideas for stories and other creative projects, and more. The longest silence lasted six weeks.

I also read every published journal and autobiography I could find, starting with Louise Fitzhugh's *Harriet the Spy*, the story of a spirited eleven-year-old girl who kept a secret notebook of her observations on the world around her, and the classic *Diary of Anne Frank*. When my best friend gave me a volume of Anaïs Nin's published diaries for my twenty-first birthday, I was hooked. Since then I've read hundreds of published journals and autobiographies. At university, I read Virginia Woolf, Anaïs Nin, Simone de Beauvoir, André Gide, Jean-Paul Sartre, Friedrich Nietzsche, Alma Mahler-Werfel, Lou Andreas-Salomé, and others.

As a graduate student of comparative literature, I found myself gravitating once again to women's personal narratives. I wrote my doctoral dissertation on the theme of language and silence in the work of Christa Wolf, a writer who keeps a diary herself and has written about its significance for her life and work. My diary became a sourcebook for my dissertation in those years, and I found myself incorporating parts of journal entries into my thesis. Also during that time, I taught a course called "Writing the Female Self," for the City University of London, in which we read, kept journals, and discussed how women write in order to forge identity. Since then diaries have become an indispensable pedagogical tool. All my students keep journals of one sort or another, and I keep a separate teaching journal myself.

Then I started the Women's Journal Workshop, with the hope of creating a safe and supportive environment in which women could explore their written voices. In recent years, I've conducted workshops in the United States and Canada, and have heard women everywhere describe in amazement how journal writing is changing their lives in ways they had never foreseen. It has been exhilarating, to say the least, to watch new diarists discover the fascinating drama of their own existence.

This book brings together two interwoven strands of my long-standing interest in journals: the personal and the scholarly. As a young woman bent on writing and self-discovery, I loved the diary for its therapeutic and creative dimensions and for the freedom it offered. As a student of literature, I read published journals and notebooks for the insights they gave into the writer's life, and into the mystery of the creative process itself. This book has come out of my fascination with women's personal writing over many years of reading and study, out of countless conversations with long-term and occasional diarists about the role of journal writing in their lives, and out of my experiences as a workshop leader. Above all, it has come from almost three decades of passionate journal writing. It is the culmination of my lifelong love affair with journals.

Taking a Journey, Finding a Voice

Over the years in which I've kept a journal, many images and metaphors for the process have occurred to me. Sometimes I have thought of it as a growing patchwork quilt in which the many pieces and fragments of my life come together to form a meaningful, sometimes beautiful pattern. At other times, I've regarded it as an unfailingly loyal and interested friend who accompanies me wherever I go. But the two metaphors that have stayed with me most vividly over time are those in the book's title: taking a journey, and finding a voice. Both are images of process and transformation.

For women these are inseparable. They challenge our long role as mute and passive objects of history, intimating both the possibility to be on the way to somewhere new, and the means of describing what we experience on the way. In fact, it's even difficult to say which comes first: the journey or the voice. And maybe it doesn't matter. What matters is that now it is our turn to be on the way to new time and space and to give word to what we discover. Odysseus is still thrusting forward to new seas and adventures, but when he returns home to tell his tale and rest up for the next voyage, the house is empty. Penelope has embarked on a journey of her own. Will her husband recognize it if it doesn't look like his? It doesn't really matter. This time, the story is hers.

The Journey

To keep a journal is to embark on a journey. The words share common roots obvious in the French jour (day), which comes from the Latin word diurnalis, or "daily." A journey was originally the distance that could be traveled in one day. Similarly, "diary" comes from the Latin diarium, or daily food or allowance. Originally the two words were used interchangeably; only more recently has "diary" carried feminine (and more trivial) connotations, and "journal," masculine. In this book, I use the two terms synonymously.

The metaphor of life as a journey is an old one. Dante was only one of many to take stock "in the middle of the journey of my life" (although we don't know whether he did this by keeping a diary). Like the journey of our lives, the journal writing journey is not linear but twists and turns and loops around to old, familiar ground, with many detours along the way. At times we feel that we are in all-too-familiar territory, that our old habits assert themselves with boring repetitiveness. Then, suddenly we glimpse, just beyond the next corner, a breathtaking vista that we have never seen before. At once, the excitement of the journey is fresh and new again. We are on to another turn of the spiral. And yet, this is a journey without a destination. There's no point of arrival because, as the feminist theologian Nelle Morton put it, the journey itself is our home. The journal writing journey accompanies our life's journey, deepening it, enhancing it, both illuminating and being illuminated by it.

When I first began to write in my diary at the age of eleven, I had no idea that I was embarking on a voyage of exploration that would change the way I thought about my life, indeed would change the way I lived my life. Whether you are setting out for the first time or are already a seasoned traveler, I hope that this proves the most exciting and rewarding journey you ever undertake. Because you are the most fascinating undiscovered territory of all.

Finding a Voice

The voice metaphor has evocative echoes for me. I am a singer, and music has always been very important in my life. Over and over during my twenties I was told that my voice had the clear, pure sound of an English choirboy's. That was not an image I identified with and, feeling it was high time to find my own singing voice, I began taking lessons.

But more important was the fact that after many years of rigorous academic work, my own writing voice—the voice that had known its truth and confidently written stories at ten—had been silenced. In its place was my best attempt to sound authoritative and erudite, dispassionate and elegant. Academic writing, I found, required me to leave out precisely what I cared about most in a work of literature— ironic, since I always wrote out of passionate affinity with a particular author or work. Where my younger voice had been spontaneous and unselfconscious, my academic voice was anxious and unsure, forever second-guessing itself in the attempt to leave no nuance unexplored, no counterargument unrefuted, no reference uncited. In the final year of writing my thesis, I promised myself that as soon as it was finished, I would get back to "my own writing," to my own voice. Then I would write to please myself.

But—lo and behold—it was not that simple. "My voice" had not just been waiting patiently for an invitation to return, and hadn't gone unaltered by my years in the academic world. Suddenly I wasn't sure what my voice was, anymore, or even whether it was still there.

It had survived, I was to discover—in my journals. There, I had freely poured out my passionate hope and despair, my daily joy and anxiety; there, I had given vent to the emotional extremes and intuitive leaps that demanded an outlet, unchecked by the pressure of having to appear other than what I was. If my thesis cast light, my journal was its rich shadow. The voice that speaks in our journals is not the voice of culturally sanctioned beliefs and values. It is something rawer, more primal, more concretely authentic. Journal writing strips away the layers of social niceties that obscure our true feelings and lays bare the powerful impulse to reveal ourselves as we really are—with all of our undefended vulnerabilities, our unreasonable hurts, our unguarded passions.

In another sense, then, the title of this book reflects my own journey through the patriarchal mode of writing I had internalized throughout the years of academic work to a way of writing that speaks more intimately, more truthfully of my own life and experience. Writing this book has been yet another turn of the spiral—one in which I've found myself turning back to recapture my earlier joy in writing, then forward to integrate that spontaneous enjoyment with the more careful, reflective capacity acquired through scholarly work. I'm still in the process of integrating. The journey is home.

How to Use This Book

The twelve chapters of this book are arranged in three sections. Chapters Two and Three complete the introductory section, which explores the relationship between women's lives and voices, and the journal writing journey. The six chapters in Part Two focus on certain broad themes in journal writing. The overall movement is from more general to more specific, but you don't have to read the chapters in the order in which they appear. My movement is spiralic; each chapter offers a variation on the book's central theme. Although there are cross-references among them, each chapter is complete in itself, and you can begin wherever you like. If one draws you more than another, start there. Feel free to skip back and forth. Browse wherever your interest takes you. As you read, you may want to look at the related writing topics in the Appendix. Improvise. These can be repeated over time, and the continuity and change in your writing will intrigue you. Finally, in the last three chapters, we move beyond the personal dimension of journal writing to consider its social and communal aspects.

More than anything else, I hope you will make this book your own and add your unique voice to the universal chorus of journal writers. Good luck as you begin the inner voyage of self-discovery!

2

~~~~~~~~~~

An Hour of Her Own

What would happen if one woman told the truth about her life? The world would split open.

MURIEL RUKEYSER, *"Käthe Kollwitz"*

The modern woman stands before a great cultural task, which means perhaps, the beginning of a new Era.

CARL G. JUNG, *Women in Europe*

You and I and the Goddess

Our culture speaks with a male voice. Collectively, we uphold values such as logical thinking, goal-oriented movement, and the hierarchical transmission of knowledge and power. These are values that Jung and others associated with the masculine half of psychic development. In itself, this is not a bad thing; these are the values that gave us Shakespeare, Bach, even Jung himself. But somewhere along the line, something essential was sacrificed for the sake of masculine achievement. We lost our concretely felt connection to the world around us, our capacity for whole-bodied attention to the present moment, for empathic identification with others.

The results of this imbalance are all around us. We have money for sophisticated military technology but not for education, health care, or programs to address the massive environmental devastation we have wrought. While many of us in the Northern Hemisphere eat ourselves to an early death, millions of our southern neighbors perish for lack of food, drink, and basic nutrients. Worst of all, most of the time we're totally oblivious to what we have done—evidence of our culture's dangerous blind spot.

And yet, many believe that this is the age of Gaia: that we are witnessing the reemergence of a long-suppressed feminine presence in the world, that feminine wisdom—in both women and men—is coming into its own and can enable us to heal the dangerous divisions that threaten our continuance as a species. The Jungian analyst Marion Woodman claims that the feminine dimension "is now coming to consciousness as a cultural phenomenon," and that we have a responsibility not only to hear but "to act on it and accept the consequences of our lives being turned inside out." Sophia, or feminine wisdom, seeks to reconcile what has been split apart: heaven and earth, body and spirit, female and male, emotion and intellect, human and non-human life; and to transform, through compassion and unconditional love, the current death-dealing, linear, one-track-minded patriarchal ethos at the heart of our global culture.

Women have a crucial role in this process. Effectively silenced in the public realm for centuries, we have a different perspective on things, one related to the fact that we are the givers of life, the daughters of the Great Mother from whose body the world is reborn over and over again. What is our part in this newly evolving holistic consciousness? In *The Heroine's Journey*, Maureen Murdock claims,

> Our task is to heal the internal split that tells us to override the feelings, intuition, and dream images that inform us of the truth of life. We must have the courage to live with paradox, the strength to hold the tension of not knowing the answers, and the willingness to listen to our inner wisdom and the wisdom of the planet, which begs for change.

Long confined to passivity, we are challenged to become active; long limited to whispering, we are asked to describe in a clear and unmistakable voice what we experience in the world around us, what we know in our innermost being.

It's clear that women's roles are changing on the societal level. Although we haven't attained the fully equal status envisioned by the women's liberation movement, there are more options available to us than ever before. This means that the choices required of us are more exhilarating and, at the same time, more terrifying. The decisions we make determine our identities. No longer willing to see ourselves through the eyes of men, who are we? Unable to suppress the urgent need for lives of our own, how do we live? Reluctant now to play supporting roles in men's ongoing dramas, how do we discover our own? Now is the time to explore the feminine voice. What does it say? Into what unexplored regions of woman's psyche (and man's unconscious) does it take us? What can it tell us about the way we experience ourselves, each other, the world? This is where the diary comes in.

Journal writing is a powerful tool for reclaiming our authentic feminine voices. The diary is truly a "no-man's-land," in which the rules of patriarchal logic, cause and effect, grammar and syntax are suspended—in unwritten territory as new as the blank page before you and as expansive as your imagination can conceive. In this place without borders, new worlds can be created: worlds of feeling and intuition, of imagination and dream. As Kim Chernin emphatically states, "If the Woman Who Is Not Yet is ever to exist we must discover ourselves as women apart from the woman we have invented to please men." In our diaries we give birth to the Woman Who Is Not Yet: to our selves. From my own journal:

If logic is a mode of perception rather than THE way of arriving at the truth, it surely is the mode of perception that we make god in this society. "Be logical." "But does that follow, logically?" "That's illogical." The ultimate determinant of importance, it seems. The trouble is, when I do have intimations of other kinds of perception, logic stands in judgment over them and tries to undermine their validity, questions the idea that they could have any value: "That doesn't even make sense." But does it always have to "make sense"? How can feelings and intuition "make sense"? Isn't that asking an apple to be an orange? Feelings, emotions and intuitions have their own "language," their own inner *rhythm and integrity that don't revolve around logic, but we discount them, subjugating them to logic's rule.*

"Women come to writing . . . simultaneously with self-creation," Carolyn Heilbrun suggests to us. Again and again, journal writing plays a key role in modern women's search for identity. Kim Chernin tells the story of Eleanor, who abruptly bowed out of her legal career one day, moving to a small oceanside cottage, where she planted a garden, baked her own bread, and kept a diary in an attempt to understand the deep dissatisfaction pervading her life. Outwardly successful, Eleanor had discovered she had no self apart from the roles externally imposed on her. As she began writing a journal and reading other women's published diaries, a sense of her own identity slowly started to take shape.

Writing a diary encourages us to explore intuitions and perceptions that run counter to "malestream" logic and to discover the concrete truth of our own experience—a well-kept secret throughout time, even from us! It also provides both a supportive framework in which to ask ourselves what it is we really want in life and the freedom to explore our own unique written voices. Along the way we will surely find, with Anaïs Nin, that we are writing the long-hidden truth of many women's lives, not only our own. "It is my thousand years of womanhood I am recording, a thousand women," Nin wrote in her journal. In the safety of our diaries, we are "hearing ourselves into speech."

What Do Women Really Want?

That we face a wider spectrum of possibilities than previous generations of women is exhilarating. But it also puts a new kind of pressure on us. To begin with, we have to distinguish our perceived obligations from our actual desires. What we feel we *should* want for the sake of those we love may be a far cry from what we truly yearn for in our heart of hearts. Then, too, we must summon up the faith that we have the courage, energy, and talent to accomplish what we dream of doing. Both tasks are complicated by lingering echoes of the 1980s myth that women can and should "have it all." Now that this is supposedly possible, what is the "all" we have struggled so long and so hard to have? Successful careers and "functional" families? Money and power? Recognition and prestige? Solitude? Creative freedom? What *do* we really want? And if we haven't managed to have it all, where have we gone wrong? These are some of the questions that lie at the heart of our journey.

We all want love and peace in our lives; that goes without saying. Most of us want a loving relationship with a partner who is an equal. The affection of those around us provides emotional sustenance in our day-to-day existence; without it we would fall into despair. Peace is harder to come by, especially for women. Often we are too torn by both inner and outer conflicts, too fragmented by society's imperative to be "faster, better, and more" to breathe the quiet air of contentment within the moment. Add to that the fact that women, by and large, provide the emotional "connective glue" that maintains human relationships, and this brings us to the heart of the conflict: What a woman needs to do for herself is often very different from what her family, whether biological or chosen, demands of her. This dilemma is evident in the following journal entry written by Robin Garber-Kabalkin, mother of four young children, in the midst of a crisis concerning her sexual orientation.

July 6, 1991
Even as I grumble about responsibility, I still delight at having a tiny child crawl into my bed with a book first thing in the morning. There was Esther. "Mommy, I want you to read me this book, that's why I bringed it. It's full of 'ventures." And indeed it was, a book of Disney adventures. We cuddled as I read, then I gave her a bath, marvelling at my tenderness as I shampooed her hair. Which is the real me? The one who wishes them away, the one who does the job and does it well even as she suffers under the "yoke of oppression"? The one who wants to be in Greece, gazing into the eyes of a dark-haired goddess, willing her to be mine? I am a coward above all else. Afraid to assert myself, afraid of rejection, afraid, afraid, afraid.

How clear the diarist's sense of being torn in two opposing directions: the path of maternal love and responsibility, and that of freedom and sexual self-discovery. In her life she has not found a way to travel both at once, but her journal can *contain* the conflict, can hold the paradox of her seemingly irreconcilable desires.

Many of us continue to negotiate a perilous balance between familial and professional obligations. Most often, we end up with the feeling that we are shortchanging both and, due to powerful feelings of guilt, what gets sacrificed is any semblance of *personal* time and space. Rather than give short shrift to those we love or to our careers, we suppress our own needs. Not surprisingly, then, hunger for privacy is a frequent theme in women's journals. Here is another entry from Robin's journal, in which her desperate longing for "personal space" is clear.

> I don't want just a room of my own. I want a house, a life of my own. An existence shaped and framed by my own needs. God, I feel so selfish—crying out for me, my, mine. But I feel as if nothing is mine. Everything I have is at the disposal of others. My books—they can take them, and do. They read them. My tapes disappear—my socks do too. It's not a figment of my imagination—what's mine is theirs—they gnaw away at me like little mice. Robbing me of possessions is not so bad but they rob me of my mind and soul as well. Who ever said children were a blessing? They clamor for so much—how can I have anything left over for me if I give it all away to them? Who are these unselfish women who give and give and keep on giving even when there's nothing left to give? Who made them? And in whose image, I'd like to know.

What else do women want? We want a sense of communal relatedness to those around us, the sense of being fully alive and engaged. We want, as Marion Milner put it, "to share things, experiences, not passively, as if sitting at a theater all one's life, but actively taking part in things." We want the chance to explore our creative potential in all areas, and confidence that we have something valuable to share with others. We want self-understanding at ever-deepening levels, in ever-broadening spheres. We want to make contact with what is real and true. At the beginning of her own journal, Milner wrote, "This diary is to discover where one can put one's faith, *as shown by experience*" (my emphasis).

A Voice of One's Own

What, exactly, does it mean to speak and write in our own voices? If we are born female, isn't our voice by definition female? Perhaps so, but the voice of the little girl we once were doesn't survive intact into our adult years, according to psychologists who have carried out studies in this area. In her attempt to illuminate the major turning points in women's psychological development, Emily Hancock discovered "the girl within": the little girl of eight or nine who knew who and what she was and confidently voiced what she wanted. That knowledge subsequently was lost to us, buried in the course of growing up female, but it survives in every woman and holds the key to her authentic identity. For each of the twenty women Hancock spoke with at length, contacting "the girl within" was the crucial step to recovering stifled spontaneity, intuitive knowledge, and joy of life. In essence, it gave her back *her self*.

What becomes of that confident little girl in each of us? Psychologists Carol Gilligan and Lyn Mikel Brown describe the adolescent girl's loss of faith in her own voice in our society. What happens to girls around the age of eleven, they ask, that causes them to abandon their own perception, disown their knowledge, and disavow their earlier confident voices? Their answer is adolescence, with its intense pressure to conform to social expectations of feminine behavior. The young girl on the brink of puberty begins to see flaws and shortcomings in herself, and to realize she will have to make some big changes if she is to play the role that is expected of her. She loses weight or gains it, attempts to be more "cool," more feminine, more acquiescent, in order to gain acceptance from adults and peers alike. Often she is beginning to think about boys, and the basis of her self-esteem shifts from the affection of family and girlfriends to how she fares with boys. She suspects she is as smart as they are, but knows also that if she is to be liked, she must defer to them, let them feel superior. If she says what she really thinks, they won't like her and she won't be popular. Is it any wonder that she no longer trusts her own voice?

> February 10, 1994
>
> Last night Carol Gilligan was on the Charlie Rose show, talking about her two books on girls' and women's voices. The eight-year-old girl is full of certainty and self-confidence, and has a sense of entitlement. By eleven, all that begins to change. Gilligan says that now that same girl "doesn't know what she knows" any longer; she loses confidence in the value of her own perceptions. Since she defines herself largely in relationship to others, she doesn't want to lose those ties and so she stops saying what she knows and thinks, for fear of offending.
>
> This morning I made a connection between what Gilligan said and the fact that so many girls start writing diaries at that age. Eleven seems to be the crucial age for women who keep journals. I have a powerful hunch that these two things are connected. Once the eleven-year-old girl feels she can't speak her mind any longer (for fear of losing social approval), she goes "underground" in a sense—into her diary. She evolves a hidden life in which she CAN continue to know and say what she really feels and thinks. The diary becomes the one place where she can be herself. (Maybe the reason boys don't keep diaries is because they don't experience this split between what they know and what society says is so. They don't need a private inner life in order to stay sane and intact.) It's not new to me that this is the function that diary writing fulfills for young girls—an assertion of identity. But I don't think I've ever clearly tied it in with the age of eleven before. Doesn't it make sense that these two things would overlap? And, of course, not all girls keep diaries. Some keep their voices alive in other ways. Music. Sports. Others adopt society's conventions and give up their own voices altogether. I wish I hadn't destroyed my own early journals.

This idea excited me. The longer I thought about it, the more sense it made. What if the eleven-year-old girl takes all the ideas and feelings she knows will not be acceptable to those around her into the safety of her journal, since express them she must? Is this the way she keeps her own voice intact, albeit in a hidden fashion? Couldn't this be seen as a highly creative way of keeping alive the "girl within," that precocious critic of the world around her and fearless champion of her own opinions?

With these questions in mind, I began to search out the ages at which women start writing journals. Over and over again I found my hunch confirmed. Many diarists begin to write between the ages of ten and twelve—precisely the time in their lives when, according to Hancock, Brown, and Gilligan, their own voices are being sublimated to the demands of the culture. In *Heart Songs*, an anthology of young girls' diaries, five of the nine girls included began writing at the age of eleven or twelve. Though the starting ages of the other four are not given, all were writing by the age of fourteen. About half the diarists in *Private Pages* also began writing between the ages of ten and thirteen. Christina Baldwin and Kay Leigh Hagan, authors of journal books, both started writing at eleven, and so did I. Consider, too, this entry from the diary of the young Anaïs Nin: "There is one thing which troubles me," she wrote at twelve. "I feel different from everybody. I notice no child in my class of my age thinks as I do. They are all alike, they are in accord. . . . I am altogether different. . . . My desires, my dreams, my ambition, my opinions, are different. Why am I not like everybody?"

The adolescent girl's experience of socialization—of being silenced through a subtle and insidious version of societal behavior modification—ushers in a period of obedience to social expectation from which some women never recover. The authentic voice is sacrificed in deference to the need to be liked. In its place, the feminine mask. But a mask can't speak out; only a face can. What follows is often years of silence in the public realm, of dissimulation in the private. Sometimes it takes a major crisis or upheaval to remind a woman of the extent of her loss: a serious illness; losing someone close to her through death or separation; a midlife reevaluation of her life. Then the journal may become a canvas for her hidden self, the mouthpiece of her stifled voice.

Among the most poignant instances I have come across is the story of Kate Danson, who describes the life crisis that gradually led her into deeply repressed memories of childhood sexual abuse by her brother. She reflects, "It was as though, having entered the shadow of death and having reemerged partial and diminished, I was at last permitted to question the rules by which my life was governed." Unable to complete her doctoral dissertation and racked with guilt for challenging the patriarchal system she had long payed homage to, Kate began to keep a journal. "By taking time to write down my dreams, my thoughts about their possible meaning, and my feelings about daily occurrences, I began to become acquainted with myself," she recalls. "It is as though I were building a friendship with myself and with it, a stronger sense of my own self-worth." Through her dreams and journal writing, Kate became aware of just how thoroughly she'd dissociated from her body's reality in order to survive, how much she had moved "into her head."

Often, as in Kate Danson's case, the silencing effects of female socialization are compounded by other traumas that render women mute. While using journals in the college classroom, Cinthia Gannett discovered that approximately half her female students had suffered some form of sexual violence, and that journal writing provided a means of bringing this abuse to expression. She notes, "Like untold numbers of women in the past, many of these students have literally used their writing and their journals to break their silence for the first time, to construct a self, to find their voices." In one dramatic example, a young woman who had filled twenty-eight spiral notebooks in five years, wrote, "Considering where I started from, I feel I have literally written myself into existence."

Women's silence within our culture has been deepened by the visceral knowledge that our words most often are neither wanted nor missed. The French feminist critic Hélène Cixous describes our experience of speaking out publicly in all too familiar terms. She says,

> Every woman has known the torment of getting up to speak. Her heart racing, at times entirely lost for words, ground and language slipping away—that's how daring a feat, how great a transgression it is for a woman to speak—even just open her mouth—in public. A double distress, for even if she transgresses, her words fall almost always upon the deaf male ear, which hears in language only that which speaks in the masculine.

But this is changing. The enormous fascination with women's lives on the part of many feminist scholars and artists in recent decades has given us back some of our lost history and, with it, new courage to speak. Through their diverse explorations, feminists have discovered crucial differences in how women and men think, experience, and express themselves. Carol Gilligan points out that while men live out an "ethic of justice" in which independence and individual achieve-ment are highly prized, women see themselves in a relationship of connection to others, manifesting an "ethic of care." She explains,

> As we have listened for centuries to the voices of men and the theories of development that their experience informs, so we have come more recently to notice not only the silence of women but the difficulty in hearing what they say when they speak. . . . The failure to see the different reality of women's lives and to hear the differences in their voices stems in part from the assumption that there is a single mode of social experience and interpretation. By positing instead two different modes, we arrive at a more complex rendition of human experience.

More women are "getting up to speak" and finding a responsive audience among other women hungry for affirmation of their experi-ence (and, too, among a growing number of men). Journal writing is often the first step toward reclaiming their voices. Maureen Murdock describes her experience of a period of descent and going inward, which occurs in many women's lives when the old patriarchal expec-tations gradually fall away and the rejected feminine values are re-claimed. Writing in her journal helped her to understand the course of this journey:

> My feminine voice became stronger as I developed the courage to let go of my reliance on linear mind. Then I was free to listen to dreams, images, and inner allies. These became my guides. When a woman reduces the emphasis on the outer heroic quest for self-definition, she is free to explore *her* images and *her* voice.

Kate Danson, at the end of her account, leaves us with these hopeful words: "I experience a new creative energy, a kind of security and playfulness within the structure of words I create. I am rediscovering in writing, with a growing confidence and pleasure, an outlet for the outpourings of my thoughts and feelings. I write. I dance. I love. I am. Today." For Kate, journal writing was a means of becoming whole.

Language of the Heart

Marion Woodman describes a dream that provided insight into her difficulty finding the right voice for the book she was writing. In the dream, a large smiling frog waits as she attempts to roll a lily pad into a pipe through which frog eggs can pass, while two men fight on a balcony behind her until one is thrown off, barely missing her head. Woodman concludes that the two men represent the internal critic disparaging her ability to write, and the frog, a suppressed feminine voice that leaps "intuitively with the imagination" and insists, " 'I want to write, but I don't want to write essays. I want to write my way.' " Afterward, she ponders the significance of the dream.

> Leap—leap—remembering my journal that looks like a Beethoven manuscript—blots, blue ink, red, yellow and green, pages torn by an angry pen, smudged with tears, leaping with joy from exclamation marks to dashes that speak more than the words between, my journal that dances with the heartbeat of a process in motion. How does one fashion a pipe than can contain that honesty, and be at the same time professionally credible? How can a woman write from her authentic center without being labeled "histrionic" or "hysterical"? Splat! Long Pause!
>
> And then my frog spoke from the mud.
>
> "Why don't you write as you feel? Be a virgin. Surrender to the whirlwind and see what happens."
>
> . . . For weeks I tried to find a syntax that could simultaneously contain the passion of my heart and the analytic detachment of my mind.

What Marion Woodman found among the colored blots and torn pages of her journal is a mode of expression different from her usual controlled and reasoned discourse. It is a language of the heart.

Sometimes it's the fear of being thought overly effusive or sentimental that keeps us from speaking our heart's truth to the world around us. With all its limitations, formal education does at least attempt to teach us the importance of thinking. Nowhere are we taught the value of our emotional life. Instead, we learn to stifle and suppress our feelings because they are illogical, inconvenient, and often messy. But just because we force them underground doesn't mean they no longer exist. It merely ensures that they will surface in other ways—generally, destructive ways. How much healthier if we could learn to express them directly, without fear or shame, if this spontaneous emotional language could permeate our everyday inter-actions with its immediacy, vitality, and passion!

Your journal allows you to explore your inner truth without em-barrassment. The language of the heart that finds expression here is not concerned with logic or consistency. It exists beyond time and space and contains its own integrity, reflecting not the laws of cause and effect or of grammar and syntax, but those of our own inner psychic process. Past and future are brought together in the eternal Now that contains everything we ever have been and shall be.

The Feminine Spiral

The Jungian author Linda Leonard writes, "I have discovered in the course of my journey that life and psychic growth move in cycling spiral rings of descent and ascent. Every new growth in myself has been preceded by a descent of the seed into the dark ground." In her exploration of women's psychic journey, Emily Hancock discovers "the striking phe-nomenon of circling back to a self obscured and reclaimed." Exploring how women find their female roots, Naomi Ruth Lowinsky observes a pattern of "looping" that "disregards linear time" and "finds mean-ing in patterns that repeat." Kim Chernin, too, concludes that all change "circles around, snakes back on itself, finds detours, leads us a merry chase, starts us out it seems all over again from where we were in the first place" (my emphasis). Many women describe the course of their life's journey as a spiral. Circling back to the familiar before sweeping ahead to the unknown, the spiral moves forward by moving back-ward, goes up by going down. In contrast to the relentless forward drive of the masculine "line," the spiral incorporates periods of re-turning to our childhood wounds before proceeding ahead with fresh insight and energy. At the best of times, this journey may involve "moving back and down" into our Shadow—our unacknowledged dark side—in order to face our demons, before moving ahead into the light of new growth.

The spiral is an archetypal symbol of the cyclical nature of life and of the unending stream of vital energy that calls all things into being. In the ancient matriarchal religion of the earth, the serpent-spiral represented the flowing process of continual transformation. Its simultaneous ascending and descending movement symbolized the double motion of the cosmos itself toward death and rebirth, the unity of spirit and matter, of the temporal and the eternal, and "the power of the above and below." It was also connected to the waxing and waning of the moon. The monthly lunar cycle, too, manifests the cosmic rhythm of birth and death and rebirth. Our capacity to bear children reminds us that lifetimes and generations overlap rather than succeed each other; that our lives are integrally interwoven with those born before and after us; that the future circles back to, and incorporates, the past. In Lowinsky's words, "We measure our lives in our mother's terms, and in our daughter's terms."

The same is true of our creative process. Over and over again, in the work of women writers, the spiral serves as the symbol of a nonlinear creativity that encircles familiar territory while moving ahead into the unknown. Sometimes the structure of the work itself reflects this movement, as Nelle Morton observes in the "Prelude" to her book. She writes,

> I have been concerned about the repetitive stories, references, and quotations. In trying to delete many of them, I began to see each one saying something different, though the words were the same, as it moved to a different level or another context. Finally it became evident that what I thought was needless repetition may be a cyclical way of thinking, movement, and writing.

In the opening pages of *Addiction to Perfection*, Marion Woodman tells us, "Linear thinking does not come naturally to me; moreover, it kills my imagination. Nothing happens. No bell rings; no moment of HERE and NOW. No moment that says YES. Without those moments I am not alive. And so, rather than driving toward a goal, I prefer the

pleasure of the journey through a spiral." What is this "pleasure of
the journey through a spiral"? I think it derives from the integration
of deliberate and purposeful movement with uninhibited and spontaneous play. The spiral combines the circle and the line, feminine and
masculine, the comfort of home and the excitement of the quest—a
powerful example of holistic process. Is it surprising, then, that
women find the diary—with its integration of the old and the new,
the familiar and the unknown—a natural companion on our life
journeys? Our diaries circle out from our present lives, at once to the
past and the future, in fluid and ever-changing ways. With each entry,
another turn of the spiral.

It has happened that while reading my old journals, I've had a
sense of going around in circles. Year after year, it seems, the same
painful obsessions, the same unresolved insecurities and unexorcised
fears. And yet, a second look often discloses that successive entries on
old themes reveal inklings of new insights, greater clarity of thought,
deeper understanding of emotion. What appears at first to be a circle
is more often a spiral, too tightly coiled for my liking, perhaps, but
not entirely closed. What may look like "treading water" is simply a
rest stop leading up to the next plunge forward into the unknown.

The journey through this book is also a spiral. I hope you will
enjoy its cyclical movement, find pleasure in variations on a theme,
and take what is most meaningful to you on each successive round.

An Hour of Your Own

Many women are so caught up in fulfilling external obligations that
they neglect their own needs and end up depleted and weary. Nor is
this limited to women with families. It's just as possible for single
women without children to be so involved with professional responsibilities that the inner life goes unattended. "The first hurdle," says
Marion Woodman, "is the inner commitment. 'Do I really believe that
I am worthy of one hour a day for myself? I who have given my life
to others, am I selfish enough to take one hour a day to find myself?
Where can I find an hour? What has got to go?' " It is a fact that all

of the potential benefits of keeping a journal are lost to us if we can't find the time to sit down with a cup of coffee—and write. In our culture, taking care of oneself is more likely to suggest fitness—having "the look"—than a quiet time for journal writing and self-renewal. For many, this seems a luxury they cannot afford. And yet, if the well is not replenished by underground springs, how long before it runs dry? If the deep-lying roots of our psychic lives are not watered, how can there be new growth?

Women, particularly those in traditional couples, are less likely than men to have an hour—let alone a room—of their own. Things are changing, to be sure. But study after study shows that it is still women who most often bear the brunt of the "second shift" and who collapse into bed, too drained even to read a few pages of a good book. With all the time-consuming responsibilities that face her, when, in the hectic life of the modern woman, can she direct her undivided, much-sought-after attention toward her own needs and desires?

Journal writing can be woven into the busy fabric of our daily lives, providing a moment of contact with our inner selves. Your journal is the most readily transportable, the most accommodating and forgiving companion you will ever have! Carry a small diary in your handbag or briefcase, and you can write for ten minutes at the Laundromat, in the car, the dentist's office, or wherever else fate has seen fit to keep you waiting. Speaking from experience (I've surely filled an entire journal while sitting in offices), I find that writing sweetens the sourness of being put on "hold." Anaïs Nin often wrote on the go. "What an ambulant diary," she says. "At times behind desks, under a mattress, in an unlit stove, in trunks, in valises, iron boxes, buses, subways, taxis, lecture-hall desks, briefcases, in doctors' offices, hospital waiting rooms, park benches, on café tables, hair-dressers' salons. The pages often stained with coffee, wine, tears, lipstick."

Some diarists use their travel time to and from work each day to write. Mary takes the express bus from Staten Island into Manhattan, alternately writing in her journal and reading en route. Some work-shop participants have made the daily twenty-five-minute Staten Island ferry trip their writing time. Upon boarding, they head immediately

to a secluded nook and pull out their journals. Traveling across water
enhances their sense of being on a significant journey, into the oceanic
inner realms.

Brenda drives her seven-year-old twins to school and, on the three
days each week that her four-year-old attends nursery school, continues on to a local café for her second cup of tea and an uninterrupted
hour with her journal. No matter how hectic her life gets, she is thus
guaranteed three weekly appointments with herself. Mary Anne, a
single working mother, claims Saturday morning as her weekly writing time. After her three teenage children have finished eating breakfast, she sends them on their way, with instructions not to interrupt
her except in an emergency. For that period of time, her dining room
with its old oak table is hers alone.

If you are having difficulty finding time to write in your journal,
consider getting up half an hour earlier three or four mornings a
week. Chances are, you won't miss that half hour of sleep, and the
sense of stealing time for yourself while the rest of the world slumbers
is especially sweet. Or perhaps you can get to bed half an hour earlier
at night and write comfortably propped up by pillows. If you have a
lengthy auto commute, try keeping an audio diary; speak your
thoughts into a cassette recorder during your drive. One of my colleagues planned an entire article on her forty-minute drive to and
from college four days a week. Many of the diarists in Life Notes write
wherever they find themselves with a free moment. One says, " 'I
have written at the kitchen table, sitting up in bed, in the car while
waiting to pick up one of my children.' " Another responds, " 'I write
in offices, bus stop curbs, the very edge of the sea, on the bus, in bed,
at the gym.' " No place is off limits as far as journal writing is
concerned!

The initial decision to start keeping a diary is yours. After that,
journal writing creates its own momentum and provides its own
justification. The longer you continue to write, the stronger your
sense of identity and entitlement—and the more likely that the diary
will become an essential part of your journey. As you write, your life
itself may change in surprising ways. If you have read this far, more
than likely you have faith that you can find an hour—or a half hour
or twenty minutes—for yourself. What next? In Chapter Three, the

"nuts and bolts" chapter of this book, I want to make some practical suggestions that should help, whether you're just beginning or have been writing a diary for years. Every journey requires preparation. In journal writing it is minimal, but there are things you can do to enhance the process, practical matters that will increase the pleasure and rewards of your inner voyage. Let's get started.

3

◠‿◠

Getting Started

Q[uestion]. *I'm not presently keeping a diary, but sometimes I do feel the need to sit down and write down my feelings. So I decide I will write a diary; I get everything ready, open the book, and then comes the question: where do I start?*

A. N. *Put yourself right in the present. This was my principle when I wrote the diary—to write the thing I felt most strongly about that day. Start there and that starts the whole unravelling, because that has roots in the past and it has branches into the future. . . . I chose the event of the day that I felt most strongly about, the most vivid one, the warmest one, the nearest one, the strongest one.*

ANAÏS NIN, *A Woman Speaks*

Getting started is easy. All you need is some paper or an empty bound book, a pen, a place to sit down, and the desire to stop and turn your attention inward. It sounds simple. It is. The best thing about starting a diary is that there's no wrong way to do it. All the suggestions I make in this chapter are intended to stimulate your imagination and to enhance your writing journey. Take what appeals to you and, for now, disregard the rest.

Many times I've heard women say the reason that they don't start a diary is because they are daunted by the thought of all the lost time they'd have to make up for. A journal is not an autobiography. You don't have to describe all the milestones of your life (although that can be interesting), fill in the gaps, or make up for lost time. What counts is always the present moment. Start there and, before you know it, you'll be drawing from the past and weaving in the future.

You could pick up your pen and write about how you feel at this very moment, in your living room or office lunchroom, the college library or local diner, wherever you happen to be. If your feelings need a minute to become clear, describe the view from your study, kitchen, or park bench. Write about the background noise in the restaurant and the smell of fresh-brewed coffee, the color of the flowers on the window ledge in front of you, the rumble of the dryers in the Laundromat, the odd-looking person sitting across from you on the train. What feelings, memories, sensations do they evoke in you?

What is in your heart right now? What's on your mind? What's the main sensation in your body? Are you comfortable? Excited? Anxious? Serene? Restless? Bored? Happy? Filled with anticipation? In Anaïs Nin's words, what feels vivid, warm, or near to you at the moment? If you're writing during the early part of the day, what is your mood like? Are you looking forward to a lunch date with a friend? Are you oppressed by the sheer amount of paperwork that must be finished by the end of the week? Anxious to complete the day's chores before your family returns, tired and hungry? Looking forward to a weekend away? Is there a lingering dream image on the edge of your awareness? If you're writing in the evening, what emotion or event of the day stands out? What is still with you? Whatever impresses itself upon your senses, bubbles in your emotions, preoccupies your thoughts, or nibbles away at your sense of well-being—whether momentous or humble—start there. You don't need anything else.

Some diarists take the question of how to get started as the topic of their first entries. Fourteen-year-old Yvonne Blue began her diary on New Year's Day like this:

January 1[, 1926]. For days I have pondered upon a fitting beginning for this glorious diary. If I intended this for publication, I should begin something like this: "I, Yvonne Blue, being in the fourteenth year of my life, and feeling that I am old enough to convey my impressions on paper, am going to write faithfully herein, and make this book a lasting memorial of me, for those who live after I die. . . ." But I most emphatically do not intend this for publication, so I shall begin merely by recording the events of the past hours instead of the past years.

Here is the opening entry from the diary of Diane Wikse, begun in school when she was thirteen years old:

Sept. 6, 1973. I don't know much about how to confess everything to a piece of paper. It might help me get everything out of my system, but I know that it will be fun to look back to see how I felt one day. All August, I was looking forward to getting back to school because I was so bored. In that long month I had time to decide that I was going to start a jogging program and cut down on what I ate. Since it's only the second day of school, I don't know how it's working yet.

Sylvia Plath, at seventeen, started a new journal volume like this:

November 13, 1949. As of today I have decided to keep a diary again— just a place where I can write my thoughts and opinions when I have a moment. Somehow I have to keep and hold the rapture of being seventeen. Every day is so precious I feel infinitely sad at the thought of all this time melting farther and farther away from me as I grow older. Now, now is the perfect time of my life.

Other diarists write a thumbnail sketch of their lives thus far or introduce themselves to their diaries as they would to a new friend. At the turn of the century, Mary MacLane began her diary thus:

Butte, Montana, January 13, 1901. I of womankind and of nineteen years, will now begin to set down as full and frank a Portrayal as I am able of myself, Mary MacLane, for whom the world contains not a parallel. I am convinced of this, for I am odd. I am distinctly original innately, and in development. I have in me a quite unusual intensity of life. I can feel. I have a marvelous capacity for misery and for happiness. . . .

Still others regard the first page of the diary as symbolic of a new beginning. Written a month after she met the man who was to become the most important figure in her life, Etty Hillesum's opening entry reveals her intuitive understanding of both the promise and the risk of honest self-disclosure.

Sunday, 9 March [1941]. Here goes, then. This is a painful and well-nigh insuperable step for me: yielding up so much that has been suppressed to a blank sheet of lined paper. The thoughts in my head are sometimes so clear and so sharp and my feelings so deep, but writing about them comes hard. The main difficulty, I think, is a sense of shame. So many inhibitions, so much fear of letting go, of allowing things to pour out of me, and yet that is what I must do if I am ever to give my life a reasonable and satisfactory purpose.

Sometimes journal writers begin by describing their hopes and intentions in the new diary. This is what the Canadian artist Emily Carr wrote on the first page of hers:

Sunday, November 23rd [1930]. Yesterday I went to town and bought this book to enter scraps in, not a diary of statistics and dates and decency of spelling and happenings but just to jot me down in, unvarnished me, old me at fifty-eight—old, old, old, in most ways and in others just a baby with so much to learn and not much time left here but maybe somewhere else. It seems to me it helps to write things and thoughts down. It makes the unworthy ones look more shamefaced and helps to place the better ones for sure in our minds. It sorts out jumbled up thoughts and helps to clarify them, and I want my thoughts clear and straight for my work.

In 1874, the fourteen-year-old French-Canadian Henriette Dessaulles began a new volume of her diary on the first day of the school year. For her, the diary played the role of needed confidante. "It receives my secrets without giving me any advice!" she wrote. "I try to ignore advice whenever I can because it is so useless. People tell you to do loads of things they won't do themselves." Edith Wharton began a new notebook in 1924 with the hope that " 'Perhaps at last I shall be able to write down some disconnected thoughts, old & new —gather together the floating scraps of experience that have lurked for years in corners of my mind.' " A century earlier, Elizabeth Barrett Browning had kept a diary for a period of one year, the only diary she wrote during her lifetime. The opening entry, dated June 4, 1831, makes clear her ambivalence at the outset.

> I wonder if I shall burn this sheet of paper like most others I have begun in the same way. To write a diary, I have thought of very often at far & near distances of time: but how could I write a diary without throwing upon paper my thoughts all my thoughts—the thoughts of my heart as well as of my head?—& then how could I bear to look on them after they were written? . . . Well! but I will write: I must write.

Many diarists begin by describing what they hope to accomplish through keeping a diary. What are you hoping to achieve? Why not start your journal by exploring the impulse that has you sitting down to write about your inner life?

Paper and Pen

As you begin, don't overlook the aesthetic pleasure of keeping a journal. It's true that an inexpensive spiral notebook and a twenty-nine-cent Bic pen are all you need. But you'll feel more inclined to write if you put some care into choosing paper and a pen that you like. A notebook or a bound book that appeals to you (they don't have to be expensive) or the weight and color of paper that satisfy your aesthetic sense will make the prospect of writing much more inviting than strictly utilitarian writing aids. Any longtime diarist will attest to the importance of finding a journal that feels "just right." In fact, many diarists are paper fetishists! Lead us into a stationery or art supply shop, and our eyes immediately zero in on the blank book section against the back wall. The paper we write on, the book we write in are not just arbitrary raw materials. They are companions on the writing journey. If supplies were scarce, I'd write my journal on used computer paper or any stray scrap I could lay my hands on. In the meantime, how wonderful to have so many choices.

The same thing is true of pens. Some will feel better in your hand than others. Anne Frank titled one of her journal entries "Ode to My Fountain Pen In Memoriam," after her pen accidentally ended up in the stove after years of fond use. "At thirteen," she wrote, "the fountain pen came with us to the 'Secret Annexe,' where it has raced through countless diaries and compositions for me. Now I am fourteen, we have spent our last year together." Cosima Wagner (1837– 1930) wrote a diary to her two young daughters, from her first marriage, with a pen she considered hallowed. On New Year's Day, 1869, she wrote,

> The Friend [Richard Wagner] has given me the golden pen with which he wrote *Tristan* and *Siegfried*, and this I consecrate to these communications of mine to you. Thus I signify to you how sacredly I regard this work of a mother's confidences and anxieties; the pen which has traced the sublimest things ever created by a noble spirit shall now be dedicated solely to the depths of a woman's heart.

Personally, I've come to prefer Pilot-liner pens with fine points that don't leak. Not long ago, I found an office supply store that sells the basic colors by the dozen. Now I use eight colors, each for a specific topic: black for dreams, purple for entries relating to this book, burgundy for workshop entries, green for special quotes and references, blue for general entries, red for special emphasis, and so on. This makes it easy to spot dreams or ideas for the book, and I like the look of multicolored pages. If you like writing with a pencil, use a high-quality lead that won't smudge or fade. And promise yourself that you won't erase anything!

The size of the pages is important, too. If the journal is too large for my lap, I can't curl up on the couch on a miserable day with a cup of tea and a quilt, to write. I don't want to be limited to my desk or the dining-room table. But I can't write in a small journal, either. If I can fit only four words on a line, my writing changes. There is an implicit pressure to be concise and get to the point. I need the sense that the page is large and generous, that it invites expansiveness and extravagance. Other diarists have made similar discoveries. Antonia White wrote, in October of 1935, "It is cheating, I know, to begin a new notebook—But the last one never felt right." And Susan Kinnicutt noted in hers, "This diary looked so inviting when I first bought it. . . . But this isn't big enough, for one thing; I feel limited by the short

page. And it doesn't open up, bend nicely, invite me to write." This is
what Anaïs Nin had to say on the issue of size:

> This volume of the diary [No. 54] is large. A large, honest expansive
> one given to me by Henry, on which I can spread out beyond the
> diary, encompassing more, transcending myself. The small notebook I
> could slip into my pocket was mine, this one I cannot clutch, hide,
> restrain or retain. It spreads. It asserts itself. It lies on my desk like a real
> manuscript. It is a larger canvas. No marginal writing done delicately,
> unobtrusively, but work, assertion.

For Nin, then, the size of the diary was inseparable from its function.
While her earlier, small diary was private and easily hidden, the new,
larger volume intimated a movement beyond purely personal writing
into a wider realm. It looked like a "real manuscript." It's probably no
coincidence that, at around this time, she began to think seriously of
publishing part of the diary.

You may want to browse through the nearest stationery shop to see
what it has in stock. While the price can range from a dollar or two
for a simple spiral notebook (more for recycled paper) to eighty
dollars or more for a book bound in leather or for marbleized Italian
paper, there is something for everyone. If you like unusual designs
and motifs, try an import store, which may have Chinese satin-bound
books or Japanese rice paper. Not long ago, a friend gave me a beautiful book from Nepal, made from the bark of the Daphne bush, or
"paper tree." Make sure that the paper is of high-enough quality that
it won't discolor or tear and that your writing won't fade with time.
Look for acid-free paper, 100 percent rag, if possible. This means it's
made of cotton fiber (rather than the cheaper wood pulp) and buf-
fered to break down the acidity that causes inexpensive paper to
yellow with age. Artists' sketchbooks are good and don't cost as much
as some of the fancy bound books. If you can, sit down with the
journal in your lap before you buy it, and make sure its size and
weight feel right. If you can't find anything you like, tell the shop
owners they are missing out on sales because they don't have enough
to offer.

Since I started writing in my little five-year diary with lock and key three decades ago, my journals have included several fifty-nine-cent notebooks, a couple of enormous three-ring binders (each holding about five hundred sheets of paper), and many bound books of all sizes and descriptions: lined and unlined, with plain and patterned covers of cloth, vinyl, and leather. When I was living in London in the 1980s, I discovered the series of reasonably priced Chartwell Students Manuscript books with brightly colored linen covers, which fit my budget and handbag. After I left England, I stocked up during return visits and twice prevailed on friends to carry a few across the Atlantic for me. Recently, I've been experimenting again and have written in two leather-bound volumes, a beautiful floral fabric-covered book, and two dark green artist's sketchbooks. Wherever I go, I'm always on the lookout for the "perfect" journal.

What suits me best, I've found, is a large but not oversized hard bound book with white or cream-colored paper, either unlined or faintly lined in blue, with a flexible binding that doesn't have to be cracked open, about three quarters of an inch thick. A second, smaller journal accompanies me wherever I go and lasts much longer, since I write in it only when away from home. All of my diary volumes have enclosures: loose pages written unexpectedly on the run and later inserted into the diary, and occasionally a photograph, a letter from a friend, a newspaper clipping, a recipe from that time. While skimming the other day through a journal from 1981, I found letters from a friend and my thesis supervisor, a treasured choral audition report praising my voice, a copy of a poem I'd written for another friend, and a magazine illustration of a white peasant shirt I'd wanted to sew. Just as surely as the words written on the pages of that volume, those enclosures remind me of what was important to me during that period of my life. Some were taped into the journal, others simply inserted among its pages. Years ago, I decorated the covers of new journal volumes with pictures, postcards, or images that had particular significance for me then. Other diarists I know have covered bound books with beautiful fabric, with dried flowers, and with their own art. Virginia Woolf wrote most of her diaries on large blank sheets of paper that she later had bound and covered with colored, patterned Italian paper. The possibilities are as endless as your imagination.

Some diarists even title successive volumes of their journals. Isak

Dinesen named one of her diaries "Honest, Honest" ("Aerlig, Aerlig"): an admonition against self-deception. A friend who felt her familiar life collapsing around her and could glimpse something new being born titled her journal "Windows." As she gained confidence to step out of the old life and cross the threshold of the new one, she titled the next volume "Doors." Recent volumes bear the titles "Horizons" and "Sunrise." In a recent workshop where the first exercise involved naming one's real or imagined journal, the titles included "Changes," "A Little Humor and a Little Grace," "What's So Bad About Mediocrity?," "The Adventures of Veronica," and "Pecking My Way Out." What a lot of stories those titles hint at!

Experiment. Enjoy the freedom to play, to indulge your sense of whimsy, to switch to a different size of book, to another color of ink. Several of my earlier journals are less than half full because I grew tired of the paper or the feel of the book, or wanted to start over. Literally, as well as symbolically, I wanted to say, "This chapter of my life is finished; I'm starting afresh." Find paper and pen that delight you. Writing in a bound book can serve as a gentle and tangible reminder that you are making a commitment to fill its pages, to keep writing. If that seems daunting, begin on a single page. Or on your calendar, if there is space. It doesn't matter where. Just start!

With time, you'll get a clearer idea about what kind of journal best meets your needs. Do you want something that fits into your coat pocket, handbag, or briefcase? Or do you write mainly at home? Does your hand like the freedom and expansiveness of a large page or the security of a smaller one? If you enjoy writing in bed, what kind of book works best? What kind of paper do you like? Some diarists prefer the comfort of lined paper; for others, it has too many associations with obligatory assignments. Unlined pages might also serve you better if you like to sketch or doodle in your journal. One diarist I know writes only on unlined pale blue paper; another, on lilac looseleaf. A friend keeps her journal in a binder and buys a different color of paper each time. You can begin with a yellow legal pad and pencil or with a leather-bound book and a special fountain pen. The choice is yours. Have fun.

When and Where?

Journal writing is an infinitely flexible practice. With time you'll evolve your own writing habits and rituals, which may involve a particular time of day, a favorite place, and more. Some diarists write before getting out of bed, fresh with dreams, before the left brain kicks in. Others prefer midday, when the day has both a before and an after. Still others like the quiet of the evening, when the day's activity has subsided. They may even set the mood by lighting candles or incense, and playing some favorite music. The author Patricia Hampl regards her early-morning journal entries as a warm-up for the day's work. "I usually begin the day by writing, swiftly, what I see out the window," she says. "It's the keyboard, arpeggios, scales, limbering." Virginia Woolf wrote during the "casual half hours after tea," and Anaïs Nin, sitting up in bed, late at night. What time of day appeals to you? When do you have time to write? Do you want to begin by writing for twenty minutes before you go to bed each night? Do you have time to stop in a café after work, to reflect on the shape of your day thus far? What about during your lunch hour? Is early morning the best time, perhaps? Where are the nooks and crannies of your day?

When I was a graduate student in Vancouver in the late seventies and early eighties, I often wrote in my favorite café, three blocks from where I lived. The Boca Bar had newspapers in eight languages and a loyal clientele of academic and artsy bohemian types. The owner was a latter-day Italian hippy who'd managed to create the atmosphere of a Parisian café in the thirties. There was one corner table that everyone wanted. Set into a little nook behind the door, it offered more privacy than the other tables, yet provided a good view of the rest of the café. Daily, my friends and I would look for one another there in the late afternoon to talk, read, and work on essays, our books and papers strewn across the weathered oak tabletop. Once, while writing in my journal (I wrote in mottled green-and-white student notebooks in those days), I got a sudden inspiration for an Ibsen paper, and wrote most of a rough draft in the next three hours, fueled by steaming caffelattes. A friend of a friend wrote his entire novel in the Boca Bar. I think we all endowed that café with magical powers of inspiration.

Some diarists like to set aside a block of time once or twice a week to reflect on what has been happening in their lives. Others find that certain times of the year offer more opportunity for soul-searching and reflection than others. Karen looks forward all year to her annual vacation in a beach resort on Long Beach Island off the New Jersey shore. For those four weeks, her husband cares for their two little boys during the mornings while she writes in her journal, a luxury she doesn't have the rest of the year. Longtime journal writers may create a ritual of writing on their birthdays or at the end of each calendar year. This can serve as a way of taking stock and articulating hopes for the new year. Several years ago I decided that instead of my customary list of New Year's resolutions, I would write about everything I had accomplished in the year just past. Although these were not necessarily impressive achievements to anyone else's eyes, I would list the things that were important to me:

> *January 17, 1992.* What did I accomplish last year? I taught six courses, including two new ones, one of which had never been offered at CSI before: Nineteenth Century European literature. I began friendships with. . . . I held eight journal workshops, including four six-week series. I was invited to teach a five-week course on women's journals at the Jung Foundation in Manhattan this Spring. I had a lecture proposal accepted for the New York Women's Studies Association Annual Conference in March. I paid off half my student loan. I completed the one-year Gestalt training course. I spent five weeks in British Columbia and we drove to Eastern Canada for ten days.

I ended up with a journal entry that amazed and inspired me. Instead of bemoaning the articles I *hadn't* written and my other non-achievements, I had before me concrete evidence of what I *had* done. It was substantial. A week later I used this as the first exercise in a workshop, and there were similar responses of surprised delight with what each participant had achieved in 1991.

Some diarists keep journals only during times of crisis. When our lives are in flux and everything we've counted on is up for grabs, the journal can become an anchor that grounds and helps us stay connected with ourselves, reminding us of who we are (more on this in

Chapters Six and Ten). Imprisoned in 1944 on charges of high treason for her resistance work against the Nazis, the German writer Luise Rinser kept a secret diary. After ten days in a women's prison in Bavaria, she discovered some aged yellow paper and a pencil hidden beneath a loose floorboard in her cell. Immediately she began to write: "22 October, 1944. . . . When I was still free and could write when I wanted and as often as I wanted, I often doubted the point of the exercise; now I consider it a great personal good. The Word mercifully cushions me, coming between me and the naked experience of imprisonment." When she ran out of paper a week later, Rinser continued on the back of toilet paper made from old lists of criminals, trembling when the diary just missed being discovered during a cell search. More recently, Migael Scherer published a journal about her painful year of recovery after she was raped and nearly murdered in February of 1988. Elizabeth Cox kept a journal from January 1986 to April 1987, the period during which her husband was diagnosed with and died of AIDS.

Other diarists find just the opposite: that when they are in crisis, words do not come. Edie found that although her journal was a great comfort as her mother lay dying of cancer, she couldn't write at all for a year and a half following the death. Since she'd assumed responsibility for her aging father and was working full-time as well, her only chance to write was while sitting in a park during her lunch hour. "Every time I began to write," Edie told me, "something would remind me of my mother's death and I would start to cry. It was just too overwhelming, too deep a wound. I got tired of trying not to cry in public, so I stopped writing altogether." Sixteen months later, it was a particularly graphic episode of the television series M*A*S*H that forced her to realize if she didn't begin to express and communicate her grief, she would become ill, physically, mentally, or both. She picked up her journal and began to write.

Sometimes it's a happy event that precipitates the "diary habit." For Gwen, it was the long-yearned-for birth of her first and only child, at the age of forty-two. And Julia began to keep a journal after she and her husband left their fast-track careers in journalism and moved onto an island in the Pacific Northwest to grow their own vegetables and write fiction.

How Much? How Long? How Often?

How often someone has said to me, "I'm not really a journal writer, because I write only when I feel like it." When else, I always wonder, do they think they are supposed to write? What most longtime diarists have in common is that they write out of desire and need rather than obligation. Journal writing generates its own momentum. As you write, you'll gradually develop your own unique writing rhythms. You may find yourself writing at fairly regular intervals, three or four times a week. Or you may write two or three times one week, not at all the next week, and every single day during the third. One entry may be two sentences long, the next, six pages. You may not pick up your diary at all for two months, then find yourself with pen in hand again one day. You may even stop for years, then begin afresh. Unlike physical exercise, where intensity, duration, and frequency are paramount, journal writing has a beneficial effect regardless of how much, how long, or how often you write.

When people discover that I've been writing a journal for three decades, I frequently hear, "How could you possibly keep it up for that long? I would never have the discipline to do it!" This always catches me by surprise. Journal writing isn't and never has been a self-imposed discipline for me; I've always written only when I wanted, needed, longed to write. On the contrary—when for some reason I haven't had time to write for a while, I yearn for nothing more than an hour with my journal. This is how I catch up with myself, understand what has been happening in my life. Gail Godwin, too, feels the need to write regularly. She says, "Keeping a diary is a part of almost every day, like swimming. It has become part of the rhythm of my life." She writes on average three times a week; however, "during times of solitude, anguish and intense creative work . . . I often write several times a day. When I am really on edge . . . I sometimes write hourly."

Like the ground beneath your feet, your journal is always there to support your connection to the world you live in. As you begin to experience its rewards, you'll be encouraged to increase your writing. In all likelihood, you'll find yourself writing more often and more daringly with time, until one day you discover that the journal has become an indispensable companion on your life's journey. About five years ago, a friend informed me that she no longer felt the need to "make things real" by writing them down in her journal. Her self-satisfied air suggested that she had evolved beyond those of us who were still "stuck" writing in our diaries. Knowing that she has a writerly soul, I didn't take what she said too seriously. Sure enough, she picked her diary up again about a year after that conversation and has been going strong ever since.

Naturally, much of what I'm telling you is what has worked best for me over the years. Some diarists do prefer a more structured approach. Ingrid, for example, regards her half hour of journal writing early each morning as a discipline that yields great benefits for both her other writing and her emotional health. Women with small children often can't afford to wait until they feel the urge to write; they have to snatch the quarter hour that comes unexpectedly, the half hour while the baby sleeps, the early-morning moments before anyone else is awake. With a little patience, you'll eventually find the best rhythm for your own writing. Don't give up. A friend who recently left her abusive husband has created a healing morning routine for herself. She rises at 5:30, makes herself a pot of tea, and takes it back to bed, along with her journal. After writing for an hour, she goes out for an invigorating early-morning walk, then showers and heads off to work. After twenty-five years of getting up early in order to send her husband and children on their way, she can finally plan the morning around her own needs. At night, she is in bed by nine o'clock and reads until she falls asleep.

Some women write only when they are upset, depressed, or unhappy. Then the journal becomes a sounding board for their woes, a means of exorcising demons. Lou Nelson confided to her journal, "When life goes well, I do not find time to write. It is only when I am blocked by some sadness, or inspired by some relentlessness that I search out a pen or pencil and open my diary to a new page." And Virginia Woolf complained, "It is unfortunate, for truths sake, that I never write here except when jangled with talk. I only record the dumps & the dismals." The German artist Käthe Kollwitz observed herself growing depressed while reading old journals. "The reason for that," she surmised, "is probably that I wrote only when there were obstacles and halts to the flow of life, seldom when everything was smooth and even. . . . Certainly there was truth behind what I wrote; but I set down only one side of life, its hitches and harassments." Other diarists, like my friend Mona, write only when they are traveling, recording their impressions of everything they see and experience. Often, the outer voyage becomes a metaphor for the inner quest; it is themselves they are discovering as they travel through foreign lands (more in Chapter Nine).

On August 13, 1980, after a spell of very sporadic writing, I wrote in my journal, "I can't believe how long the intervals between the times I write in here, lately. It seems to be true that the more I'm doing, the less likely I am to have time to sit down and reflect on it." Sometimes we find ourselves in the old predicament that when life is full and exciting, there's no time to write, and in periods when we do have time, there's nothing compelling to write about. Diane Kendig had this experience; in April of 1970, she wrote,

> I have been promising myself for over a week I would begin a journal again. Then I decided last Wednesday that it was the day. My mind was shot full of new ideas from new people. But a dorm discussion lasted till 3 A.M., and I was too tired. So why do I write today of all days—an almost meaningless day; I mean, nothing has happened. But then, "nothing" happens most days, so why not start out with the usual.

Sometimes the urge to write may strike, the time is right, and still —as in the quote above—we lack inspiration to begin. What then? Where can we go from there?

Finding Inspiration

If you find yourself—like the person at the beginning of this chapter —wanting to write but stuck for something to say, never fear! There are many possibilities for breaking through. Anaïs Nin's suggestion— write about what feels warm, near, or strong in the present moment —may provoke a flood of feelings and associations, especially if you haven't written in a while. Another useful, all-purpose opener is the basic Gestalt exercise: "I feel . . . I need . . . I want . . ." Write for ten minutes on each of these and you'll be well on your way. One diarist found herself writing "I need a whole new life." This prompted her to ask herself, "What would this life look like?" which, in turn, led to a longer journal entry, on the sources of her discontent. Since both of these exercises focus on your inner experience, they will take you as deeply inside as you are willing to go on that day. You only have to pay attention to the endless chattering of your mind to find ample evidence of what is occupying you at this moment. Most of the time we aren't even aware of how rich the undercurrent of our psychic lives is: how full of thoughts and emotions, feelings, intuitions, and images. Tuning in provides rich material for your journal. Just sit quietly and try to empty your mind of all thoughts and feelings for ten minutes, and you'll see what I mean!

Another great source of inspiration is reading, especially published journals. Whatever moves you has power to inspire your own writing. Whatever engages your interest and empathy has a correlate in your own life. Write about it. It's almost impossible to read someone else's journal without entering into a kind of inner dialogue with the diarist in which your own experience is brought richly to bear. What follows is a passage from the class journal of Sandra Miller, who wrote this entry just after she'd read Carolyn Heilbrun's *Writing a Woman's Life*.

April 30, 1994. I was attending Philadelphia General Hospital School of Nursing in the early 1960's at the time Carolyn Heilbrun took a pseudonym and started writing detective novels. She was living, what appeared on the surface, the life of an independent woman, a life of choice and self-expression, the perfect life for a woman during that time. She was a wife, a mother, and even had a career; she was a tenured professor at the university. Yet she wanted psychic space, which writing detective novels would allow. . . . As I remember that time in my personal history, I wonder, what did I know of psychic space, let alone what claiming my Self by name meant in the larger scheme of the 1960's. Life, for me, was a fast-paced blur of trying to maintain sanity in the violence of a city hospital. I remember blood, lots of blood, burned flesh, cancer breaking through skin, organs torn by bullets, dead fetuses, endless draining of pus and the wretchedness of life seen only in the bowels of a welfare hospital. I learned quickly that my psychic safety depended on the undaunted nurse's smile given to those who are dying before they have even lived. What did I know of psychic space? . . . Yet, perhaps, there is something in the horror of this remembering that has a place in the dismantling of my history as a woman.

If you don't already read published journals, why not follow up one of the writers quoted in this book? The bibliography will give you some ideas, and Chapter Ten focuses on the process of reading journals. The Appendix contains writing exercises related to the themes covered in Part Two. They've all been tested by workshop participants. In addition, there's a wide range of writing books available. Whether or not they focus specifically on journal writing isn't important. The main thing is that they trigger your imagination and get you writing. There are even writing books that focus specifically on childhood memories, on women's relationship with food and our bodies, on coming to terms with crisis and grief. If you enjoy the company of others, you might consider joining a journal workshop (Chapter Eleven). The group writing energy, the discussion, and the sharing will all inspire you.

For Your Eyes Only

What about privacy? What steps will you take to ensure that your diary is for your own eyes only unless you decide otherwise? If you live with others, they may be very curious about your diary, especially if you've never kept one before. You may want to explain to them what you're hoping to accomplish and that in order to achieve it, you need to know that they'll come to you if they find themselves overwhelmed with curiosity about your journal's contents. Alternately, you might consider carrying your diary with you, storing it in a secret place, or investing in a briefcase or wooden box with a lock and key. You could even use a small suitcase, but you'll probably need one with a customized lock.

I've come to believe that there are really only two options here: either you trust those around you to respect your right to privacy or you don't. It's that simple. If you do, all is well. If you don't, you must do whatever it takes to ensure that the confidentiality of your writing is preserved. Ideally, we could all rest assured that what we write in private is sacrosanct to those who know of the journal's existence. But in reality, more often it appears as a tantalizing secret document, promising illicit secrets to those who peek. Sometimes the temptation is strong. Remember: *You and only you* can ensure that no one else reads your journal!

Remember, too, that a diary placed on a coffee table in a shared room sends a very different message than one tucked away in a private drawer. Years ago, my friend and housemate often left her journal on our ironing board. One day, against my better judgment, I opened it. The unflattering description of myself that I found in her most recent entry paid me back in full for my sins, and I couldn't rest easy until I had apologized to her. Without excusing my behavior, after twenty years I now wonder whether the strategic placement of her diary was deliberate. Once you start writing a journal, it becomes your private affair, in every sense. Take care that this is obvious in your actions as well as words by removing temptation from curious eyes.

One workshop participant reported that no matter where she hid her journal, her husband always managed to find and read it, and then would let drop some reference to its contents. This so infuriated her that she in turn began to direct barbed comments at him in her diary as a way of getting even. We all brainstormed and came up with some ideas about how she might handle this situation. But nothing changed. After this issue had come up repeatedly over a period of months, it became clear that, despite her complaints, she had a stake in allowing the pattern to continue. What began as her personal journal had turned into a forum for unspoken resentments, since she knew full well that he was sure to find and read her diary as soon as she left the house. It occurred to me that if a lack of communication was the real issue, they could deal with it in a cleaner, healthier fashion—by keeping a shared "journal" in which both could air grievances and hard-to-articulate resentments without infringing on the other's right to privacy. This would eliminate the element of stolen mutual titillation in their illicit game of hide-and-seek. Once you know in advance that someone will read—against your will—what you write in privacy, you are no longer writing for yourself. I would even question whether what you are writing is truly a diary. How can authentic self-disclosure be possible if you are anticipating someone else's reaction as you write?

What about voluntary sharing? It's your diary, after all; why shouldn't you read from it to whomever you choose? One important factor is your motivation. What is prompting you to share something that you wrote for yourself alone? Are you hoping to create greater intimacy with a friend? Is your intention to affect her or his behavior in some way? Are you hoping to get feedback on your writing? Most important: Are you prepared for their possible reaction? My own intuition says *don't do it*, especially at first. Your psyche needs to know that you are safe to say whatever you want and need to say. This can't happen if you are writing with thoughts of sharing what's in your diary. Before I began working on this book, all I'd ever shared from my journal were dream-work entries with my husband and workshop members. In some instances, I've said almost the same thing in almost the same words to a close friend, but what I wrote in the diary has always been for my eyes only.

Styles, Modes, and Techniques

Style in journal writing is like personal bias in conversation and accent in speech. We all have one, but most of the time we're not aware of it. It's much easier to notice the next person's than our own. If you keep a diary, you have a writing style as surely as you have a thumbprint of your own. Whether you write in fully formed sentences or in short phrases joined by commas and dashes; whether you write in the first person or address yourself as "you" or "she"; whether you proceed by logical progression or through images and associations— these are only a few of the characteristics that determine your particular diary writing style. But unlike your thumbprint, your style will most assuredly change and evolve as you pay attention to it and continue to write. You may want to experiment with other voices, perspectives, and modes of writing. Perhaps you'll find yourself writing with more feeling, as time goes by, or giving more room to your poetic intuitive side.

What about writing techniques? Insightful journal writing is, above all, a matter of asking ourselves the right questions: those that niggle away at us and won't be easily put aside. If we can figure out what those are, we are well on the way. My approach to journal writing focuses on themes, rather than on techniques. But I do want to summarize the main diary writing modes, with the hope that you will try them out, altering and embellishing as you feel inclined.

Whether we speak of techniques or devices, strategies or modes, the possibilities are endless. If you already keep a journal, no doubt you'll find—as I did when I began to read journal books—that you've spontaneously used some of these techniques in your writing all along. All of them are fruitful if you come to your journal with an attitude of honest self-searching, the willingness to look truthfully into your own heart and soul. Without that will toward honesty, the techniques described below become simply abstract exercises.

Free Writing, Flow Writing, Rapid Writing

Free writing (also called flow writing) is what we commonly think of as journal writing. It consists simply of starting with a thought or feeling, an idea or a word, and writing as long as you want, without stopping to reread or correct, order, or analyze. In other words, allow your thoughts to move associatively, organically, without attempting to stick to any particular topic. Interestingly, what emerges is often extremely lucid and beautiful.

Rapid writing consists of a series of several short bursts of free writing that quickly get the creative juices flowing. The topics may be either related in some way or chosen randomly. It doesn't matter. In either case, the psyche creates continuity, almost without fail. This exercise is easily adapted for your own use. Start with one of the topics in the Appendix, and begin writing without stopping to think about what you're going to say. After ten minutes, go on to another topic. Don't stop writing to plan what you want to say next; make the process part of the journal entry. Excerpted here is what one workshop participant, Robin Garber-Kabalkin, wrote during a rapid writing exercise using the words "color," "journey," and "image."

1. Color: In the lines—beyond the lines: who made the lines? Who broke the crayons? waxy smell, tearing paper, breaking rules, color, back to color cornflower blue, my favorite crayon because the crayon was two things—a crayon *and* a flower—early love of complexity— ambivalence about the rules—don't break the crayon, don't tear the paper off, don't, don't . . . seeing, feeling, creating, all one action— pink air, blue skin—anything I want to do, do it as I will—paint on paint, exhibitionist soul dancing across the canvas, leaving tracks, outrageous tracks for all the world to see—to see and feel and know that freedom dwells within. . . .

2. Journey: Cave-Dweller: Winding path, highs and lows, toward discovery of a self long hidden, long despised.
Journey: Cave dweller, come out into the sun, and learn of the world outside, where caring overcomes fear.
C: Hard trail, rocks, landslides, pitfalls at every turn.
J: Cool lakes, lush valleys, food for the mind and soul—travel with me.
C: I am afraid, but I shall try, with halting steps. See, I cringe at every obstacle. . . .
J: Push yourself, the journey is now—if you stop, your world will stop; darkness will descend. . . . What do you see as you travel?
C: Wonders—Self—Strength—Poetry—Acceptance.

3. Image: Desert darkness. The cave dweller struggles through a narrow pass and sees a light ahead. It is the Journey woman, come to guide her through an especially tough patch of life's highway. Yech—go on to something else, Robin, you don't really want to do this.
Dragonfly. Multiplies the image a hundredfold and changes one's perspective, Lightens the mood and permits the creation of many, breaks the rules.

What is interesting here is the organic relatedness of these three entries, their common theme of wanting to break through the barriers of inner fear and external authority in order to experience freedom and spontaneous self-expression. During the third part of that exercise, Edie Scheie wrote the following entry:

> *Images*—horseback riding, playing conga drums, writing. Rhythm. A pounding of a heart—a heart, small, red, throbbing appears in my right hand—valves, too. Cholesterol buildup. The tides of the sea, the ocean, blue, white wash of clouds, a fading bath house, rushes dunes, sand. The pounding of woman on top sex. Need, gratification. Living. Pounding of waves. Flying. In my left hand, coalesces into a key. An ancient metal key. I taste it—taste of cold metal. A white screen door appears, old. Leads to a hot house of flowers. Uncle tells me to come in—I am little and he is expecting me. He wants me to sit in his lap. I get older and taller and tell him to get out, I can come back and deal with him later, but I don't want him here now. Place vanishes.

In a subsequent telephone conversation, Edie and I discussed the content of this piece of writing further. She later sent me a written commentary on what she thought it meant:

> . . . Memories of childhood days by the beach inspired ideas and fears that had been on my mind a long time. The reference to sexual abuse is not a memory; it is a possibility that haunts me. An uncle molested three female relatives when they were young children and teenagers. It is not known if he also molested his daughter and granddaughter. I do not remember being molested, but since I was exposed to this person as a child, it is a possibility. . . . To be alive is to experience not only the joy of living, but also the grief of loss or the inertia of depression. It is also a cycle.

I have used rapid writing exercises with exciting results in many workshops and college writing classes. There's something about being limited to ten minutes on a given topic that stimulates rapid and unselfconscious writing. Students who might chew their pens nervously during a longer writing session often write just as much or more when they know their time is limited. You can easily create your own rapid writing exercise. Sometimes a word or phrase will jump out at you from something you are reading. Language is sensual. Perhaps it's the shape of the word that delights you, its texture, the feel of it through your lips, across your tongue. When a word vibrates with unusual intensity, it's a key to some subconscious association that holds meaning for you. Why not follow it and explore what that meaning might be? Try free writing on "peace," "blue," "roads," "tears," "circles," "windows," "mistake," "light," "enemies." Make up your own list of words that glow, and start writing.

Spiral Writing

Spiral writing is a variation on rapid writing. Start with a ten-minute rapid-write on any topic whatsoever. Then read what you just wrote, and pull out one sentence or even a phrase that stands out. Rewrite it at the top of a new page. That becomes the first sentence in your next round of writing. Repeat this process three or four times, as often as you like. On any given page of your journal, there'll be at least one or two sentences that catch your eye because of their evocativeness, because they contain a striking image or metaphor or seem to leave something unfinished. Begin with that sentence and proceed from there. You can even expand the spiral by continuing this process for a week or more. This mode of writing guarantees organic flow and continuity in your writing, yet always takes you in unexpected directions.

One diarist began by free writing about conscious choices she had made that day. From her first journal entry, she pulled the sentence "We split the bill three ways but now I wish I'd paid Anne's share." Thus began the second entry. Ten minutes later, she again reread what she had just written and chose, as her next lead-in, "Sometimes I get the feeling that people don't really see each other at all." What began as a concrete description of the day's intentional activities led to a more intimate entry, about a friend who had run into hard times, then a reflective piece about the diarist's frustration with humanity at large. Although we went on to a new topic at that point, she felt that she could easily have continued.

The spiral writing exercise can be a useful way to counter the occasional blank feeling you may experience when you sit down to write. If nothing in your day feels "warm," "strong," or "vivid," read back through some old entries until you come across something that strikes you as questionable, unclear, or incomplete. Rewrite it as the first line of this day's entry, and start writing. See what happens. Often, the physical process of moving your hand across the empty page will dispel the blankness and get you moving again. You can also do this on a broader scale, by carrying over an evocative sentence from one journal to the next. Reread a few pages of an old diary, until you come across a passage that leaps off the page. Use that as your point of departure, making sure to include the date of the original entry. Invent your own variations. You may surprise yourself.

Unsent Letters

What about writing a letter in which you can pour your heart out, unchecked, knowing no one will see it? The unsent letter combines the immediacy of direct address with the guarantee of confidentiality, providing an ideal vehicle for clarifying feelings and thoughts. You can write a letter to someone—whether living or dead—for whom you feel admiration and gratitude, someone with whom you are angry or have unfinished business, a person from your past who has recently appeared in a dream, or to an unknown dream figure. Your recipient may not even be a person; it could be your own Shadow, a beloved animal, or the Earth Mother herself. Several years ago, my friend the writer Nancy Linde suffered a recurrence of an affliction that had haunted her years earlier. In her effort to understand its roots and to heal herself, she wrote a letter to her agoraphobia in her journal. Here is a passage from that letter.

Hello old friend, sister, tormentor, mistress:
I've been your slave for too long. I'd like to be your friend instead. I push you away and you own me, I'm your creature . . . a poor wimpish cowardly thing, like the slobbering hunchback servant, Igor, in *Frankenstein*, drooling, "yes Master, can I get you any more living human brains, Master? Can I get you any more human sacrifices, can I lay down and die for you?" I'm so afraid of going mad, being incapacitated, being a fool, being out of control. When people talk about their

fear of going crazy, it triggers my fears and I hyperventilate and get dizzy. I become a dizzy dame.

. . . Will you be my friend? I want to be friends with myself, with all parts of myself, with my death, my weakness, with my potential for illness, with all my feelings, all my potentials, good or bad. My talents, my skills, my strengths, my weaknesses, my potential for failure, my potential for success. . . . You've made my life a lot harder, a lot less fun, a lot lonelier. But maybe, like those who have found their serious illness a path towards enlightenment, you can lead me away from hope and fear into the blessings of the moment. Will you be my friend, my sister?

Writing a letter will clarify your feelings. It may even cause them to shift. It's the process of getting the words down on paper where you can take a look at them that is important. Sometimes, the person with whom you have unfinished business may have died before you could make your peace with each other. For Robin, the topic "Write about the orphaned child within" took the form of a poem and letter to her mother, who had died earlier that year.

December 12, 1991

With blue-green flowered silk
You prepared to go—
Notches matching, darts aligned
Zipper set with near-perfection
You vanished
Without a word
Without a trace
Then there were none.
Lonely child
Cut off like a laddered stocking
At the end of a harlot's day
Watches in silence.

Mama, why did you leave me that day? Didn't you know that I would never recover from the abandonment? You left me all alone in the world with no one to reach out to: fear, worry, doubt and pain kept me company while I tended to your children. I am scarred for all eternity by your action.

In the first part of this entry, the inner orphan is the writer's younger self, spiritually abandoned many years earlier when she was left to tend her younger brothers and sisters while her mother went out on the town. In the second part, it is Robin's adult self, made motherless ten months earlier and full of unresolved anguish and sorrow over her loss.

Several years ago I planned a series of workshops based on material in Judith Duerk's *Circle of Stones: Woman's Journey to Herself*. One evening the writing topic was "How might your life have been different if, as a young woman, you'd had an older woman to sit with in your depression and darkness, one who could accept, witness, and attend to your pain?" Although I don't usually write during the workshop itself, I do all the exercises in advance. What I wrote began as a letter to the Great Mother from the viewpoint of my much younger self, who had longed desperately for such a place of acceptance. Here are some excerpts.

> Where are you, great Listening One, Loving Ear at the Heart of Creation? I long for your embrace, your loving, all-encompassing gaze, your unconditional love.
>
> I find myself despicable—loathesome—can't find a place inside myself to reside in, to "take up residence" and be at home in. I don't see myself reflected anywhere with love.
>
> Let me weep into your lap and howl out my pain. Let me be heard and not alone. Touch me with tenderness and show me myself. Let me be real and not just a shadow.
>
> Tell me you know and that I can survive and come out whole and not the sum total of a thousand pinpoints of pain. Soothe me, heal me, bless me.
>
> But, above all—listen to me. Let me pour out my heart's loneliness and anguish. Let me not carry it all alone. It's too heavy and too awful.
>
> If I had known there was someone there, it would have taken the dread and terror out of the depression and darkness.
>
> "Hello darkness, my old friend. . . ." Depression, hello, I know you. I've seen this country before. You're not so awful, at times. You come, you stay, and you always leave. Only—what's the old joke?—"Come again when you can't stay so long!" Just the three of us: Darkness, my mother-friend, and me.

I'm not a freak and it's all alright. I'm not alone and it can't be so bad because someone is willing to sit here with me and witness it.

Does that mean I have to take it—myself—seriously? How can I hate myself when all I see on Her radiant face is love—just that. Solid, unquestioning, implacable bedrock love.

It would have made a difference.

Because letter writing is so conducive to intimacy, some diarists write their entire journals as series of letters to a real or imaginary friend who serves as an empathic witness to their lives. Perhaps the most famous is Anne Frank. On June 20, 1942, less than three weeks before the Frank family entered the "Secret Annexe" where they were to spend two years hiding from the Nazis, Anne wrote, "In order to enhance in my mind's eye the picture of the friend for whom I have waited so long, I don't want to set down a series of bald facts in a diary like most people do, but I want this diary itself to be my friend, and I shall call my friend Kitty." Fanny Burney (1752–1840), as a girl of sixteen, addressed her diary to "A Certain Miss Nobody" because she was convinced that "to Nobody can I be wholly unreserved." George Sand (1804–1876) wrote to "the very learned and highly skilled Dr. Piffoël," an imaginary male figure who represented her own masculine side.

To whom do you have something to say? What unexpressed words of love and admiration well up within you? What unresolved conflicts haunt your daydreams? What letters do you want to write in the safety of your diary?

Invented Dialogues

Do you find yourself having imaginary conversations in your head where you wonder what the other person might say? Perhaps you even take both sides in the discussion, arguing back and forth with yourself. Why not try to capture these voices on paper? Invented dialogues go one step beyond unsent letters, requiring an act of empathic identification with two often opposing points of view. Like the unsent letter, the dialogue may involve someone else, whether living or dead, some part of yourself (a habit, physical characteristic, or subpersonality), an object, a dream, an emotion or mood, anything at all. This mode of writing likely originates in the Gestalt "empty chair" exercise. Here the person literally speaks first from one chair, then moves to the other one and responds from a different perspective. The aim of this exercise in Gestalt therapy is to bring about a deeper understanding of two needs, impulses, or inner voices at cross-purposes with each other, with the hope of integrating them. The same thing can be achieved through a written dialogue. Here is one diarist's invented dialogue between her masculine and feminine sides.

Masculine: Why don't you push harder in your life? Go out into the world and sell yourself—write, publish, do what you have to do to get ahead in the world. It isn't going to just come to you, you know!

Feminine: I don't want to be single-minded, goal-oriented, or any of those male things that we are supposed to be. I don't work in a line— I work in a spiral. So maybe it takes me longer but I need to dwell in and among things. I don't just move from here to there without breathing in awareness of where I am and how it feels to be there. And —I don't want to have a heart attack at fifty!

M: You are overdramatizing things. As usual. You just want to smell the flowers and stop to chat along the way. There's more to life than that! If that is all anyone ever did, nothing would ever get done. It's fine and dandy to "pour the tea slowly," but someone has to be out in the world doing things, running the country, manning the stations!

F: Yes Yes Yes—I know. My god, what would happen if the stations went un-manned! Disaster? Catastrophe? Collapse? Actually—it sounds like an interesting experiment. What would happen? Then again, maybe you do have a point about not only stopping to smell the flowers. But —if that was really all I ever did, I would never have made it as far as I have in my life. Of course I know you don't think it's far enough. I know I can't "sell myself" well. . . .

Sometimes writing the dialogue brings about a degree of reconciliation between the two sides. At other times its value lies simply in clarifying the conflict by giving each side a voice. Lila, another work-shop participant, wrote a dialogue between two possible lifestyles: the preconceived pattern passed on to her through her upbringing, and the more authentic life that she was struggling to realize. What follows is an excerpt from that entry.

> *Pattern:* I could give you such security, such stability—such a good life. I could guarantee you a happy old age, a pension plan, and all of those wise and foresightful things. All you have to do is play your part; stop fighting me, let me take care of things—and you will be safe.

> *Authentic life:* I'll be safe alright—safe and "dead." Braindead. Heart-dead. My route is much more difficult. I'm not always even sure of where I'm going and everything seems uncertain, scary. There are no guarantees. I really could end up a bag lady: no pension plan, no children to take care of me, and a stranger in a foreign land.

> *Pattern:* I could give you prestige, recognition, and financial security. There's a lot to be said for these and you know it!

> *Authentic life:* I need air, space, independence, breathing room. Of course, I want to have it all. Who wouldn't? But I've had to test every step out alone and build the path, then traverse it on my own. It has taken time, energy, pain, sorrow, regret and, perhaps, wasted efforts. But here I am—in my life!

While writing this dialogue, Lila realized that more work remained to be done on this issue and resolved to continue the dialogue over time to see where it would lead her.

Altered Perspective

We can all use a break, at times, from ourselves. Writing from an altered perspective provides some psychic distance from our usual point of view. This can take the form of writing in the second or third person (as "you" or "she"), projecting ourselves into a different time and space, or speaking with the voice of someone or something else.

The results can be enlightening, poignant, humorous. The voice that speaks from this altered perspective may come as a great surprise. For one workshop, I prepared an exercise in which we explored the question "If your tears could speak to you, what would they say?" As usual, I did the exercise before the workshop, and this is what I wrote:

October 9, 1991. I am the water of life that softens your edges and eases your pain. I let you know when there is too much or too little—of stress, pain, anxiety, grief, loveliness, love, nourishment, stimulation, boredom. I show you your dissatisfaction with your life, and the potential for change; the possibility of something else. I wash away the encrusted attitudes, beliefs and assumptions, and bathe you softly in hope and optimism. I lubricate your life and make you human, soft, permeable. Sometimes, I am your longing—for more love, joy, nurturing. Sometimes I'm your immeasurable relief that, after all, there is someone there to comfort you when you fall and get up bruised; when you bear the brunt of some unforeseen cruelty. (I cried, and someone came. How many times did I cry, as a child, and no one came?) I am your unfathomable oceanic sadness that you cannot heal your mother's wounds nor make up for her losses. You cannot give her back her mother—nor can you *be* her mother, although you've surely tried.

Here, too, is an excerpt from a long journal entry written by Rita Miller, a workshop member, after a painful breakup with her lover. Rita began the entry in the second person but switched to third in the next paragraph, writing it as a narrative that happened to someone else.

There comes a time when you've just got to decide you can't take it anymore. You know it's that time when you're left feeling empty, numb, the tears won't come. You're dried up. You're emotionally dead. Why do you let him do this to you? No! It's "why do you do this to *yourself?*" No one can make you do anything. You've chosen to allow yourself to be used, abused, and neglected.

She kept typing, dreamily, the light, hollow rap-tapping of the keyboard acting as a cathartic salve for the painful din she'd been harboring in her being.

What follows this excerpt from Rita's diary is a narrative describing the couple's last painful time together. The entry closes with "She left. Drove home in a fugue state. Got into her cold little bed for one." The second and third person points of view afforded Rita just enough distance to get down on paper what would otherwise have been too painful to describe.

On a lighter note, during a workshop exercise that involved writing a lie about oneself, Sheila Byrd Smith invented her ancestral origins and her arrival on Staten Island. "I am not an American," she wrote. "I am a direct descendent of Nairothina, the noblest of African queens. . . . When I was four months old, there was a plot to exterminate all female children of the village so that the Scurajete tribe would die out. My mother, being light-years ahead of all civilizations, came up with the idea of transporting me to the United States. . . ."

Another variation of altered perspective involves writing with metaphor. Write down "My life is . . ." and "My life is like . . ." and go from there. Another possibility: What kind of fruit are you? What kind of vegetable, flower, bird, animal? From my journal:

I'm an apple—golden delicious, full of juice and flavour, crisp and tart. I'm a butternut squash, golden in flavour and shape, glowing with colour. I'm a rosebush, prickly and poignant and glowingly crimson. I'm a dandelion growing off the beaten path—no one's idea of a rose or a gift worth giving. I'm a chicken, content to hatch my brood in privacy, hoping for a long, range-fed life before I go to hen heaven. I'm a singing warbler—my throat shivers with ecstasy when I sing, the pure delicious joy of it. I am a butterfly—alighting on one branch, then fluttering off to another. My wings are brilliant turquoise, black, and gold. I am a monkey, peering through ancient and curious eyes. I am a tomato—solid, ripe, fleshy and succulent, heading juicily into the best Greek salad on earth!

Lists and Outlines

When Luise Rinser ran out of paper toward the end of her months in prison, she wrote down a list of key words, with the intention of fleshing them out into journal entries at a later date. But when the war was over and she set about preparing the journal for publication, she decided not to change anything after all; those skeletal entries conveyed the stark truth of her prison life.

We tend to think of lists and outlines as purely practical measures and forget that they are also a form of writing. In fact, writing a list or an outline can be an effective way of brainstorming, of getting to the bare bones of a situation, of capturing a lot of information in a small amount of time and space. Take, for example, the following "likes" and "hates" Antonia White recorded in her diary in a stock-taking exercise she did on December 30, 1935.

Likes
Clean clothes . . . Being out of debt . . . Sitting at café tables . . . Starting a relationship . . . Sound of crockery when someone is getting tea for me . . . Summer and summer clothes . . .

Hates
Feeling fat . . . Dirt: especially in my clothes . . . Colds and draughts . . . The hours between lunch and tea . . . Meeting people in the street unexpectedly . . . People who automatically ask first "How are the children?"

In one recent workshop exercise, I asked everyone to create three lists, with the headings "I am," "I am not," "I would like to be." Here are excerpts from one diarist's journal entry.

I am . . .   heavy and solid as the earth
                          pulled down by gravity and flying high with ideas
                          a singer of songs and an unsung melody
                          a poem about to write itself
                          filled with intuition and suspicion
                          an outspoken woman and a headstrong woman . . .
I am not . . .   willing to be silent any longer when things are wrong
                          confident that my perspective is always truthful or
                              accurate
                          always thrilled with the sound of my own voice
                          the only woman who thinks it's time for a woman
                              President

sure the human race will be around forever
as expressive, productive, tolerant, flexible as I'd
    like . . .
I would like to be . . . completely at peace in and with myself
more energetic, motivated, and industrious
less concerned about other people's opinions of me
twenty-three again, for a week
thirty-three again, for a month
traveling around the world with a friend
a mother, and a wise and tenderhearted crone,
    someday

Although these lists are sketchy, they provide an outline and a frame-work for a longer entry. Had Denise written in complete sentences and paragraphs, she would never have captured so much detail in twenty minutes of writing. Dorothy V. Claire, in her journal, wrote,

> I am thistle, pink, salmon with a hint of lavender, textured like velour, sensual and subtle, part of the sky, flowers, skin. I am basic nude life itself in the shining sun joyous, celebratory. My five top values. Being closer to nature, creative problem-solving, honest caring relationships, freedom and responsibility for myself, a healthy, sensuous body.

Short and succinct as this list of attributes and values may be, it gives us a powerful glimpse of the writer's personality. Why not make some lists of your own?

Guided Visualizations

In the guided visualization or meditation, one person reads or speaks an exercise intended to induce a state of profound relaxation, bypass the inner critic, and tap into the rich imagery of the unconscious (many are available on cassette and in printed form). Because they evoke images rather than words, guided visualizations call on the creative-intuitive right-brain functions rather than those of the rational left brain. The results can be powerful, especially for those of us inclined to be overly cerebral and analytic. In addition to a wide range of emotions, some people experience strong bodily sensations, vivid scenes, smells, and sounds. The imagery evoked when you are in a deeply relaxed and meditative state will surprise you with its suggestiveness and beauty.

The guided visualization may be as simple as imagining yourself in a different setting, or it might involve a quest or a journey in which you may encounter the following elements: a choice of paths, an obstacle, a lesson or truth, a teacher or guide, and an insight or gift to "bring back." It calls for a receptive frame of mind; the destination, at the outset, is always unknown. Workshop participants often find this exercise both liberating and exciting, because it can evoke all kinds of unique and unexpected imagery. I often introduce a guided visualization at the end of a day-long workshop, when the rational mind has depleted its resources and needs replenishment from the underground springs.

Allowing your imagination to take you on a journey from which you return in some way transformed, or to conjure a vision of your "ideal" life or career, can provide a powerful impetus to make small but concrete changes in your life now. One exercise, a favorite among workshop members, asks you to project yourself into the future— one, two, five years from today—and imagine what your life has become in the interim. Whether I use a printed meditation or create my own, I try to engage all of the senses in the course of the exercise, knowing that individuals have differing levels of sensitivity to visual imagery, sound, hearing, smell, and so on.

The Appendix includes a guided visualization that I have used frequently in workshops. You can read it or, better yet, record yourself reading it or have someone else read out loud to you as you relax, then write afterward. There are many books and tapes available now with beautiful meditations that will evoke rich material for your writing. Here follow excerpts from a journal entry that Ellen Schwimer wrote after an imagined meeting with her future self.

Green trees, shade, a brown path, a slight incline, sunlight causing speckled shadows on the undergrowth. Cool clear fragrant air of the woods, moist, sweet, clean and pungent too. A slight breeze, the light touch of moisture in the air, a bit of warmth when I walk through a patch of sunlight. I see someone ahead of me on the path. The person I want to be. My future self. Who is she? Kind and wise. . . . What she gives, she gives freely and does not feel depleted. She feels content with herself. She feels secure in her self knowledge. I become one with her. I sense her inner calmness. I am alone, but not lonely. The solitude is a delight. . . .

This future self can look back at who I am today and see the things that I am learning through my present struggles. This future self can see the insights I am gaining and can assess their value in her life. They are what has made her the being she is right now. A being forged by fire. Finely honed sense and insight born of my pain today. She is glad now to have gone through that pain for it has tempered her wisdom. She knows what is truly important because of my suffering. She has chosen to be who she is through this process. My pain has purged all conceit and falsehood from her life. She is a pure being whose integrity is unquestionable. . . . Knowing who I will be gives me the strength to bear up under what life and circumstances are imposing on me in the present.

During another guided visualization, Hyla Kuhlman found a scroll that contained a message for her. As she approached it anxiously, she discovered, "I was being welcomed. It said, 'You are lovable.' " The insight Hyla received at the end of her journey was "Be yourself and stop along the way to observe silently and enjoy."

Visual Journal Keeping

Your journal need not consist of words only. Many diarists draw, sketch, and doodle in their diaries. And I'm not talking only about the artists among us. Perhaps what you experience in the course of the guided visualization is more readily sketched than portrayed in words (one workshop participant drew a gift she'd received during a journey meditation: a stone water fountain with two beautiful carved birds at the top). Gabriele Rico, the author of several writing books, advocates the use of "Word Sculptures," which consist of "a rapid, kinesthetic movement of your hand" across the empty page that produces a visual image expressing your overall felt sense at that moment.

After your hand creates the initial outline on the page, you can fill it in with colors, words, and phrases. The way you embellish the original outline may reflect your sense of being "brimming with emotion," "tied up in knots," or "full of joy." Through the shape and colors you bring to its design, the word sculpture becomes a visual metaphor of your inner psychic state at that moment.

But that's only one approach to visual journal keeping. There are others. Hannah Hinchman's "illuminated journal," for example, contains pencil sketches and watercolors of vegetation, animals, and people, as well as calligraphy practice and different kinds of lettering. *A Life in Hand*, her book on drawing and writing about the world around us, is one of my favorites. George Simons, author of *Keeping Your Personal Journal*, describes an exercise he calls "Soul Country," in which you draw a map of your inner world, then embellish it with images and colors. You may experience yourself as a continent or an island, a mountain or lake. I have often used this in workshops, always with interesting results. Another visual experiment that workshop members have liked is Solly and Lloyd's mandala exercise, where a circle is divided into four quadrants, which can be filled in with designs, patterns, or meaningful reference points for your life. The mandala is an ancient symbol of wholeness, consisting of the combination of a circle and square. Often we enhance the visual content of our diaries without even thinking about it. For example, my journals of the past few years, written in multicolored ink, provide a different rereading experience than do the earlier ones, written all in blue. And when a dream image begs to be set down on paper, I try to oblige, usually with a written commentary just below it.

In the course of a day-long workshop, I usually include one exercise with a visual component. Recently, I described an exercise in which we would express our inner worlds on paper in some way other than words. As always, there were some nervous protests, such as "I can't draw to save my life!" "That doesn't matter," I said. "I can't either. Try it anyway. You don't have to show us what you do." Half an hour later, with everyone quietly engrossed in their work, I asked how it was going. To their amazement, almost everyone in the workshop was delighted with what they had put on paper, and wanted to share it with the group. Artistic ability is not the issue. The imaginative interplay of shape and color, texture and form is forever proceeding all around us and within us. We just have to tune in and let it move through our arms and hands.

The modes of journal writing described in this chapter will give you some ideas for getting started. Experiment, and see what each has to offer, which ones most enhance your own writing. Trust your intuition, follow your own creative impulses as you write, and you'll invent others along the way. The journal writing journey is one of personal fulfillment and creative satisfaction. Enjoy it, immerse yourself in it, and anytime you aren't in the mood, don't write! You'll come back to writing when you are ready.

PART TWO

The Inner Journey

4

⟨ ⟩

Writing Below the Surface

To awaken, to open up like a flower to the light of a fuller consciousness! I want to see and feel and expand, little book, you holder of my secrets.

EMILY CARR, Hundreds and Thousands: The Journals of an Artist

I had felt my life to be a dull dead-level mediocrity, with the sense of real and vital things going on round the corner, out in the streets, in other people's lives. For I had taken the surface ripples for all there was, when actually happenings of vital importance to me had been going on, not somewhere away from me, but just underneath the calm surface of my own mind.

MARION MILNER, A Life of One's Own

To write is to descend, to excavate, to go underground.

ANAÏS NIN, The Diary of Anaïs Nin, Volume Five, 1947–1955

Journal writing can be many different things in your life. Your journal may become your closest confidante and a safe place to vent your emotions and feelings. Writing a diary can be a cathartic process that leaves you feeling lighter and freer. It can also be an ongoing channel of creative expression or a form of meditation whereby you explore your relationship to the mystery of life. Over time, your diary may even become a memory album that preserves written images of your past selves. All of these facets of journal writing have something essential in common. In each, keeping a diary becomes a process of expanding awareness of yourself and your purposes in life. As you explore feelings and thoughts, intuitions and sensations in your journal, you increase the breadth and depth of what you know about yourself. We can see this above, in the journals of Emily Carr, Marion Milner, and Anaïs Nin.

Self-awareness has many dimensions. It involves being in touch with our emotions and feelings, positive and negative alike. It means understanding our own thinking process, trusting hunches and intuitions, even when they run counter to the prevailing "malestream" logic. It includes being able to tune into our bodily sensations, so often at odds with what our minds tell us. It means acknowledging our own vulnerability while refusing to close ourselves off to the risk of heartache. It involves recognizing the influence of the past upon our present life without being trapped by it, transforming it instead in such a way that it enriches the present. It means being able to distinguish the roles we play from our authentic being.

On a deeper level, self-awareness involves coming to understand the conscious hopes and the subconscious needs that propel our lives and the lives of those we love, and allowing this understanding to fill us with compassion toward ourselves and others. It means regarding dreams as benevolent carriers of important psychic material from the unconscious. It means recognizing the presence of critical internal voices that undermine faith in our own value and hinder spontaneous self-expression. It entails realizing that where we have outlawed certain feelings or sensations, there's something in our lives that we are not willing to face. Not least, self-awareness involves acknowledging that we all have blind spots. Try as we might, we cannot see ourselves clearly.

Etty Hillesum knew this with absolute clarity. "We carry everything within us," she said, "God and Heaven and Hell and Earth and Life and Death and all of history. The externals are simply so many props. . . . We must know what motives inspire our struggle and we must begin with ourselves, every day anew." It is this insight that enabled Etty to say on New Year's Eve, 1941, even after the Nazis had begun to harass and persecute the Jewish population in Holland,

[This is] the last evening of a year that has been my richest and most fruitful and yes, the happiest of all. And if I had to put in a nutshell what this year has meant . . . I would say: greater awareness and hence easier access to my inner sources. . . . I listen in to myself, allow myself to be led, not by anything on the outside, but by what wells up from within.

For women today, the quest for self-awareness has special urgency. Many voices, both inner and outer, are only too eager to tell us what we ought to be and do and feel. Engulfed by what others need and want from us, we are often unfamiliar with the landscape of our own desires. Torn between the conflicting demands of our personal and professional lives, we are the ones who stay home with a sick child, cancel a social engagement to take care of an aging parent-in-law, lay our work aside to prepare Thanksgiving dinner. Throughout time, we have been all things to all people.

But it doesn't take a visionary to see that, for both women and men, things are changing. Many of us, both women and men, are discovering that, in order to be whole, we need to embody the full spectrum of qualities within all of us: both hard *and* soft, strong *and* vulnerable, rational *and* emotional. When Jung spoke of the fully individuated person, he was referring to one in whom all of these capacities have found acceptance and integration. But what does it mean to be both active and passive? To be led by both reason and emotion? To experience ourselves as strong and vulnerable at the same time? Enter here the journal writing process.

As we imagine our lives beyond stereotyped feminine and masculine roles, journal writing becomes a process of exploring and discarding the old assumptions and habits of ritualized femininity, and creating ourselves—as women—anew. Not in the sense of tabula rasa, of course, since we can't simply undo the past. But I think we can transcend it, move beyond it in a new turn of the evolutionary spiral. In contrast to the archetypal male voyage that thrusts into outer space, what will launch us all, women and men alike, on the crucial journey to self-awareness is a change of direction. This is a journey *inward*. And what we encounter along the way is not an unknown life form or even an "evil empire," but rather the full range and extent of our own humanness, of the feminine and masculine qualities within each of us. When the goal of the journey—the coming to selfhood—has been achieved, these qualities will no longer be at war within us. Instead, their integration will make us whole.

Journey to Inner Space

Journal writing is a way of paying attention to our lives. When all the external demands and stresses of life are pulling us out and away from our inner realms, it brings us back to ourselves. It helps us remember ourselves. Writing in your journal, no matter how briefly, allows you to catch your psychic breath in the course of a busy day. It provides a moment to tune into your felt sense of how the day is going and to replenish inner resources, even if you have time to write only a few lines describing your feelings about the next task at hand.

Years ago, I found myself stuck in an unchallenging summer job in order to pay my university tuition for the following semester. To cope with the boredom, I often retreated into my journal during noisy coffee breaks filled with cigarette smoke and loud chatter about who had been out to which disco the night before. Fifteen minutes of writing allowed me to air my frustration and replenish my psychic resources, and this would tide me over until lunch, when I had an hour to walk or read a book, or until the workday's end. The presence of a small bound journal tucked into your coat pocket, briefcase, or backpack reminds you that beneath the hectic activities of the day, there is a quiet well within you, filled with the riches of your inner life. Then you can jot down an idea that occurs to you during a busy moment, an endless meeting, or in transit. How many times have you made a mental note about an inspiration that came to you on the run, only to discover it was completely gone when you finally had time to return to it? All it takes is a line or two, a penciled sketch, or even a key word or phrase to trigger your memory and imagination at a later date.

The very notion of turning inward in order to replenish our psychic resources is at odds with our usual way of functioning. We assume that we know what we think and feel at any given moment,

or if we don't, that it isn't important or can wait. Imagine a society
where everyone regularly pauses to become aware of his or her feelings, a political leader who allows herself to be guided by the wisdom
of her dreams. Imagine corporate executives who begin board meet-
ings with a moment of meditation, in order to stay mindful of global
concerns more urgent than short-term financial gains. It sounds radical, doesn't it? It might just be transformative!

To be sure, everyone has some measure of self-awareness. Without
it, we wouldn't recognize our own emotions, wouldn't know when
our feelings have been hurt or what our minds and bodies experience
in new situations. But self-awareness exists on a continuum. Describing my feelings of anger toward a close friend who has hurt my
feelings will surely be cathartic. But what if—once the heat of emotion has passed—I could see beyond my present hurt feelings to the
unhealed wounds and unresolved issues from childhood that are still
with me? What if I could focus on my felt sense of that emotion and
contact its bodily sources? That kind of self-awareness would cast light
on more than just my immediate emotional crisis. It would provide
me with an insight into my psychic process itself.

There is no better way to reach this deeper level of self-awareness
than to keep a journal. Often, simply describing the experience will
bring some clarity and a different perspective on the situation. Once
you begin writing, you will likely feel the emotional tug and pull of
related experiences, and this is where things get really interesting.
Here is one example of how journal writing deepened my understanding of a situation that had been troubling me. Some years ago,
several weeks into the semester, I was not happy with the way the
College Writing class I was teaching was going. There was little discussion and considerable extraneous chatter in the back row. Even
though I'd discussed the situation with my colleague Margery, I was
still troubled, and found myself walking into class with a vague sense
of dread. I had an inkling that something deeper was at stake here and
finally decided to take time one morning to explore it in my journal.
This is what I wrote.

Part of the problem is my need to be liked. Way down deep I'm not
entirely convinced that I am worthy or lovable. I seem to need that

kind of affirmation from outside sources. So I tend to be unduly influenced by external feedback and input. When a class is unruly or disrespectful, for example, I immediately assume it reflects on me in some way. "What am I doing 'wrong'?" And if, when I take a firmer stance, things don't greatly improve, I criticize myself even further. "Was that the wrong approach? Did I make a fool of myself? Does the class think I'm an ogre now? Do they 'hate' me?"

What I want is to feel confident and grounded in my role in the classroom. I want to state quietly and with complete conviction what is and is not acceptable behavior, and leave aside the whole issue of whether a particular student "likes me" or not. I need to get clear my own expectations and boundaries in the classroom. At some bedrock level, I must still have a distorted perception of myself: I'm either perfect or dreadful; wonderful or hopeless; the most gifted and inspiring teacher around, or an utter failure.

Clearly, my discomfort in that classroom had more to do with my own projections and unfinished business from childhood than with the behavior of the students in that class. It seemed my body recognized that this was something I wanted to address because, as I wrote, the feeling of muddy dread turned into one of anticipation. I felt a powerful surge of adrenaline, just short of giving me a headache. That afternoon I walked into the classroom without the usual uneasiness and told the students calmly and in no uncertain terms exactly what I expected from them. As I spoke, there was silence; everyone was listening. That never became one of my favorite classes, but a different dynamic was introduced with that talk.

Marion Milner, a British writer and psychoanalyst who used the pseudonym Joanna Field, wrote a fascinating book about her attempt to understand her inner workings, titled *A Life of One's Own*. In her early thirties, having attained everything she had thought she wanted, Milner found that happiness eluded her, seemed always just beyond her grasp. She began to keep a diary in which she recorded the best parts of each day, with the hope that examining her happy moments would increase them. Abandoning the idea that books or experts could give her what she was seeking—a vivid and embodied experience of her own life—she observed and explored her own reactions, and wrote in her journal.

Six weeks later she sat down to add up the "facts" of her life as they had revealed themselves in her diary. To her amazement, she discovered that happiness was not a matter of winning praise from others or of attaining worthy goals, as she'd always assumed. Neither did keeping the journal provide her with a clear direction for the future, as she had hoped. What had evolved instead was a whole new way of looking at her life. "Writing down my experiences," she wrote, "seemed to be a creative act which continually lit up new possibilities in what I had seen. . . . I felt an urge to go on and on writing, with my interest gradually shifting from what to do with my life to how to look at it." The longer she wrote, the more essential her diary became to her quest for self-awareness. "It was as if I were trying to catch something and the written word provided a net," she reflected. Astonished by these insights, Milner continued writing for seven years. And, through observing her own mind at work over time, she found it was the quality of her awareness rather than the content of her experience that brought contentment and happiness. Her diary played the crucial role in her quest for self-understanding.

For the writer Burghild Nina Holzer, this kind of self-awareness is essential in any kind of creative endeavor. She claims, "The reason so many people block themselves from writing, from creating, is that they are not here. They have a head full of blueprints for the goal, they have elaborate outlines of how to get there, but they have never taken a conscious walk from their bedroom to their bathroom." And here is the New Zealand writer Sylvia Ashton-Warner, reminding herself to stay conscious of the present moment: " 'Now' is the real time," she wrote. "Don't let the past and the unknown future clutter the simple 'now.' Live true and deep, O my Self, fast and hard, the effervescent life that is 'now.' Crowd out the curse of fear, the remorse looking back, the concern looking forward."

Keeping a diary is the gentlest and most accessible means of increasing self-awareness that I know of. At any given time, we explore only as deeply as we want and discover only what we are ready to see. No expertise is required, there are no minimum time requirements, and, in contrast to diet or exercise, we don't lose the benefits if we miss a week or even a month. The only guidelines are those that we create ourselves. This is your journey. You chart its course!

Becoming Self-Centered

In December of 1941, Etty Hillesum wrote in her journal, "If only I listened to my own rhythm, and tried to live in accordance with it. Much of what I do is mere imitation, springs from a sense of duty or from preconceived notions of how people should behave. The only certainties about what is right and wrong are those which spring from sources deep inside oneself." So often, we live "outside ourselves." In many different ways, we are under duress to do and say what others find acceptable. After a time, our passionate childhood certainty about what we feel and want is dulled. Instead, we know what we should feel and want. Eventually we can no longer tell the difference.

A friend with a wicked sense of humor once sent me a postcard depicting a chain of paper dolls below a caption that reads, "In order to discover who you are, first learn who everybody else is—and you're what's left." I love this postcard, because just beneath its obvious ridiculousness lurks a hint of something familiar. As women, we are indeed frequently more attuned to other people's feelings and needs than to our own. Somewhere along the line—as a result both of how we are socialized and our genuine desire to be sensitive and nurturing—we have developed what Gloria Steinem calls "empathy sickness." We know other people's feelings better than our own. We are like ships adrift on turbulent waters, tossed about with no firm anchor or direction. We lack grounding in our own being.

When did self-centeredness take on the negative connotations it has today? How has it come to be synonymous with narcissistic self-preoccupation? Where else is there for you, or me, or anyone else to be centered, after all, other than in ourselves? In her book *Composing a Life*, Mary Catherine Bateson says, "If women were brought up to be more centered on themselves, many of the conflicts and discontinuities that disrupt their lives would be irrelevant, peripheral to the central definition of self." What would it be like to be truly *centered in ourselves*? To begin with, we would make our own needs and desires as important as those of the people we love most, and give ourselves the same care, respect, and nurturance. Ironically, I think that this would make us *more* able to see others as they really are rather than as we need them to be. Perhaps we'd come to see our interactions with others as symphonies of shared understanding rather than as solo performances competing for center stage.

Journal writing allows us to ground ourselves in our own experience. Instead of my focusing on other people's perceptions of me, the journal encourages me to ask, "Where am I in my life, right now? What am I feeling in this moment?" In our diaries, we experience self-centeredness from the inside out. The following journal excerpts show the attempt of one workshop member, Jarda Bailey, to find such a place of groundedness within herself after a traumatic marriage breakup.

September 8, 1992. Since I started to keep a journal last year, I asked these same questions. A year has gone by and I still have not found any answers. In fact, I don't think I have even found all of the questions yet! I have an emptiness inside and I'm trying to fill it up. . . .

November 5, 1992. I need to ground myself and learn to take care of me. I like the idea of having my tea in bed and writing in my journal instead of rushing around trying to get everything done at once. I like spending this special time with myself. . . .

February 21, 1993. . . . Deep within I know what my needs are, but I've been suppressing them as insignificant and answering to outside criteria. I was looking for someone else to fix all my needs and wants. That can't be, because only I know what needs must be met within myself. . . .

February 25, 1993. I am like a chameleon! Always trying to be what is needed of me. . . .

September 30, 1993. For the first time in my life I have found someone who will take care and protect me—ME. For so long I thought other people should do it for me. Now I know it's only me for me. I think I am really beginning to feel a difference in me. I am beginning to feel a sense of safety with myself. . . .

November 4, 1993. . . . My writing helps to define me. I strive to find a sense of balance in my life. . . . I draw sustenance from within my soul. It's the place that supports my dreams.

What began as a sense of emptiness and self-absence evolved over those fifteen months into Jarda's steady assurance that she could recognize and take care of her own needs. Many of her questions continue, but she has discovered a place inside from which to nurture herself as she waits for the answers to unfold. No longer seeking approval from others, she is finding a way to give it to herself.

Keeping a journal is an effective way of overcoming "empathy sickness" and bringing you back to your own experience. This is your life—to explore and to question, to celebrate and to grieve, to expand and to experience. Become self-centered!

Suspending Self-Criticism

If you hope to gain greater self-awareness through keeping a journal, you will have to suspend judgment about what constitutes acceptable qualities, behavior, and writing. Like Marion Milner, you must see yourself and your writing as fully as possible. This means your flaws, weaknesses, and unfair prejudices as well as the qualities that you value and cherish in yourself, such as your generosity, humor, and creativity. The only way that I have found to write honestly about my life is to put aside self-criticism and to regard myself as intrinsically interesting and worthy of close attention. I don't always manage to do this, of course. Sometimes my journal shows my derisive and unforgiving inner critic in full gear, making me feel my feeble efforts at self-understanding are not worth the paper I am writing on. From repeated experience, I know that once the dynamic of alternating self-criticism and self-defense takes over, I might as well close my journal and do something else. At times, however, when I do manage to come to my journal with a kind spirit toward myself and the world, I know simply that my life is filled with richness and value. The most beneficial attitude to bring to your journal writing is one of interest and hopeful expectancy, as you would bring to a friend who has just returned from a long journey, or to a speaker whom you have long wanted to hear. Your life is a drama unlike anyone else's, and it increases in fascination the more you attend to and care for it.

This means accepting whatever comes. Journal writing is not a matter of submitting yourself to an internal critic. This sort of critic —mine is male—will never be satisfied, because you are only human and he thinks he is God! Send him or her on a long vacation, and let the only measure of what you write be its truthfulness and authenticity. Your diary is the one place in your life where all of the inner voices that clamor for attention can speak and be heard. Most of them have been suppressed for so long that they won't speak out at all if they anticipate harsh criticism. Be gentle with them.

Your writing, too, deserves unconditional acceptance. In his fascinating book *Free Play: Improvisation in Life and Art*, Stephen Nachmanovitch describes two inner figures that coexist in all of us: the muse and the editor. The muse, he tells us, is the living voice of intuition, while the editor "criticizes, shapes, and organizes the raw material that the free play of the muse has generated." The muse, or source of creative inspiration, can take many shapes: the female muse of Greek mythology (her roots in the Earth Mother) or the male muse of Blake's poetry; a spontaneous discussion with a friend; or our own inner child, "the self who still knows how to play." But if the editor kicks in prematurely, "the muse gets edited right out of existence" and we experience writer's block. "The judging Spectre," or the negative face of the editor, is the internalized voice of all the sources of external authority in our lives since childhood, beginning with our parents. Sometimes it can be downright vicious.

It is the muse that speaks in journal writing. Many times, after a woman has shared or read something aloud in the course of a workshop, another woman will shake her head and say, "What I wrote isn't anything like that. I think I did that exercise all wrong." And yet, as in spontaneous musical improvisation, it's precisely the variations on a theme that manifest the presence of the muse. If I could give you just one piece of advice for your writing journey, it would be simply this: Suspend judgment about what is good and bad, right and wrong. Welcome whatever comes to you as if you were having this thought, emotion, or idea for the first time. Give your muse some breathing room. Open yourself to the fascinating drama of your own existence. No one else can write your story. You are an original!

Remembering: The Presence of the Past

One of Marion Milner's crucial discoveries was that immediately below the surface of her thought world lay a rich substratum of memory. Writing in her diary, she found,

> . . . only the first sentence or two were concerned with the present and then I had plunged into memories of fifteen or twenty years ago, memories of things I had not consciously thought of for all those years, memories that I never knew I had remembered. . . . It seemed that I was normally only aware of the ripples on the surface of my mind, but the act of writing a thought was a plunge which at once took me into a different element where the past was intensely alive.

We draw on memory as we write. The more we write, the more we remember. And the more we re-member and integrate forgotten and abandoned bits of ourselves into our present lives, the greater our self-awareness, and the more whole we become.

The past is inscribed upon our bodies. If we want to be whole, we need consciously to integrate the past into our present lives. If it remains repressed, it will surface in other ways. Dreams and nightmares, psychosomatic symptoms, and even flashbacks often point toward unresolved issues from earlier years. That's why memory plays such an essential role in many forms of therapy. Some psychologists even claim that our earliest conscious memory is a major factor in our psychic development. With this in mind, I devised a journal exercise in which each participant was asked to describe her earliest memory in as much detail as possible. As we discussed these writings afterward, some striking correlations with the women's present lives became apparent. Laura's earliest memory, for example, was of being given a sandbox for her second birthday and not knowing what the word "sandbox" meant. An archaeologist now, she remembers feeling, while digging in a pit for the first time, that it was like playing in a giant sandbox! Edie, an English major, recalled walking to the library with her father to pick out books. She remembered cuddling up on his lap while he read to her and the excitement of beginning to sense that the alphabet he had been teaching her was related to the sounds he was making as he read, and to the marks on the pages of the storybook. What is your earliest memory? Can you detect threads of continuity and connection with your life today?

In a very concrete sense, we *are* what we remember. The tragedy of Alzheimer's disease, for example, is the way it robs its victims of identity by stripping away all memory. In his fascinating studies of patients with neurological disorders, Oliver Sacks shows how amnesia forces the patient into a permanent moment-by-moment existence. He describes the dramatic case of Jimmie, who suffered total memory loss of everything that had happened to him between the ages of nineteen and forty-nine. Jimmie's memory span was approximately twenty seconds, and life was not much more than an ever-repeating present moment. From one minute to the next, literally, he would forget himself. It is memory that gives our lives depth and meaning. Without it, we'd be unable to trace coherent patterns in our experience. Because of his neurological disorder, Jimmie didn't even know anything was missing from his life. It isn't like that with us. Though we may find ourselves in an environment with no meaningful associations, we are capable of remembering past situations that *do* have meaning, and the contrast can be painful. This is precisely what homesickness is: grief over the lack of meaningful relatedness to our environment. Nothing is linked to anything else; therefore, nothing has meaning.

Your memories, vivid and cloudy, joyous and painful, are yours forever. As you write in your journal, you may find that memory is both your treasure chest and your Pandora's box. Having lifted its lid, you'll be surprised by its contents. And once you plunge deeply into your own life, you will never again see yourself as dull or colorless. As Florida Scott-Maxwell concluded, looking back at her own life, "You need only claim the events of your life to make yourself yours. When you truly possess all you have been and done, which may take some time, you are fierce with reality."

Envisioning: The Presence of the Future

The German poet Rainer Maria Rilke said, "The future enters into us, in order to transform itself in us, long before it happens." Whether or not we believe we are born with a specific destiny, the future is with us in ways we are often unable to see. And just as our memories remind us of where we have been, our desires and aspirations tell us something about where we are going. In your diary you can dialogue with your ongoing hopes and dreams, and explore possible paths into the future. Journal writing can help you clarify both immediate and long-term goals. Recurring entries about your personal and professional aspirations offer symbolic signposts for where you want to go in life. Inventing scenarios in your journal about how you want to live your life five or ten years from now engages your subconscious in attaining those ends. Envisioning the future, you can help bring it into being.

Oftentimes, your journal knows more than you do. Recently, I leafed through the pages of my journal from 1969. I was sixteen years old and had been writing a "novel." In my journal I read,

> I wish English teachers required their students to keep a daily journal as part of a term assignment. It would be interesting to see one's thoughts in daily form after two or three months. I wish they would allow more time for creative writing, experiments in creativity. I love writing even when it's just rambling on and on like this. Someday I will read it and wonder if I ever really thought like that.

As far back as I can remember, I wanted to write. When I was twelve years old, I tucked one of my stories into a magazine and read it aloud to my mother as she prepared dinner. When she began to cry (I liked sad endings), I guiltily confessed that this was not a "real story" but one that I had written. She was so amazed that her tears stopped. I had no conscious thought of studying literature or becoming an English instructor, in 1969. I certainly didn't have any inkling that I would go on to get a doctorate in literature and assign class journals in my own teaching, much less write a book about diaries one day. At least, not consciously! And yet, looking back at these two entries and others like them, it seems that my journal knew even then what I came to know only years later: that literature, journals, and creativity would become my vocation.

The imagination plays a powerful role in helping us to attain our hearts' desires. If we think about something often enough, our minds begin to make it real. But there is a paradox here. There are times when we need to let go of our goals and desires in order to experience the larger shape and direction of our life's journey. In Marion Milner's attempt to discover the meaning of her life, she made the astonishing discovery that her purpose might be to *abandon* her assumed goals in life in order to open herself up to something wholly new. In her words, "I began to have an idea of my life, *not as the slow shaping of achievement to fit my preconceived purposes, but as the gradual discovery and growth of a purpose which I did not know.*"

So when do we forge ahead, and when surrender? Do you feel yourself drifting without direction? If so, this might be the time to formulate some goals in the pages of your journal. Do you feel yourself driven toward ever-greater achievements? Perhaps your challenge is to draw back temporarily and let go. Explore your motivation and reconsider the day-to-day quality of your life in your diary. As you bring your thoughts and feelings more sharply into focus, you'll develop a keener sense of the necessary balance in your life.

Recognizing Your Bodily Experience

From the time we learn to think, we are taught to obey our minds' perceptions and to ignore, even override, what our bodies feel. As children, when our stomachs ache, we cry and are comforted. Then we grow older and learn the power of painkilling medications. We take coffee as a pick-me-up, aspirin to dull a headache, and antacid to quell a queasy stomach, as if those symptoms were unrelated to our overall state of well-being. To be sure, it may still be comfort we crave, as adults, but now it's harder to find a lap onto which to climb. Instead, we stifle the symptoms. We kill the distress signals that our bodies try to send us.

Subjecting our bodies to rigorous workouts and training programs, we exercise and diet endlessly in pursuit of the ideal body shape. And yet we are neither a sensual nor even an embodied culture. Our lovemaking skills may be technically flawless. But something crucial is lacking. Our capacity for mental activity has all but blinded us to the creaturely needs that we share with infants and animals: the need for bodily warmth and closeness, physical comfort, and time for unselfconscious stretching in the sun. When do we stop needing physical tenderness that isn't sex? When do we stop feeling at home in our bodies?

As a young girl growing up in a devout evangelical Christian community, I learned that our bodies are the containers of souls, which are our essence, and that, at death, we cast off the body for a purer realm of being. The split between body and soul is not limited to any one religion, of course, but underlies all of Western thought. Mind and matter are divided in such a way that the former dominates; our "brains" rule our bodies. The philosopher Steven Rosen claims that,

> [M]odern philosophy, in essentially maintaining the Renaissance way of knowing and being, remains dualistic at bottom; implicitly if not explicitly, it presupposes an unbridgeable separation of mind and matter that obscures the concrete wholeness of experience. So it seems that if we are going to approach the problem in a genuine manner, somehow we will need to lift the repression imposed at the time of the Renaissance, recover something of the original, pre-Renaissance sense in which there was no problem, because mind and matter had not yet been starkly, categorically, separated.

But, as Rosen makes abundantly clear in "The Paradox of Mind and Matter," we cannot go back to that earlier wholeness. Nor can we "simply leave the province of intellect, cross the boundary of mind and immerse ourselves in flesh, for such boundary crossing is itself an act of simple division expressive of the intellect." Our task, instead, is to re-member—that is, re-embody ourselves in a way that will take us from "body-as-opposed-to-mind" to an integrated "bodymind." This is our challenge.

What does it mean to be a body? Not to have one, but to be one? On the first evening of my training course in Gestalt therapy, the instructor asked each of us how we were feeling. She began with me. I felt expectant and curious, I said, and a little apprehensive facing a new situation and a roomful of strangers. Where, in my body, did I feel these things? she asked. I had a hard time answering, since I'd always assumed my emotions were controlled by my mind, but finally began to sense some tremulousness in my chest and abdomen. What an amazing discovery: emotions are experienced in our bodies! When you feel exhilarated, you feel it in your body. Your heartbeat picks up, your eyes sparkle, and you can't sit still. Conversely, when you're depressed, your bodily processes slow down. And when you are anxious, that knot in the pit of your stomach is not only a metaphor! Chances are, your digestive juices are working overtime. Everything you feel originates in your body.

Journal writing allows you to tune in to your bodily experience and wisdom. The first step might be simply to describe all of the physical sensations that you are aware of (for example, my head feels as if someone were squeezing it between their palms, my arms and legs are drained of energy, there's a sharp pain in my left knee). Dialogue with symptoms of distress to explore what they want to tell you. Often, you'll discover a surprising correspondence between a physical symptom and a psychic state. A headache, for example, may indicate an inner conflict, a feeling of nausea, point toward something in your life that literally makes you sick. A sense of tightness in your chest and constricted breathing might embody the fear of opening yourself up to the environment or to emotions that seem overwhelming in their intensity. I am not for a moment suggesting that bodily distress signals are "in the head" and don't require medical attention. A feeling of constriction and dull ache around the heart may indicate acute emotional distress or may in fact be symptoms of a heart problem. In my experience, when a period of reflective journal writing has lessened or dispelled my symptoms, they've been brought on by stress rather than disease. But in the event of a persistent symptom, I would certainly consult a physician in order to rule out the possibility of a physiological problem.

The most effective way I've found to tune into my body's experience is a technique called "focusing," developed by the psychologist Eugene Gendlin. Gendlin approaches experience holistically, seeking a "felt sense" that is broader than thoughts, feelings, or sensations alone. When you think of your sister, for example, you experience an aura of feelings and associations that encompasses everything you know, and feel, and intuit about her. Your body's felt sense of "everything about Jane" is always deeper and more truthful than what your mind tells you. You can incorporate this awareness into your journal.

The Roles We Play

Women's roles have changed dramatically in the course of this century. Many of us find ourselves leading lives that have little in common with those of our grandmothers or even our mothers. For the most part, the changes have been a blessing. The women's movement opened many doors that had been firmly closed to those before us. But there is also a hidden, often painful underside to our good fortune. Women today not infrequently have the anguished sense that in making our own life choices, we invalidate those our mothers made, often with far fewer alternatives. As Kim Chernin so poignantly puts it,

> A handful of cherished recipes, perhaps, a lifetime of broken dreams and disillusion—that is what most women alive today can receive from their mothers. We are a generation who, with every act of self-assertion as women, with every movement into self-development and fulfillment, call into question the values by which our mothers have tried to live.

I know that Chernin's words hold true for me; my own life has differed greatly from my mother's. A reluctant German immigrant to Canada in 1950 at the age of nineteen, she was sent ahead to earn money so the remaining five members of her family could join her. Lilli, my mother, worked as a chambermaid and then as a housekeeper, saving every penny for her family's passage. Two years later she married my father, a new immigrant himself, and by the time she was twenty-six, they had three little ones. She never saw her own mother again. My grandmother, Pauline, died on the train en route to the ship that was to carry her to Canada in 1952. She was forty-three years old. When next my mother saw her father, younger sisters, and brother again, in 1959, it had been almost a decade.

In the years that followed, Lilli cooked and baked, gardened and mended, and generally made ends meet with great ingenuity, although her health left much to be desired, throughout. While her formal education consisted of six years of sporadic schooling in wartime Germany, she reads avidly books and articles on holistic health and naturopathic medicine, as well as religious publications. How different my own life! After attending a religious college for two years and working for a year, I began what turned into a fifteen-year stint of academic work in four countries. From time to time I yearned for the apparent security of marriage, but bowed out whenever things appeared to be headed in that direction. Instead, I studied, traveled, and made friends in many countries, the "gypsy" in a family only too happy to stay put after many forced displacements during the war.

Both the inner and outer circumstances of my mother's life and mine differ greatly. While she has found meaning in her religious faith and family ties, in creating a beautiful home, and caring for others, I have looked for fulfillment in friendship and travel, music, and intellectual pursuits. And yet, I also see similarities now that I couldn't see ten years ago. In the enjoyment I experience as I prepare beautiful cakes for my Wednesday evening workshop, I see a reflection of my mother's pleasure at the sight of a kitchen counter covered with enormous loaves of bread baked from grain she grinds herself in a stone mill in the basement. In my own hypercritical moments, I hear echoes of her voice in my childhood, readier to criticize than to praise. And in her intolerance of social chitchat, I recognize my own impatience with conversations that don't quickly turn meaningful.

Our struggles, too, have differed. Hers were those of the new immigrant adrift in a strange land, without language or money to ease the way. The death of her mother was the cruelest blow. The opportunities available during the 1950s were limited, and I think she has often felt frustrated by the limitations of her role as wife and mother. My own difficulties have been more intangible. Like other women who find themselves where they had never expected to go, I've fought the "impostor syndrome" in my academic life. In the

wider world, I've experienced the insidious pressure to "have it all."
But there's no question that I've had opportunities beyond her wildest
dreams. Perhaps the biggest luxury of all has been the time to think
things through, to ponder what it is I really want. Earlier generations
have had less scope for doing this and fewer examples of women who
had done it before them. If, as Carolyn Heilbrun says, we live our
lives by the stories we have read, they had fewer stories to live by,
fewer narratives available for enactment. What *was* available was primarily the old marriage plot in which the woman subordinates her
own needs and desires to those of her husband and children. But the
time has come. "A woman must break out of the old mold," Judith
Duerk tells us.

> She must risk disobeying the given decrees, those dictated from outside
> as well as those written within her by her past. She must confront her
> internalized patriarchs and break out of the role of good girl, good
> woman that they have scripted for her. She must submit to the dread
> that breaking the old commandments will bring.

If the shoe of patriarchal commandments doesn't fit, don't wear it.
Many of us are throwing out "old shoes" and other outdated attire in
the process of writing journals. Here we explore new stories, new
possibilities of relationship, new tones and modes of being. And in
the process, quite literally, we write ourselves—as women—into
being.

But the roles we play are not determined solely by society's definitions and dictates. If only it were that simple. According to Jung,
women and men alike have a persona, or public face, which we rely
on throughout our daily interactions. It expresses how we want to
appear to ourselves and to other people, consisting of everything from
our dress and mannerisms to our demeanor and position within
society. But, ironically, the persona conceals who and what we really
are. Marion Woodman says, "All day the mask, or persona, performs
with perfect efficiency, but when the job is done, those frenzied,
foreign rhythms continue to dominate body and Being. There is no 'I'
to call a halt, no strong, differentiated ego to gear down to the natural

rhythms." If we confuse the persona with our inner being, we lose touch with our bodily reality. The mask is taken for the face, and our real lives go unlived. "We all have a thousand faces," Anaïs Nin wrote in her diary. What are yours? What are mine? What happens when we step out of the roles society has assigned us and those, too, that we freely choose to play? Who are we when we are not concerned with how we appear to someone else?

One of the recurring themes in Nin's diary is the discrepancy between the mask she wore throughout the day and the shadow side of her personality that emerged at night in the safety of her journal. "The false person I had created for the enjoyment of my friends, the gaiety, the buoyant, the receptive, the healing person, always on call, always ready with sympathy, had to have its existence somewhere," she wrote. "In the diary I could reestablish the balance. Here I could be depressed, angry, disparaging, discouraged. I could let out my demons." Although her artist friends urged her to abandon her journal, Anaïs knew it alone could encompass the paradoxes and contradictions among different facets of her personality, and sustain her quest for self-realization. Throughout her lifetime she insisted, "The real Anaïs is in the diary" and, as the unexpurgated version appears in print, we begin to see just how true that is!

Many women describe this sense that their "real self" is far removed from what they project to others. Ruth Benedict confessed to her diary,

> What was my character anyway? My real *me* was a character I dared not look upon—it was terrorized by loneliness, frozen by a sense of futility, obsessed by a longing to *stop*. No one had ever heard of that Me. If they had, they would have thought it an interesting pose. The mask was tightly adjusted.

Another diarist describes her powerful sense of being split into two women:

> Through the Diary I became acquainted with another woman whose voice I feared yet revered, since she spoke all those truths I shunned.

Timid, she was not. And, I in my timidity admired her and dreamed of one day being like her, having her voice, her boldness, her ability to dream. Slowly, that day did come and, again, through the Diary I was able to see the merging of the woman who lived only in the Diary with myself, the woman who lived outside its pages. Our voices have become one.

Marion Woodman likens the journal to a mirror. "When we first look into it, the blank pages stare back with ominous emptiness," she writes. "But if we keep looking and trusting in what Rilke calls 'the possibility of being,' gradually we begin to see the face that is looking back at us. . . . Journal writing is a way of taking responsibility for finding out who I AM." Keeping a diary reveals an identity richer and greater than the sum of the roles you play. If you manage to stay truthful—even in the midst of uncertainty, doubt, and paradox—you will begin to see your own face and hear your own voice.

What are the roles you are called upon to play in the course of your daily life? You are certainly someone's daughter and granddaughter, and most likely, someone's friend. You may also be a sister, mother, lover, wife, grandmother, niece, aunt, and godparent. You will likely be an employee and possibly an employer, a homemaker, perhaps a mentor, a citizen, and on and on. Explore these in your journal. To begin, you might simply sit down with your diary and complete the sentence "I am . . . / I am a . . ." in as many ways as possible. Keep going for as long as you can. You will probably be surprised by the number of different hats you wear in life.

In addition to the external roles we play, we all contain a host of subpersonalities, distinct aspects of our being that carry their own life-energy. Within each of us, there may be a little girl who still cherishes the hopes and dreams of her childhood, an adolescent who hasn't decided what she wants to be when she grows up, a free spirit who wants to wander around the world, a crabby queen who wants her own way now!, an Earth Mother who nurtures and embraces those around her, a cynic who has seen it all, and more. In October 1991, I wrote in my journal:

Tonight I feel like a wistful little girl with my nose pressed against the window of other people's lives, which look fuller, more important, more consequential than my own. The lonely little stranger who yearns to be lifted into the heart of things, to be made welcome, to be cherished and loved. Do Steve and I honour and love each other's "little strangers?"

Get acquainted with as many of your inner figures as possible. Dialogue with them in your journal. Ask them what they love and hate, desire and fear. They have much to teach you.

A Self of Your Own

Marion Milner observes that early in her quest for self-awareness, "People said: 'Oh, be yourself at all costs.' But I found that it was not so easy to know just what one's self was. It was far easier to want what other people seemed to want and then imagine that the choice was one's own." Sylvia Ashton-Warner made a similar discovery. On November 19, 1943, she wrote in her journal, "I've finished playing a role. Now I'm me. There's been an incredible tendency in this last shaking year to imitate those I admire. . . . Patterning myself on other people . . . where would I get and what would I be? A carbon copy of other people? I'm determined to stay how I am and be damned." Your life's true drama is greater than the sum total of the roles you play. This is where journal writing provides "one place of truth" and a "dialogue without falsity." It gives you an opportunity to make contact with the self at your core that contains but is larger than all of these roles. When you lift your pen to the pages of your journal, all of the masks, costumes, and camouflage can drop away. Here you write from your essential self. The ultimate goal is to write below the surface of our lives in order to express as much of our core as possible. As Jung stated,

A "complete" life does not consist in a theoretic completeness, but in the fact that one accepts, without reservation, the particular tissue in which one finds oneself embedded, and that one tries to make sense of it or to create a cosmos from the chaotic mess into which one is born.

In the next chapter, we will look at some of the specific ways in which the healing dimension of journal writing can help us toward this end.

5

Healing Dimensions
of the Journal

My writing is the glue that holds my fragmented self (selves) together.

ANONYMOUS DIARIST

I feel as if I have healed myself with my own words. I am making myself well. Writing is my cure.

CAROLE BOVOSO

To create wholeness in our lives is to heal ourselves. The etymology of the words makes this clear. They derive from the Germanic *heil* (from the Anglo-Saxon *hale*), or whole, with its variations *heilen* (to heal) and *heilig* (holy). In other words, *to heal is to make whole, and to be whole is to be holy*. Perhaps it's only our own era, strongly influenced by scientific materialism, that separates psychic wholeness from spiritual perfection. Other cultures have seen them as the same thing. Even Freud used the word *Seele*, or soul, rather than the more secular "psyche," as the German is usually translated. And indeed, for many people, psychotherapy—with its attempt to heal the painful conflicts that block the flow of life energy within us—has taken the place of religion. Since Freud and Jung codified the rich workings of the individual and collective unconscious, we have been fascinated with and have come to revere the hidden face of our psyche. We seek redemption at the altar of self-understanding.

For who among us doesn't seek healing? At some point in our lives most—probably all—of us will seek help from a therapist, in the attempt to heal the unresolved losses and sorrows in our lives. Whether it's allergies or migraine headaches we suffer from, depression or panic attacks that haunt us, we all have vulnerable areas in body and soul. The Swiss psychoanalyst Alice Miller tells us, "Our true, repressed life history is stored up in our body, which attempts to recount it and to be listened to, by way of symptoms." Sometimes these symptoms become chronic. Perhaps not severe enough to debilitate us entirely, they nevertheless cast a gray shadow on our day-to-day existence. In extreme instances, they may consume all our energy, even our lives. Often it takes the onset of a serious illness before we stop to look at the roots of our dis-ease. Whatever form it takes, we live with it as long as we can; then we turn to the professionals. We seek therapy. "Therapy" comes from the Greek *therapeuein* (to take care of), with its root prefix *dher-* (to hold up or support). Since women have traditionally been the caretakers and providers of emotional support in our society, is it any wonder that we are in need of therapy ourselves?

Feminist psychologists in recent decades have shown how women's psychic structures and processes are different from men's. Our wounds differ also. Kim Chernin's quest to discover the origins of her own anguish forced her to "finally admit, in the most radical possible way, that I as a woman did not exist." What she discovered during her descent into the psychic underworld was that buried beneath her terrible sense of emptiness lay "hidden knowledge, old memory, another possibility of being female." In the image of the Great Goddess, the embodiment of feminine divinity, Chernin uncovered "a forgotten possibility of female power." Journal writing can put us in touch with the Goddess archetype deeply buried within us, and the feeling-values she represents; much that we have repressed, disowned, and forgotten, whether out of shame or neglect, can be reclaimed in the sanctuary of our diaries. As we give words to long-suppressed feelings and intuitions, we heal our estrangement from our own feminine natures. Jung said, " 'One does not become enlightened by imagining figures of light, but by making the darkness conscious.' " As we articulate our repressed rage and violence, our stifled creativity and capacity for joy, the darkness is transformed by the light of conscious understanding and we further the work of healing. When we sort out society's projections of the feminine from our own inner truth, and discover who we are as mature women, we complete the necessary task of individuation. Marion Woodman, too, says that this is the essential task of woman today: "This is the new consciousness, the giant leap, the healing in her own life which she is being called upon to incorporate."

The Journal as a Therapeutic Tool

Ask a diarist "Why do you keep a journal?" and the most likely answer will be "Because it's therapeutic." Indeed it is, and not for our psyches only. Long recognized as an invaluable means of releasing emotional tension, journal writing is listed in *Prevention Magazine*'s "Dictionary of Healing Techniques and Remedies," because it can also help to mobilize the body's defenses against *physical* illnesses. Lydia Temoskok and Henry Dreher, co-authors of *The Type C Connection: The Mind-Body Link to Cancer and Your Health*, go so far as to suggest that for cancer patients, keeping a personal journal can "lift depression, enhance meaning, and spark actions that contribute to recovery." That's quite a claim!

Even in the conservative medical establishment, there's a growing recognition of the interconnectedness of body and soul, of physical and emotional well-being. Dean Ornish, who created an unorthodox program for reversing heart disease through diet, exercise, and meditation, describes a series of fascinating studies that demonstrate the physical benefits of personal writing. In an experiment conducted at Southern Methodist University in Dallas, Dr. James Pennebaker asked a group of students to write for twenty minutes a day about trivial matters of no emotional importance to them. A second group was asked to state the facts about traumatic experiences they'd had in the past. The third and final group also wrote about trauma, but were to include their feelings as well as the facts. Researchers measured the heart rates and blood pressure of all involved, at the beginning of the study. Their findings were fascinating. While the students in the third group initially had increased blood pressure, blood samples taken six weeks later revealed that their immune systems were functioning at *heightened* levels. Those who disclosed *trauma they'd previously kept secret* had the most dramatic rise in immune-cell strength. Six months later, they had been ill less often and visited the student health center on far fewer occasions than those in the first two groups. The researchers concluded that "holding feelings in puts a chronic stress on the heart and on the immune system." In contrast, pouring feelings onto paper contributed to a healthier state of being.

But the belief that writing can promote well-being, even healing, is not new. The journal scholar Cinthia Gannett reminds us that "writing to heal, or 'iatrological writing,' is both an ancient and an honorable aim of rhetoric." Since the time of Plato and Aristotle, she says, "rhetoric has been interested in 'the emotional, as well as the moral and political health of its audience.' " In our own time, the psychologist Ira Progoff was among the first to advocate the use of journal writing as a therapeutic tool. In *Healing Voices*, a collection of essays by feminist therapists in Canada, keeping a diary is often mentioned as an essential part of therapy. One client, Chris Watson, found that the combination of psychotherapy and journal writing eventually led to graphic memories of sexual abuse when she was a little girl of three and four. Looking back, she recalls,

> Much of my journal writing from that period is a welter of emotions. Alone in my room, usually on Saturday mornings, I would wake, write down the dream I'd emerged from, and go from that point into other recollections from my childhood. Sometimes when I'd write it would be almost as if the child-me were writing the experience as it happened. What I remembered amazed me.

Through the combined support of journal writing and psychotherapy, Chris Watson was finally able to get to the origin of her inconsolable sadness: the trauma and violence perpetrated against her tiny three-year-old body by her father and uncle, who had both repeatedly raped and abused her.

Marion Woodman, who writes for an hour every day, tells us,

When the mood grips us, that is the time to write—let it pour out of the unconscious. Journal writing fulfills the need to pour out the heart. Most people find intimacy very difficult, even intimacy with themselves. Since the whole point of analysis depends on that intimacy, journal writing is crucial to recognizing those parts of ourselves that we have shunned. Unconsciousness needs the eye of consciousness; consciousness needs the energy of the unconscious. Writing allows that interchange to take place.

Although I'd been keeping a diary for more than fifteen years, my journal writing took on important new roles in the winter of 1982, when I saw a psychotherapist over a period of several months. It helped integrate the work of the therapy itself, sustaining and grounding me between weekly visits at a time when my whole life seemed up for grabs. Every Thursday morning after my session with Michael, I stopped in a muffin shop across the street from his office. There I wrote out my emotional residue and impressions of the morning's work, before heading out to campus for my afternoon graduate literature seminar. This quiet period of writing helped me assimilate the work of the previous hour and provided a buffer zone between two very different spheres of my life. I had never paid much attention to my dreams before that, but after my first appointment with Michael, I confided in my journal, "Dream last night: Increasing confusion and terror as huge waves of water swept by, swept me around, finally left me with about a foot of breathing space, when I awoke. I felt alone in the dream, as if it was literally 'the end of the world.' I don't remember much else, just the feeling of panic." Looking back now, it seems clear that the dream manifested my fear of being overwhelmed by the amount of unconscious material stirred up in the therapy session, which now threatened to engulf me. And indeed, we plunged in quickly and deeply. Two weeks later I wrote,

> It seems to me that Michael is right and I have "eaten a lot of shit" in my days. The good old Christian insistence that anger is a terrible sin is just crazy. I'd like to know how many ulcers, strokes, heart attacks and cancers are caused by people's inability to express anger. Literally, I feed myself my anger instead of directing it at its object. My anger festers inside me, and then I eat more and more and it's never food I

want inside me but peace and self-acceptance and relaxed insides. When I think of all the food I have eaten for every reason besides hunger or appetite, it seems incredible to me. Now *that is the real sin* in all of this!

But it was the next day that some floodgate burst inside me. Sitting in the university library on a beautiful afternoon, I felt ill, physically nauseated for no obvious reason. Then I asked myself, anticipating Michael's probable question, "What are you sick of?" An hour later I sat back in exhaustion, having written seven long single-spaced pages in the grip of a powerful guilt complex that had tormented me for years, allowing me no inner peace. In contrast to the usual thoughtful, measured style of my journal entries, these pages seem literally to have poured out of me without conscious direction or control. I was a graduate student in literature at the time, so I surely knew what a run-on sentence was, but the guilt complex that held me in its grip wasn't concerned with punctuation or grammar. When I finished writing, the feeling of nausea was gone. Here are some excerpts from those pages.

February 6, 1982. . . . Snide, sarcastic, bitchy, miserable, depressed, in-secure, inadequate, unlovable, endlessly inferior, never to catch up— and what if I succeed and prove it's possible to feel good—can I still belong to this family? How do we handle joy here? . . . God will punish me so I learn humility. But he doesn't have to punish me, I'll do it myself, with my guilt and my misery and my fat. What am I afraid of anyway—failure or success—and what does it mean? And no matter what they say or how terrible I feel I have one thing left they can't take it away from me, my integrity but if I say what I mean they don't like it, it's better to put it in my journal while I'm thinking it all out and I think and I think all night and I read and I can't sleep and I read Camus and it makes me upset but I can't stop reading but the pastor at Church says Christianity has all the answers and if Camus shakes your faith, don't read Camus. But I can't close my eyes if he's an imposter why do I feel he's writing my thoughts or I'm thinking his books?

I can't leave Vancouver I love Vancouver all my friends are here and what if someone dies while I'm away it's terrible to think that death can sneak up on you—every time I go on a trip I wonder if I'll see everybody again or if God will play a terrible trick on me and I'll get a telegram and discover that while I was sitting in a café drinking cappuccino and reading or talking with friends and lovers—someone I love was dying in Vancouver and I'll cheat someone out of my grief and sorrow. . . . It is strange, writing and writing and writing—such an urgency, and in my "regular" journal I try to reason things out a little more and put them in order and here I just write it all down and I hope I'm not unconsciously creating fictions of the past but if this isn't how it happened it's the memory I carry now.

"Unconsciousness needs the eye of consciousness." What poured out of me in the grip of that complex was beyond my control. It was the voice of my terror and anguish finally daring to utter itself, in the certainty that with Michael's compassionate ear, it would at last be heard. After our next session, I wrote,

> *February 11, 1982.* I had a "nervous rash" on my throat today—Michael says it is anger slowly beginning to surface—maybe I'll get there in small steps. I read him my monologue and he listened—told me to pay attention to all those voices that are not my own, and to "have it out" with them—Who are you? What do you want?—to listen to them, engage with them, then argue back.

Then four days later, "I'm a little nauseated again, this morning—don't know why—my stomach feels aflutter and I sense a thread of hostility, anger, what else? I look very unappealing to myself in the mirror—am deathly tired of my weight problem. Michael says when I feel like this, just to write." I wrote and we continued the therapy. Rereading those raw pages now, I experience a visceral memory of the painful conflicts that finally drove me to seek help. I also remember vividly the healing power of the therapy and the quiet hour of reflective writing that followed before I reentered the busy workaday world.

Those three months, full of emotional blockages and break-throughs, major and minor insights, had a tremendous effect on my life. Echoes of the therapy sessions stayed with me as I continued the healing process in my daily writing. Although I'd been pouring my emotions and feelings into my journal all along, the writing took on a different quality once I began to do it consciously, with a clearer understanding of how bringing buried material to light could help heal me. "Journaling is an ongoing mirroring process," Woodman tells us. "Seeing, not seeing; naming, unnaming. . . . The journal becomes a psychic home where the ambiguities that lie at the heart of the mystery are expressed, not explained."

If you are currently seeing a therapist, you may want to ask her or him to suggest some writing topics relating to the issues you are working on. Begin recording your dreams if you aren't already doing so (Chapter Seven). Dialogue with people and events that come up in the therapy sessions. Read published journals of other women in therapy, and do the writing exercises in the Appendix that are for this chapter.

Healing Dimensions of Journal Writing

In his study of creative process, Stephen Nachmanovitch says,

> I have never ceased to be astounded at the power of writing, music making, drawing, or dance to pull me out of sadness, disappointment, depression, bafflement. I am not talking about entertainment or distraction, but of playing, dancing, drawing, writing my way through and out. This process resembles the best in psychotherapy.

You don't have to be in therapy to experience the powerful healing benefits of keeping a diary. Through consistent and honest journal writing, you can become your own therapist. The advantages are obvious. You don't need a referral or an appointment. You don't have to go anywhere, and you don't have to wait for weekly visits in order to carry on. Your therapy is always portable, and you don't have to discontinue it if you fall upon hard times. As one diarist observed, "Journal keeping is often cheap therapy." But there is another important benefit as well: While a poor therapist can conceivably do more harm than good, journal writing has the lowest risk factor imaginable, psychically as well as financially, providing you with the gentlest and safest of therapies. At any given point, you reveal only as much of yourself as your comfort level permits. According to the Gestalt therapist Muriel Schiffman, "You have a built-in, self-protective mechanism that keeps you from uncovering an emotion you are not yet strong enough to feel without undue anxiety." This means that if you are not able or prepared to write from your gut one day, the worst that can happen is that you bore yourself and put your journal aside.

One dramatic example of the self-healing potential of journal writing is that of Alice Koller, who wrote herself out of a suicidal existential despair. Hour after hour and day after day, for three months, she pounded the typewriter, trying to reach the truth about her life, something that would give her a reason to go on living. Beginning, she reflected,

> I'm here to understand myself, deliberately to turn myself open to my own view. I know, as I sit here, what I must have known for many years: that I can recognize what's true about myself when I see it. . . . I'll write down everything I can remember, so that I can see the full extent of it, pick out some patterns in what I've been denying for so long. So that's first: to get it all written, no matter how ugly.

Near the end of the three months, having arrived at some painful truths about her own existence, Alice has written through her despair to a new possibility of living in the world, and has discovered "[a] sense of newness now . . . that the script is gone. I find myself thinking. I find myself talking. My words don't follow a prearranged pattern. They surprise me, even as I speak or think. Their unexpectedness catches my own attention, and, examining them, I discover what I mean to say."

Another diarist, Bibi Wien, similarly discovered how crucial her journal was in her attempt to regain emotional health and equilibrium. She tells us,

> For about four months, I had been suffering from a severe depression, unable to write or concentrate or even remember what was actually

happening from day to day. The journal was part of the struggle to surface, the struggle not to succumb. I forced myself to type at least one journal entry daily (at first), as a way of getting back in touch with reality, sorting out my conflicting feelings. . . . It was a major force in my return to health and work.

For Bibi Wien, the journal was the fixed point of each day, her attempt to make contact with a reality beyond her disabling depression.

In 1986, May Sarton began her journal *After the Stroke* thus: "It may prove impossible because my head feels so queer and the smallest effort, mental or physical, exhausts, but I feel so deprived of my *self* being unable to write, cut off since early January from all that I mean about my life, that I think I must try to write a few lines every day. It is a way of being self-supporting." Indeed, May Sarton accredited journal writing with enormous life-saving powers. "Six of the good poets of roughly my generation have been suicides," she reflected. "If I have survived it may be because I can write novels, journals, and so on in the dry spells. I have the tools for climbing out of depression as I am doing now."

For me, the healing dimension of journal writing has taken many forms. My diary has readily accepted all my emotional fallout: ranting and railing, weeping, venting anger and resentment, I have poured everything out—with no fear of boring or hurting, insulting or infuriating this friend. Sometimes I've used it as a security blanket, endowing it with near-magical power to comfort and heal, to vindicate and to assuage grief. In its nonjudgmental pages, I have done massive self-justification and, in recent years, recorded dreams, cherishing the gifts of my unconscious that come as images at night.

Many of the published diarists in *Life Notes* became their own therapists in the course of coming to terms with their lives. Carroll Parrott Blue writes, "Sometimes I can heal myself just by writing to myself about myself as I go through the world. My journal keeps me going to my core; to the heart of my vision, to the beat of my wisdom." And Melina Brown reflects, "My journal has also been my therapist. When no one else was around, or when I couldn't pull myself together enough to talk to anyone, I could release my thoughts and emotions without worrying about being judged. My journal would accept it all, and save my words until I was ready to read them." In the diary, as in therapy, healing is not a one-time thing, but a process that takes time and patience, and willingness to dwell within the dark while the seed of new growth forms.

Catharsis

Catharsis, for Aristotle, was "the purification or purging of emotions by art." In psychoanalysis, it refers to the "release of tension and anxiety by emotionally reliving the incidents of the past, especially those that have been repressed, and honestly facing the causes of difficulty." The experiment conducted by Dr. Pennebaker was a direct outcome of his personal experience of cathartic writing. In the midst of a crisis early in his marriage, he became very depressed, and began to drink and to isolate himself from others. Then, according to Temoskok and Dreher,

> One day, out of desperation, he turned to his typewriter and began pounding out all his feelings about his marriage, parents, career, sexuality, and death. After doing this every day for a week, he felt fatigued but also much freer. For the first time in years . . . he was in touch with the meaning and purpose of his life. This led him to realize his deep love for his wife, and enabled the two of them to resurrect their marriage.

What Dr. Pennebaker stumbled upon in his spontaneous writing marathons was the healing cathartic function of personal writing. We've all known the relief of getting things off our chests by putting powerful emotions into words. Half an hour of passionate scribbling across a blank page can offer tremendous emotional release. Angry exclamation marks, emphatic red underlining, tear stains on the page—all are marks of the diarist's intense emotion.

In her journal, Sylvia Plath observed, "Fury jams the gullet and spreads poison, but, as soon as I start to write, dissipates, flows out into the figure of the letters: writing as therapy?" And here is Emily Carr, writing on a day when life seemed impossible:

March 5th [1940]. The world is horrid right straight through and so am I. I lay awake for three hours in the night and today as a result I am tired and ratty even though the sun is as nice as can be. I want to whack everyone on earth. I've a cough and a temper and every bit of me is tired. I'm old and ugly, stupid and ungracious. I don't even want to be nice. I want to grouch and sulk and rip and snort. I am a pail of milk that has gone sour. Now, perhaps, having written it all down, the hatefulness will melt off to where the mist goes when the sun gets up. Perhaps the nastiness in me has scooted down my right arm and through my fingers into the pencil and lies spilled openly on the paper to shame me. Writing is a splendid sorter of your good and bad feelings, better even than paint.

Anne Frank, too, was aware that her diary could contain the anger she was not free to express directly. As she reread past entries on January 2, 1944, she reflected on "how it came about that I should have been so brimful of rage and really so filled with such a thing as hate that I had to confide it all in you," noting, "this diary is of great value to me." At fourteen, she already understood the cathartic function of her diary. "I can shake off everything if I write," she adds. "My sorrows disappear, my courage is reborn."

Sometimes the wounds that are healed through cathartic writing are the result of prejudice and discrimination. Shamara Shantu Riley, an African-American lesbian, reflects, "Writing gives me some sort of voice to articulate my thoughts about my identity in a world where people constantly try to deny me the right to have my own identity. Writing in my journal is also cathartic because it enables me to survive, to heal many of the wounds that have existed in my life." "Black lesbian warrior poet" Audre Lorde kept a journal of her experience of breast cancer, hoping that her words would "underline the possibilities of self-healing and the richness of living for all women." The journal bears witness to Lorde's anger and despair, and her determination to turn her disease into an impetus for the "transformation of silence into language and action." On November 19, 1979, she wrote, "I want to write rage but all that comes is sadness. . . . There must be some way to integrate death into living, neither ignoring it nor giving in to it." Lorde reflects that preparing *The Cancer Journals* for publication became a process of writing "to sort out for myself who

I was and was becoming throughout that time, setting down my artifacts, not only for later scrutiny, but also to be free of them." Catharsis, again.

Your diary provides a gentle setting in which healing can take place. What unfinished business is there in your life? What hidden wounds beg for recognition and healing? Are you carrying old resentments around with you from one day to the next? Are there unresolved grievances nagging away at your sense of well-being, undermining joy and spontaneity in your relationships? What lies unforgiven in your heart? The next time you are furious, hurt, or simply welling up with some nameless emotion, sit down with your journal for twenty minutes and write. Begin with the first word that comes to mind as a description of how you feel—betrayed or angry, elated or sad—and freewrite. Describe the heaviness of your exhaustion, the force of your wrath, the depths of your confusion. At some point you'll likely feel some kind of bodily release. Your breath may deepen and flow through your body more freely, the muscles in your throat may relax, your headache fade away. You will feel lighter, as though relieved of an oppressive burden. There may be the sense that you can step back from your problem, now that it exists in black and white on the page before you. Perhaps it can even be put aside for a day or two while your subconscious processes it.

If you do this spontaneously, without censoring yourself, your writing will have passion, urgency, and life. And you'll feel different when you stop writing. There may still be traces of the original emotion, but something will have shifted inside you. An unexpected insight may come in the very wording of your problem; a different perspective may emerge. As you write, your emotion may be dissipated or may turn into something else: anger into fear or sadness, for example; anxiety into excitement. Perhaps you'll discover associations with other facets of your life: another relationship or an earlier event that turns out to be the real heart of the matter. If you feel upset for no apparent reason, a round of spiral writing may bring you closer to the source of your agitation. Freewrite for ten minutes; then reread what you wrote and do a few rounds of spiral writing. This will allow you to explore various aspects of the feeling and may bring you nearer to the core issue. And watch for slips of the pen. They're revealing, because your subconscious always knows more than you do. If you write "love" instead of "hate," or "don't" instead of "do," do not cross it out; instead, write what you thought you intended to say above or below what you actually wrote. This kind of "slip" is a telling manifestation of just how easily a feeling can flip over into its opposite.

Exploring Hidden Emotions

Journal writing provides a way of getting at "hidden emotions": those we are unable or unwilling to see. We all carry within us an idealized map of who we are that tells us how we ought to conduct ourselves toward others, but human relationships are characterized by ambivalence. Sometimes we hate those we love; we need them, but want to be free of them. How do we integrate our conflicting, seemingly contradictory emotions? And how do we reconcile our idealized self with who we really are?

The fiercest taboo for women is anger. Men get furious; women get sad and depressed. Men explode in temper tantrums; women dissolve into tears. An angry woman threatens many. This has had pernicious implications, for, as Carolyn Heilbrun observes, "If one is not permitted to express anger or even to recognize it within oneself, one is, by simple extension, refused both power and control." Following this to its logical conclusion, she states, "Forbidden anger, women could find no voice in which publicly to complain; they took refuge in depression or madness." The psychologist Harriet Lerner makes a similar point. She says, "If we are guilty, depressed, or self-doubting, we stay in place. . . . In contrast, angry women may change and challenge the lives of us all . . . and change is an anxiety-arousing and difficult business for everyone, including those of us who are actively pushing for it." Despite great changes during the last thirty years, many women still have difficulty acknowledging anger. We are far more likely to talk ourselves out of it, turn it against ourselves and fall into depression, even develop psychosomatic symptoms. That's where journal writing comes in. As Alice Miller tells us, "As soon as the truth can be slowly explored, thanks to the conscious experience of once-repressed feelings, the language of symptoms becomes super-fluous. They simply disappear." When the inhibition against direct expression is too great, writing is a powerful first step in helping us to recognize and name our anger. In time, we learn to channel it directly.

The Jungian analyst Janet Dallett describes a period of her life in which her inability to articulate her feelings bore devastating results. After her physician convinced her to have an unwanted tubal ligation at the age of thirty, she'd been a model patient, "calm and unemotional in the face of crisis, cheerful and cooperative, perfectly obedient to doctor's orders." But that was not the end of the story. More than twenty years later, Janet's suppressed feelings took their toll in the form of nightmares. "For several weeks I awoke screaming in the night," she remembers, "swept by emotions that had waited twenty-one years to be heard. What had I done to my body by repressing my reactions for so long? Would the years of silence make me sick?" After three of her close friends were similarly plunged into crises resulting from years of unnatural silence, Dallett resolved to write a book about "women struggling to find their voices, trying to say real things instead of what we imagine our men want us to say." She found her long-lost fountain pen, bought "four lined yellow tablets at the office supply store," and returned home. Then, she recalls, after a long dry spell, "I picked up my fountain pen and began to write."

If women's anger in general is outlawed, there's no greater taboo than a mother's anger toward her children, so deeply entrenched is the myth of self-sacrificing motherhood. Mothers are expected to provide unconditional love and untiring support for their children. Adrienne Rich was among the first writers to challenge the "masks of motherhood." She tells us that the journals she wrote when her children were small are full of despair at her own inadequacy and rage at the extent of the sacrifice called for. Her book Of Woman Born begins with one such entry:

November 1960. My children cause me the most exquisite suffering of which I have any experience. It is the suffering of ambivalence: the murderous alternation between bitter resentment and raw-edged nerves, and blissful gratification and tenderness. Sometimes I seem to

myself, in my feelings toward these tiny guiltless beings, a monster of
selfishness and intolerance. Their voices wear away at my nerves, their
constant needs, above all their need for simplicity and patience, fill me
with despair at my own failures. . . . And I am weak sometimes from
held-in rage. . . . I *love them*. But it's in the enormity and inevitability of
this love that the sufferings lie.

The truth is that, contrary to the myth, every mother has felt at one
time or another that it was all a big mistake, that she hates her child
and would like nothing more than to walk away from her maternal
obligations. Here, too, the journal can serve as a safe sounding board
for pent-up frustration and a temporary refuge from the demands for
perpetual selflessness.

And what about envy, fear, and anxiety? A person beset by the
green-eyed monster is seen as petty, grasping, and mean-spirited. Yet
exploring this emotion rather than simply denying it can tell you
something important about what is lacking in your life. Envy over
someone else's accomplishment, for example, may provide a clue that
this is an area in which you have talent yourself. Provided it causes
you to stop and trace your feelings to their roots, envy can be a
teacher. Although fear and anxiety don't carry the same social stigma
for women as anger and jealousy, each of us has private fears we
would rather not acknowledge, anxieties that suggest neurotic conflicts we'd prefer to deny, even to ourselves. Audre Lorde claims, "As
women we were raised to fear. But instead of being crippled by it, we
can turn it around, forcing it to yield self-knowledge," she reflects.
"For then fear becomes not a tyrant against which I waste my energy
fighting, but a companion, not particularly desirable, yet one whose
knowledge can be useful."

Exploring one emotion may lead you to another, more deeply
buried one. For example, the Gestalt therapist Muriel Schiffman tells
us that depression "is not a real emotion like anger, fear, hurt, jealousy,
but a *disorder*, a symptom, a mere cover for some genuine emotion." In
her two excellent books on self-therapy, Schiffman offers several paths
to hidden emotions, including a writing technique that she finds
highly effective. In the midst of an emotional experience or immediately afterward, Muriel suggests, write in a quiet corner with a soft

pencil and answer the following questions: *"What am I feeling?"* (If you aren't sure, describe your physical symptoms.) *"What happened?" "What might have been bothering me?"* and *"What does this remind me of?"* You may have to come up with a number of different answers before you reach something that strikes you as true. She concludes: "How do you know when you have peeled away a layer and discovered the hidden feeling? It feels at least as intense as the apparent emotion with which you began, and completely displaces it: you remember the apparent emotion but you no longer feel it." Schiffman advocates destroying the paper as soon as the underlying emotion has been felt, but I prefer to do the exercise in my journal or to place it at the back of my filing cabinet, where it is safe, even from my own eyes, until I decide to look at it again.

Throughout the 1992 Winter Olympic Games in Albertville, France, I was powerfully drawn to the figure skating competitions. By the third evening, tears were rolling down my face as I watched, and the next morning I wrote a journal entry about it. Not surprisingly, something else emerged.

> I woke up this morning with the figure skaters on my mind again—I could weep at the thought. I don't know what it is but they obviously touch something very deep in me. I think it has something to do with the beauty of it and the way each skater puts her/his entire soul into the performance. I can see it so clearly on their faces as well. The Russian couple who skated so beautifully to Bach's "Air on a G String" —it seemed to be a spiritual experience for them. It must also trigger some projection in me. Maybe something about not being young anymore, not feeling I am expressing or creating enough beauty in my life. There's the sewing (patchwork quilts) which does serve that function. I feel that I create something lovely out of nothing there. But where else? The Workshop. There is a palpable beauty when each woman is absorbed in her own writing, music in the background, and a collective calm and peace in the room. However, I'm not making music, such an important source of beauty in my life over the years— and I don't find my environment beautiful. What else makes up this longing? Youth—Beauty—Pouring one's whole soul into a perfor- mance. Holding nothing back. Dreaming of the future. Having all one's adult life still before one. Maybe even—being the "darling of the

crowd?" Yet, somehow I don't think I've got it entirely, yet. There's something more going on.

Two weeks later I had a similar experience during a concert in Manhattan.

> There's something important here that ties together my emotional reaction to the Olympic figure skaters and my feeling yesterday at the concert—tears when Alexis Weissenberg played, as his encore, "Jesu, Joy of Man's Desiring." So beautiful. Steve says I create beauty around me. But I don't feel that, not strongly enough. I need something else.

Writing in my journal I discovered that the intense longing I felt watching the figure skating and listening to the concert was an indication of my own hunger to create something beautiful in my life. It was no accident, either, that both occasions involved classical music. While doing my doctoral work in London, I had begun to study voice, then decided that having been a student all my life, I couldn't bear starting over at thirty-five. Although I didn't make the connection then, this was also around the same time that I began thinking seriously of writing this book.

Journal writing allows us to examine the complexities and paradoxes of our emotional lives and, in Marion Milner's words, to let our thoughts "write themselves." In the safety of the journal's pages, we can examine what lies beneath our "apparent" emotions, trace the past and present associations that interweave in our emotional lives, and get closer to the real heart of the matter.

Taking Care of the Child Within

Anaïs Nin said in 1973, "In all of us there is a man, a woman, and a child, and the child is usually an orphan. So we have a tremendous task to do: we have to take care of this orphan in ourselves and in others." A great deal has been written about the inner child who lives on in each of us, usually abandoned and forgotten, often mistreated and brutalized, and always desperate for comfort. Whether this child is described in the language of Jungian archetypes or in the jargon of pop psychology, it is more than a metaphor. Indeed, its ongoing existence goes a long way toward explaining the primal emotions and irrational hurts we experience as adults that seem more appropriate to a young child.

For some therapists, the child within us holds the key to healing. For Alice Miller, it is where everything begins. Describing her own encounter with the child within, she says,

> She took me by the hand and led me into territory I had been avoiding all my life because it frightened me. Yet I had to go there; I could not keep on turning my back, for it was my territory, my very own. It was the place I had attempted to forget so many years ago, the same place where I had abandoned the child I once was. There she had to stay, alone with her knowledge, waiting until someone would come at last to listen to her and believe her.

And so, decades later, Alice Miller made the profound and life-changing decision to place her trust in the child within her, "this nearly autistic being who had survived the isolation of decades." She claims, *"We are all prisoners of our childhood, whether we know it, suspect it, deny it, or have never even heard about the possibility."* If we hope to become whole human beings, we have no choice but to face our repressed past and come to terms with what was perpetrated against that child. This is especially true in the case of childhood abuse and incest. Naida D. Hyde, a psychologist who works with incest survivors, writes, "It is the inner child of the past who holds the secret of each woman's abuse in a sacred but deadly trust with her offender. Suicide often seems a more viable option than breaking that trust." One woman who'd survived incest wrote a letter to the little girl she had been, comforting her and assuring her that things would get better. "Dear little ten-year-old girl," she wrote, "I speak to you from your future, surrounded by women, strong women, women who have suffered. The thing I want most for you to know is that you are a survivor. . . . All of the hurts, fears, and anger you are having to store up in that little body of yours will have an outlet some day in the future."

Another diarist expressed her sorrow for her lonely and terrified inner child in a poem, excerpted here.

> . . . I grieve for the lost child
> the child that still lives in me
> the child that cannot ask for life
> for love,
> for she knows it will not be given to her
> so she withdraws in fear
> praying for some sign of love . . .

Kate Danson (see Chapter Two) experienced the full extent of her childhood wounds through a series of dreams and nightmares that repeatedly revealed a little girl being starved and raped. She writes,

> Here, in the grief of my inner child, was the source of the strange sadness that overcame me whenever I attempted to write my thesis. Now that I understood the cause, I simply let the grief happen; I kept a special journal in which I poured out my love for the little child, and comforted her. I kept a picture on my desk, the only picture I had of my infant self, a picture of a child holding flowers so tightly one might have thought she was afraid someone would take them away from her.

Recently, many women have written about encountering the child within. Having written a doctoral dissertation on Christa Wolf, I find no account more fascinating than Wolf's *A Model Childhood*. In this multilayered autobiographical novel of her attempt to come to terms with her long-buried childhood in Nazi Germany, Wolf discovered that the child she had been was almost beyond retrieval, so effective the repression. She reflects,

> It hurts to admit that the child—aged three, helpless, alone—is inaccessible to you. . . . You abandoned the child, after all. After others abandoned it. All right, but she was also abandoned by the adult who slipped out of her, and who managed to do to her all the things adults usually do to children. The adult left the child behind, pushed her aside, forgot her, suppressed her, denied her, remade, falsified, spoiled and neglected her, was ashamed and proud of her, loved her with the

wrong kind of love, and hated her with the wrong kind of hate. Now, in spite of all impossibility, the adult wishes to make the child's acquaintance.

At the end of the book, Christa Wolf still isn't sure whether or not she has been able to comfort the child she'd abandoned almost half a century earlier. On the last page of the book, we read, "The closer you are to a person, the harder it seems to say something conclusive about him; it's a known fact. The child who was hidden in me—has she come forth? Or has she been scared into looking for a deeper, more inaccessible hiding place?" The truthful answer to her question can only be "I don't know."

Whether it is childhood abuse or other trauma she harbors, this inner child holds the key to our identity as mature adults. Astonishingly, she is also the source of spontaneity, creativity, and vitality in our lives. She may even be the most potent muse of all. "The poet, musician, artist continues throughout life to contact this child, the self who still knows how to play," Stephen Nachmanovitch tells us. "Improvisation, as playful experiment, is the recovery in each of us of the savage mind, our original child-mind." Emily Hancock describes how the gradual recovery of her own "girl within" was essential in moving her through writer's block while writing her book. She found, "Young Emily was a girl I had sealed off long ago because she did not fit the usual female stereotype. . . . Now that I recognized her and knew of her significance I could embrace her as the keeper of my original identity. Her memory galvanized my energies: I resumed writing this book."

You can get to know your inner child in the pages of your journal. Some therapists believe that writing with your nondominant hand takes you back to the point at which you were just learning how to write. Unsent letters and invented dialogues are also effective. Perhaps, like the diarist above, you want to write a letter to your younger self, offering the comfort and reassurance that she yearned for. Is there something that she wants to tell her mother or father that she couldn't say earlier? Even if they are no longer alive, it's not too late. Allow her to say it now. Perhaps it's someone else she wants to address. Write a dialogue between them. Let her have her say.

One exercise that may evoke powerful feelings involves working with photographs of yourself at various early ages. Choose photos that move you in some way, that elicit an emotion, a memory, or a bodily recollection. Perhaps you experience a sense of poignancy, sadness, or fondness when you look at them. You might even have a visceral response as memories locked in your body for years are activated. Start with a photo of yourself as a young child and describe what you see there. What do you feel, looking at the image of that little girl? What is she experiencing? Does she look happy, excited, shy, fearful, impassive? What kind of world does she inhabit? Who are her friends? What are her needs? Freewrite whatever impressions, feelings, or thoughts come into your head. Then, choose another photo of yourself, taken five to ten years later, and do the same thing. What changes do you see? What do you feel about her now? What does she feel? Let your two younger selves dialogue with each other. What do they have to say to each other? What do they have in common? How are they different?

My own inner child first surfaced when I was in therapy. From time to time, Michael would ask me what she was feeling and what she wanted from me. At first I resisted. Intellectually, I knew what he was talking about, but on an emotional level, I was embarrassed to be carrying a needy child inside me. If she had to exist at all, I just hoped she'd politely keep quiet during the therapy sessions, and then leave me alone. One day Michael asked me what she needed at that moment, and I had an immediate bodily sense of a little girl yearning to be stroked and cuddled. Much of my healing would come, he suggested, through paying careful attention to that child. I'm still working on it. Get to know your inner child. What is she like? What does she want to tell you? What does she most need from you? What would you like to give her that she never had before?

Self-Esteem

Low self-esteem plagues many if not most women today. When no less a big sister of modern feminism than Gloria Steinem writes a book about her own lifelong crippling sense of a lack of self-worth, the rest of us may feel vindicated. But this doesn't solve the problem. Low self-esteem obviously isn't a biological trait. It is not genetically inherited, although parents who suffer feelings of inferiority are likely to have children who follow suit. Nor is it simply related to whether or not we are successful in the eyes of the world. Its roots lie much deeper than that. What is it, then, and where does it come from?

The fact that low self-esteem is endemic among women suggests it is a social issue rather than merely a personal neurosis. Mary Catherine Bateson claims that "the issue of female inferiority still arises for virtually every woman growing up in this society." She speaks from experience. Despite being raised by two enlightened parents, Bateson herself spent many years putting her husband's concerns before her own. She says,

> For at least twenty years, whenever I interrupted my husband when he was busy, he finished what he was doing before he responded. When he interrupted me, I would drop what I was doing to respond to him, automatically giving his concerns priority. . . . By now, Barkev has learned that both of us need to be on guard against my willingness to sacrifice my time and my space, as if my goals were automatically less important than those of other members of the family.

Cultural myths of female inferiority are powerful. Often, they are so deeply ingrained in us that we don't even see their full effect. We assume that we're simply deficient, in some way lacking. But intellectual understanding of the problem alone won't solve it. Marion Woodman intimates that there is an archetypal dimension at play here. After 2,500 years during which the feminine has been denigrated, she suggests, it's no wonder that the "negative mother complex" rages out of control. She tells us,

> If you hear a voice deep in your body or in your dreams that says you are no good, that you are a failure, that you don't have any right to live, you may think it's you talking. In fact, it's the voice of the complex. You have to become strong enough to say, "This is the complex talking here. I do not have to submit to it." To stand up and hold your

self-esteem while that voice is doing everything it can to pull you down is not easy.

These critical voices within us affect our psychic functioning in dramatic ways, as the writer Deena Metzger discovered, doing battle with them as she tried to understand the reasons for her cancer. "The voices besiege me," she writes.

> "You've done your work." "You haven't done your work." "You've done too many different kinds of work." "You haven't focused on your own work." "You work too hard." "You never cease to work." "You don't work hard enough." "You neglect your real work." "You don't play, it even spoils your work." "There's nothing more important than your work." And didn't the inner hag cackle, "Even if you get cancer, you won't make the necessary sacrifices to write." Didn't the bitter inner critic shriek, "Die!"

We all have internalized self-defeating voices that tell us we can't do it even before we begin, and threaten us with mediocrity, failure, and ridicule if we go ahead despite them. One common manifestation is the impostor syndrome, where success is seen as a lucky fluke and we live our lives in fear of being "found out." No amount of external recognition can save us, either, because at the heart of the syndrome lies a deep-seated conviction of our own essential inadequacy, which persists in the face of all evidence. The impostor syndrome is so widespread that the term has entered mainstream vocabulary. Peggy Orenstein, author of Schoolgirls: Young Women, Self-Esteem, and the Confidence Gap, describes her experience, at twenty-one, of becoming paralyzed with fear of being "found out" as she wrote her senior thesis. "You feel like an impostor?" her adviser queried. "Don't worry about it. All smart women feel that way."

Men are not immune to the impostor syndrome, either, but studies have shown that by and large there's a difference. While they tend to attribute their success to personal merit and ability, we are more likely to explain it in terms of luck and fortunate circumstances. Conversely, when things go wrong, men are apt to blame external factors; women, themselves. Of course, such generalizations offer only a partial truth. But it's a telling one.

Women's lives, in fact, are divided in two by a mixed message that is hardly reasonable: Strive for success but don't surpass your husband; give all to the company, but don't neglect your children; demonstrate excellence, but be prepared to be judged by your looks; strive to gain a competitive edge, but don't be unfeminine—that is, aggressive. We are forced to switch back and forth between two opposing value systems and to live schizophrenic lives. No wonder women often feel like impostors; we're trying to serve two gods!

How does journal writing come in here? Exploring these nebulous, often deeply rooted doubts and anxieties in your journal is a gentle but effective way of raising them to a conscious level where they can be examined and challenged. The diary provides the ideal forum to dialogue with the internal voices that sap your confidence and tell you anything you accomplish is just a lucky break. One way to eavesdrop on the inner critic is to set up a dialogue between your conscious self and the voice of your "impostor." Play the role of an interested and sympathetic interviewer. Don't attack the impostor. She has been in hiding for too long. Let her finally have her say.

The very fact that you keep a journal speaks to your positive self-esteem. Putting pen to paper reflects an intuition, however tentative, that your life has value. The more you discover of your own hidden depths, the stronger the incentive to keep writing. A positive cycle ensues. Over time—six months, two years, five years—your journal witnesses to a self who is making a passionate effort to live with awareness and integrity. In the end, that is all any of us can do. It is no mean accomplishment.

Healing Our Bodies

And what of our all-too-often despised and abandoned bodies? Marion Woodman describes a time in her life when, near death, she learned compassion toward herself. During an out-of-body experience, she suddenly saw her physical being lying on the ground, waiting trustingly, like her dog, for her return. She remembers,

I thought, "I wouldn't betray him, but I would betray my own body."
Suddenly I realized what that betrayal meant—to have been given a
life and then decide it's not worth living. That seemed to be an ultimate
betrayal. I thought, "I wouldn't do this to my own dog, and I can't do
it to my own body." I was overcome by the sweetness of this patient
thing trusting that I would come back. I decided then to take responsibility for the life I was given—it wasn't mine to throw away.

Woodman's near-death experience symbolically mirrors both our culture's disdain for the body's integrity, and the broken link between
body and soul. For women, this is twice true: What, in all of Western
cultural history, has carried as much symbolic baggage as the female
body? Today, more than ever, the female body is allowed to exist only
as an abstract ideal, a fleshless construct of perfect lines and angles.
And it's this construct that supposedly defines who we are, what we
are worth, and what we can be in our lifetimes. The irony is that
women's real bodies have never been allowed to exist in and for
themselves.

Taught everywhere to objectify our bodies, how can we inhabit
them? To say that many of us have troubled relationships with our
bodies doesn't begin to intimate the depth of the wound. There is
nothing in our culture that encourages girls and women to accept
themselves in their unique beauty. As a result, that acceptance is won
only painfully and over time. Sometimes it doesn't come at all. The
writer Michele Murray, at forty, described her anguished relationship
with her body in journal entries that she wrote in the last six months
before she died of cancer in 1974:

A good part of my life has been determined by my conviction that my
body was ugly. As much as possible, I have avoided using it because I
have hated it so much. . . . The mastectomy and hysterectomy only
underlined the utter despicable quality of my body, but this wasn't a
new feeling. I'm not talking about my face here—but that too is
unsatisfactory. Like an ugly mask hiding the real me, thick lips, bad
skin, thick glasses, nothing shape. It could be said that all my cleverness
and intellectual activity was a way of compensating for and drawing
attention away from a body that was only a disgrace and an embar-

rassment. . . . And the culmination of all of this is that I am right—my body has failed me and in the most terrible way possible.

What painful self-objectification is laid bare in this journal entry. And how tragic that this self-loathing gave the writer no respite, even during the last weeks of her life. Yet, sadly, her suffering is not unusual.

I remember thinking throughout my teenage years and most of my twenties that if only I could get ten or twenty more pounds off, my life would fall into place. Until then, I was just putting in time. Nothing that I did, counted; nothing, including my body, was real. I did lose weight and there were dramatic changes in my self-image but, of course, things did not suddenly fall into place. Indeed, my body was no more my own than ever. For a time, the results of my early-morning weigh-in determined the mood of the day. I wish I could say that by my thirtieth birthday, my eyes were opened and I finally saw the light of self-acceptance once and for all. But it didn't happen like that. For some women it never ends; witness the number of gaunt, bleached-blond sixty- and seventy-year-olds trying to look thirty. And yet, somewhere along the way, I did begin to differentiate between the feminine ideal I was striving to emulate and the concrete reality of my own body. And despite my addiction to external reinforcement, I knew that I wasn't prepared to spend the rest of my life under the tyranny of the scales. If this meant my weight would fluctuate, so be it.

Part of our self-rejection comes from the fact that we generally don't see other women's bodies. Thus we measure our own by an impossible standard, and buy into society's fantasies of the perfect breasts and buttocks, turning ourselves into objects in the process. I remember the awe I felt the first time I shared a shower with other women in my swimming class. Here was a woman of at least sixty-five (I was in my late twenties then) with soft curves and skin that revealed the rich living of her years; there was a young woman of perhaps twenty with long, smooth body and hair. Both were complete within themselves; each had her own loveliness. As Gloria Steinem urged so eloquently, "A little natural togetherness would show us, the Family of Woman, where each of us is beautiful and no one is the same."

That was the first time I sensed that perhaps my body, too, was acceptable just as it was.

For most of us, self-acceptance is a slow and gradual process. Accustomed to putting others' needs before our own, we may take our bodies for granted until confronted with a bodily crisis or breakdown. Then the link between body and soul manifests itself with unmistakable clarity. Several months after her mastectomy in 1979, Audre Lorde wrote in her journal,

> It is such an effort to find decent food in this place, not to just give up and eat the old poison. But I must tend my body with at least as much care as I tend the compost, particularly now when it seems so beside the point. Is this pain and despair that surround me a result of cancer, or has it just been released by cancer?

But along with despair, Audre Lorde also experienced "the whole terrible meaning of mortality as both weapon and power," and "the large sweetness of the women who stayed open to me when I needed that openness like rain, who made themselves available." Healing, in the midst of trauma. In February 1977, Deena Metzger, too, tried to decipher the meaning of her breast cancer in her journal. "This is the moment of danger, I know it," she wrote. "What shall I decide about being responsible for my own life? . . . If transformation of my life holds the possibility of health—and it does, it does—then what are the consequences of old habits and blindspots?" For both Audre Lorde and Deena Metzger, the cancer that claimed their right breasts was more than a freak accident of cellular dysfunction. They saw it as symbolic of the toxic poisons, both chemical and emotional, that surround us from all sides, and accepted it as an opportunity for self-transformation at the deepest possible level. Healing came, not through radiation or chemotherapy, but through ruthless soul-searching, intensive journal writing, and the love of friends. The title of Metzger's work, *Tree*, like the tree she had tattooed on her scar, stands for the "transformative and revolutionary love" that can preserve the body from harm despite every threat of aggression. As she put it, "It's what we do for each other that heals." Audre Lorde, for her part, claimed, "I say the love of women healed me." What more powerful witness to our undivided bodysoul could there be?

What meanings does your body hold for you? What defining moments have determined your sense of bodily identity? How have you celebrated your body's beauty and integrity, its immeasurable capacities? Where have you abandoned it, betrayed, or despised it? What story does your body want to tell?

Adrienne Rich makes a passionate plea that we women take back our own bodily experience and begin to "think through the body," claiming,

> We need to imagine a world in which every woman is the presiding genius of her own body. In such a world women will truly create new life, bringing forth not only children (if and as we choose) but the visions, and the thinking, necessary to sustain, console, and alter human existence—a new relationship to the universe. Sexuality, politics, intelligence, power, motherhood, work, community, intimacy will develop new meanings; thinking itself will be transformed.

Adrienne Rich is describing a state of wholeness in which thinking is brought back to its bodily origins, in which body, soul, and mind are no longer experienced as opposing aspects of a being at war with itself. As I said at the beginning of this chapter, to heal is to make whole: to unify what was separate, broken in pieces. For many women, the journal offers one place in their lives where, literally and symbolically, all of the pieces of themselves finally come together and they can be whole. Elly Danica, a writer and visual artist who survived a horrifying childhood of sexual and psychological brutalization by her father, wrote over two thousand pages of journal notes about those years and then, in a period of three weeks, wrote a book based on those journals. She reflects,

> I used my extensive journal writing to search for a voice, for an "I" who could speak with authority about the Self. For me, the daily writing was where and how I worked towards a re-integration of the aspects of Self which had been fragmented. So it was a search, a quest,

to find the pieces and then a long process of writing them into a *whole*
I could live with.

The wholeness we seek is not a fixed point of arrival, however. It
is a fluid process, "a never-ending striving toward individuation on
first this frontier and then that frontier of self," writes Stephanie
Demetrakopoulos. Growth, she says in *Listening to Our Bodies*, "ought to
be an ebb and flow that seeks new channels, new shores." The process
of seeking new shores, of continual transformation, which the journal
writer enacts over and over again, ultimately affects everyone around
her. In closing, as Judith Duerk put it, "The wholeness manifesting in
the life of one individual becomes a microcosm of wholeness effecting
an alchemical change in the macrocosm of the outer realm . . . wholeness begetting wholeness."

6

Reinventing the Self

It's not so much the imperfect words on these faint blue lines, as the feeling, time and again, of returning to a place from which one can continue to spin one and the same thread, where one can gradually create a continuum, a continuum which is really one's life.

ETTY HILLESUM, An Interrupted Life

Writing has been the constancy through which I have reinvented myself after every uprooting.

MARY CATHERINE BATESON, Composing a Life

It is possible that when we travel deep enough, we always encounter an element of sadness, for full awareness of ourselves always includes the knowledge of our own ephemerality and the passage of time. But it is only in that knowledge—not its denial—that things gain their true dimensions, and we begin to feel the simplicity of being alive. It is only that knowledge that is large enough to cradle a tenderness for everything that is always to be lost—a tenderness for each of our moments, for others and for the world.

EVA HOFFMAN, Lost in Translation

Things change. Nothing stays the same for long—an obvious truth, yet one for which our hearts and psyches seem curiously unprepared. Life itself is flux, transience, mutability. Like the coming and going of the seasons, of bumper harvests and times of scarcity, our individual lives have their own cycles of abundance and loss, their own rhythms of constancy and change. During our lifetimes, each of us will undergo myriad changes, large and small. These may range from births and deaths of those we love the most, to the endless changes of lesser consequence that we absorb every day of our lives. Many of the changes we experience bring new challenge, growth, stimulation, excitement, joy, and celebration. Others are accompanied by heartache and loss, identity crisis, and a sense of having no solid ground under our feet, a feeling that the novelist Milan Kundera described as "the unbearable lightness of being," in his novel with that title. Our bodies' continual replacement of cells provides a metaphor for the working of our psyches: forever changing, forever the same.

Often, we prefer the security of the known and the comfort of the familiar to the challenge of the new and strange. We may even insist on maintaining the status quo against our own best interests. Because, as studies have shown, any significant change, even one we welcome, carries a high stress quotient. (In a recent survey of lottery winners, for example, many said they were actually less happy than they had been before their big windfall, a discovery that probably leaves most of us with the feeling that we might have done better, given the opportunity!) Why is change—even desired change—so stressful? To begin with, it requires psychic energy. It threatens the routines, habits, and fixed points of reference that provide comfort and stability in our daily lives. We are creatures of habit. During a time when most of the traditional support structures that once held families and communities in place have collapsed, any further upheaval in our lives can threaten our sense of having a secure identity. Then, too, it's never a single contained event. Our lives are complex tapestries of delicately interwoven threads. A tug in one direction usually has unforeseen consequences for the whole; change can alter the entire woof and warp of our existence.

What is fascinating is that psychologists claim the degree of satisfaction and well-being we experience over time depends less on what actually happens to us than on the meaning we give it, the extent to which we are able to weave it into our evolving life stories. Change always brings the possibility of chaos—and of transformation. In her extraordinary book Composing a Life, Mary Catherine Bateson takes a close look at the lives of five women who turned the many upheavals in their personal and professional lives into creative steppingstones to new and expanded identities. Bateson claims that change is inevitable in our lives today. "The circumstances of women's lives now and in the past provide examples for new ways of thinking about the lives of both men and women," she tells us, then asks,

> What are the possible transfers of learning when life is a collage of different tasks? How does creativity flourish on distraction? What insights arise from the experience of multiplicity and ambiguity? And at what point does desperate improvisation become significant achievement?

With these unusual questions, Bateson gives us a fresh way of thinking about the role of change in our own lives. We often think of learning as a predictable linear path, one step leading to the next, more challenging, one. But what if the most fruitful learning lies, instead, in the unmapped spaces between those steps, between the known fixed points of our lives? If that were the case, a different way of looking at the disruptions and dislocations in our lives might reveal their hidden gold. This is where the journal comes in.

Change and the Journal

The Greek philosopher Heraclitus said that we can't step into the same river twice. Of course, it's not only the river that changes. Who we are today is not who we were yesterday, and none of us knows who she will be twenty or thirty years from now. Like Mary Catherine Bateson, many of us reinvent ourselves after every uprooting, through writing. Keeping a journal provides an experience of continuity in the never-ending flux of life. It affirms that we are not leaves tossed around haphazardly by autumn winds, but embodied beings with depth, substance, and solidity. It reminds us that, come what may, through every major and minor upheaval in our lives, paradoxically we remain ourselves. The diary mirrors the paradox of Heraclitus' river, forever changing while remaining the same. It provides stability and captures who we are in a given moment at the same time that it helps us understand and accept the many fluctuations, desired and unbidden, that we experience. As you contemplate the possibility of changing your career, your marital status, your home, it functions as a patient sounding board, allowing you to weave the changes into the larger fabric of your life. To borrow Bateson's metaphor, it's the internal gyroscope that keeps us centered, affirming continuity "among various stages and commitments" even while it testifies to change.

Some changes are inevitable during our lifetimes. People are born. People die. We move, form primary relationships, couple and uncouple. We complete our education and embark on careers. We change careers. Time passes, and we observe our bodies aging. One way or another we lose those we love—family members, friends, and colleagues, perhaps a cherished animal. In a sense, all change implies a loss of some kind, a loss of the known, the familiar, the comfortable.

"An Effort Against Loss"

Anaïs Nin began writing her legendary diary at the age of ten, aboard the ship that carried her across the Atlantic, away from Barcelona and her beloved father to a new life in New York. Years later, she reflected, "Over and over again I discover the diary is an effort against loss, the passing, the deaths, the uprootings, the witherings, the unrealities. I feel that when I enclose something, I save it. It is alive here."

Like Anaïs Nin, many of us anchor our lives in some form of writing practice, hoping to preserve what we have cherished, on the blank page. Keeping a journal provides a means of coming to terms with the loss we experience. Its pages absorb our desolation and anguish. Through giving our grief a voice, rather than denying or suppressing it, we begin to integrate it into our lives. The poet Rainer Maria Rilke admonished us not to waste our sorrows by desperately "trying to foresee their end." Instead, he says, we must recognize them as "our winter foliage, our sombre evergreen, one of the seasons of our interior year." This, we can do in our diaries.

Oftentimes, women start keeping journals precisely in the midst of sorrow, yearning to find solace, clarity, and a sense of meaning in a life disrupted by tragedy. Here are excerpts from the diary of Wilma Shore, whose husband had died only weeks before.

> July 14. His death spills over into everything. The most trivial things become tragic. I stepped on a wasp under the flowering crab and it became: *My husband died and I was stung by a wasp.* And then it was, *My husband died and the market had no apricot juice.* I keep crying. If I happen to be at a mirror I sometimes look at myself and see in my eyes the helpless rage that I remember from the blue eyes of crying babies.

> July 15. I'm tired all the time. Today I could hardly talk to the kind friends who called. Until a widow called and then I was lively. Could it be that I'm angry at the women who still have husbands?

Two weeks later, Wilma wrote, "Yesterday I got dressed up and I looked pretty good, and I went out and saw friends I hadn't seen for years, and I felt fine. And when I got home he was still dead." Here the casual enjoyment of visiting old friends coexists alongside the inescapable finality of her husband's death. The diarist has begun to integrate the reality of her enormous loss into her daily life.

Mary Shelley, whose husband, Percy, drowned before her twenty-fifth birthday (following the deaths of three of their four children), also poured her bitter loneliness and despair into her journal. Three months after his death, she wrote,

> Oct. 2. [1822] Alas! I am alone. No eye answers mine; my voice can with none assume its natural modulation. What a change! O my beloved Shelley! how often during those happy days—happy, though chequered—I thought how superiorly gifted I had been in being united with one to whom I could unveil myself, and who could understand me! Well, then, now I am reduced to these white pages, which I am to blot with dark imagery.

Two years later, Mary Shelley was still full of anguish over her loss, and barely able to cope. "Writing this is useless," she wrote, "it does not even soothe me; on the contrary, it irritates me by showing the pitiful expedient to which I am reduced." Nevertheless, she continued to lament her losses in the journal. Obviously the ongoing expression of her grief was cathartic.

Perhaps no one has described the journal's essential role in times of loss more eloquently than Elizabeth Cox. Describing her sense of unreality and need to mourn in the days following her husband's death of AIDS in 1987, she recalls,

> One night I got out my journal. And its words rang true and strong. I wanted to hold its words, organize them—create with them something coherent and concrete that would help me remember, help me make sense of the unexplainable. . . . I wanted to immortalize my loss. I wanted to find a place to put the anger I felt at the cruelty of life. These were the feelings that had prompted me to keep a journal in the first place. These were the feelings I had as I read and reread my journal through the night. My journal helped me grieve my husband.

In *A Time to Mourn*, Rebecca Rice reflects on the role of the journal she kept during the final stages of her husband's brain cancer. In March 1985, three months after his death, she wrote,

> In my journal, which I have almost filled since I began it last December, I write of how Len's cancer swelled in his brain for eight and a half months before he died and how the passages into and out of life are not, in the end, so different. . . . Both are natural events rooted in a mystery over which we ultimately have no control. What I wonder is this: Where will I be when my nine months of mourning are finished? At the beginning of my life or the end of it? All I know for certain is that I am moving toward some new phase.

Even in her sorrow, the journal allowed Rebecca Rice to envision her life beyond the finality of her husband's death, thereby enabling her to make the essential transition from death to life. It also served as the basis of a series of essays and her book, *A Time to Mourn: One Woman's Journey Through Widowhood*.

When the beloved one's quality of life has long since diminished, the experience of his or her death may be double-edged. May Sarton described this experience poignantly in her published journal *At Sev-*

enty. On December 22, 1982, she wrote, "Judy died last night. I have prayed that she might be allowed to slip away, and now she has. But it is always so sudden, so unexpected—death—and so final. . . . There have been other great loves in my life, but only Judy gave me a home and made me know what home can be."

One of the most devastating losses for all women, regardless of age, is the death of their mothers. Often this becomes a turning point, prompting extensive soul-searching and a reckoning with all that remains unresolved. For Nancy Esther James, journal writing was a way of coming to terms with her guilt over the fact that she wasn't at home when her mother died, and of working out grief over a relationship that would never be salvaged now. "What did I think yesterday morning?" she berated herself on November 25, 1969.

> Why didn't I know, and stay home? Or did I know, and only half-know I knew? On the other hand, what could I have done—except, no doubt, panic and do and say all the wrong things, or just be paralyzed? . . . Still, I can't help feeling that I really failed her by not being there —as I suppose I have more or less consistently failed her, in some way, all my life.

For Le Anne Schreiber, the journal served a different function. It affirmed her own ongoing life while providing a means of facing her mother's imminent death with honesty. She tells us,

> During the last month of my mother's life, this journal was my means of survival. In part it gave me a saving distance, reminded me that I was a witness to dying, not the one dying. The journal was also my weapon against denial, my way of looking in the presence of so many averted eyes, my way of remembering in the face of so much forgetting.

The loss of a sister, too, can plunge us into unprecedented grief. Here is Emily Carr, writing ten days after the death of her older sister, Lizzie, in 1936. "How hard it is to fill up a hole that somebody has gone out of! The empty feel, the hollow quietness, that ache that you can't place as if one were sickening for something you don't quite know what." Cleaning out her sister's house, Carr experiences only absence and silence. "The sitting-room is dead now," she laments. "The walls give no echoes. Taps don't drip. No clocks tick. No fires crackle. 'Finished' seems to be written on everything, on our baby-hood and girlhood and womanhood, on our disappointments and happinesses, tendernesses and bitternesses, joys and sorrows." Two years earlier, the young Anne Morrow Lindbergh, too, had lost a beloved older sister, named Elisabeth. A week after her sister's prema-ture death at thirty, Anne tried to anticipate how this sorrow might be absorbed into her life.

> I must write it all out, at any cost. Writing is thinking. It is more than living, for it is being conscious of living. At this moment I do not worry about losing Elisabeth. I shall never lose her; I have the rest of my life to think about her, to realize her. No—what I must work out is my life without her, going on without her. The person I was with her I must keep intact, because it is a denial of her to let it go. It is failing a trust. I must be what I was with her, for, as always and with everyone she touched, the truest clearest person came out at her touch. She had the gift of clarifying you, a creative sympathy.

As painful as all loss is, however, the one we find most difficult to accept is that of a child, a loss that threatens the natural order of things and undermines our belief in an underlying cosmic justice. In February 1993, Sheila's seven-year-old daughter was struck by an automobile as she darted out between parked cars during a snowball fight. For ten days she lay in a coma, her life hovering in the balance. Then, one day while I was visiting Sheila and her daughter in the hospital, Elana opened her eyes. Ten months later, this little girl, whom no one had expected to make a full recovery, was doing accel-erated math—until one December afternoon when, without warning, she died of respiratory arrest. In a sense, her family lost her twice. Sheila is convinced that Elana came back out of the coma for those ten months because she still had something to teach those around her, especially her family. What follows is an excerpt from Sheila's journal, written on December 12, 1993, the day of her daughter's funeral.

People are laughing outside, the television is on and my daughter is dead in the cold cold ground. I sit here on my bed trying to deal with this fact. I just returned from the cemetery, where the men in my family placed the small pine box with Elana's bodily remains into the frigid snowy ground of a Farmingdale plot—where my mother bought 4 plots side by side. . . . Now I sit getting it all down while people I love eat Chinese food at my table outside my bedroom.

In the months that followed, Sheila kept up a running conversation with Elana, pouring her terrible grief and longing into the journal.

January 13, 1994. Thursday. I miss you Elana. I miss holding you and feeling your soft lips kiss mine. I miss your smoothest of smooth skin on the sweet hands I loved to hold and felt so much comfort in. Where are you—you left so quickly—you said bye to me when I went to the Post Office and I never saw you again. . . . I miss you my little girl— part of my heart was buried with you. . . . Sweetheart, even in spirit form I kiss your face and hands and lips and tell you to hold my love like I did that day in the car when you cried when I dropped you off at Daddy's. I have my suspicions that perhaps you were supposed to leave when you got hit but I wouldn't let go of you. I sat at your side in the Intensive Care Unit and I told you to take your time but said you gotta come back—it was clear and adamant, I needed you, you could not leave. And so I prayed more with my act of loving you than my words. . . . We travelled so far, Lani, why did you go when we had come so far?

October 7, 1994. Describing what Sheila went through last year brings it all back: the jubilation and relief when Lani came back whole, and the shock when she died so unexpectedly. The last time I saw her was at the Quaker Thanksgiving Pot Luck last year. I was hugging a friend, and Elana looked up at me and said, "Don't forget about me." I bent to embrace her but held her delicately, worried that I might disturb the tracheotomy tube that allowed her to breathe. I sensed she was still fragile, but not why.

While putting the final touches on my doctoral dissertation in London in April 1988, I received a devastating letter from my journal writing friend from university days. Shira had learned only weeks before that her three-year-old son, Chase, had brain cancer and the prospects for his recovery were not good. What follows is an entry from her journal of that time.

> March 18, 1988. I've wasted away my time off—putting off yet again writing down—trying to write down about it! "IT." Chase's disease: collapse January 23rd, his diagnosis—malignant brain cancer, his prognosis—"kids don't survive this kind of cancer." My pain—my overwhelming, all consuming pain! I talk and talk and talk about Chase, I do what I can and what I must and it lies in me like a lump I cannot shed, flee, pass through or face up to. I haven't written because I cannot—I am crying as I write even this "report" of events, this summary of events that have torn our family, and my heart wide open. . . . I feel so lost, so separated from myself. I feel hollow as if I was only half awake or half there. . . . Everything I've done has been because I must continue "normally" for Chase's sake. Inside, I am half dead from grief—as flat and featureless and formless as a drowning victim—as charred and dusty and dead as a burn victim.

So many expressions of loss. So much heartache entrusted to and eased by the journal. When we lose someone we love, journal writing allows us to say good-bye to that person and to mourn our loss; to capture something of their essence, thereby immortalizing them; and to continue a dialogue with them even in their physical absence. With time, as many of the diarists quoted above found, we find healing in the process.

> October 7, 1994. Working on this chapter is making me weep. How can I read these journals about suffering and loss without identifying with the writers themselves? Maybe this is the answer to my question in Chapter Ten about whether or not reading someone else's diary is voyeuristic. I think empathy is the crucial factor. Without it, we eavesdrop on someone's most intimate outpourings and take what isn't ours. A published journal is a gift to the reader, the diarist's heart and soul offered on the page. How can we come to it with anything less than compassion and tenderness?

When it involves the end of a long-term romantic relationship or cherished friendship, our experience of loss may evoke mixed emotions. The relief of ending an intolerable situation may be mixed with sadness for all that once was, anxiety about the future, and exhilaration over the new beginning. The writer Marlene Nourbese Philip says, "I started writing when my first marriage broke up some twenty-two years ago—I began to keep a journal. I was really a closet writer. And through writing I think I actually kept my sanity during that difficult time."

Loss forces us to start over. It also makes this *possible*, since it is often accompanied by a new beginning of some kind. The new mother forfeits her freedom in order to care for her infant and, through her child, sees the world with fresh eyes. Another mother, bereft after her child leaves home, may for the first time in years have a room of her own and time to write in her journal, draw, or make music. The end of a marriage brings the chance to break out of stale patterns of thought and behavior, and to reinvent one's life. A grieving friend described her mother's death as unexpectedly liberating, because it no longer left her any excuse not to live her life the way she wished. There are individuals who have managed to make chronic, even terminal illness the opportunity for rebirth. What are the losses you need to acknowledge and mourn in your journal? What do you need to release and let go of in order to enter the next stage of growth? What new beginnings can you glimpse on the near horizon of your life? What is attempting to be born? Welcome it in your journal.

On the Move

Whether we move to a new home, a different city, or even country, leaving a place where we have lived, especially one we've loved, means abandoning a setting rich with associations and memories, a place where things are more than meets the eye. The spaces we inhabit are dense with meaning. The park at the corner is not just any park; it's the park where you jogged for the first time or the park where your children always played. Each visit to a favorite restaurant carries the memories of other occasions, echoes of other conversations held there. In the new place, things are only what they appear to be. There is no rich underlay of past association, and sometimes it can feel as if we are truly starting from scratch. "Pattern is the soil of significance," Eva Hoffman observes, "and it is surely one of the hazards of emigration, and exile, and extreme mobility, that one is uprooted from that soil."

My journal has been my sole companion throughout seven major moves among cities, countries, and continents. Since most of those moves were to cities where I didn't know anyone, I could not rely on family or friends for support. Here, more than ever, I counted on my journal to help me remember myself. While writing my dissertation in London, I traveled back and forth between England and Germany to do research. As every multilinguist knows, one translates not only one's thoughts, but oneself, into the new language. In Germany, I eased the frustration of not feeling fully myself by writing often and at length in my journal. And at some point I evolved a kind of settling-in, journal writing ritual. Even before I had unpacked my bags in Marbach, I'd walk through the little town, bring back a loaf of bread and some flowers, take out my journal, and write. This became a ceremony of transition—from one country and language to another. During one extended stay in the residence, in the summer of 1985, I wrote,

> I was thinking again that wherever two or more women meet, they form a community. One brings out the coffee or the wine, another brings the biscuits, another a tablecloth and a candle, another proposes an outing together—it's amazing but it seems to happen all the time. I find that where there are three women, there is a community; where there are three men, there are usually three lonely individuals. Women seem to "commune" in order to share, whether their experiences, or resources. Men get together for external purposes: sport, business, war. Always, as they say, "goal-oriented."

Two years later, when I first arrived in New York to join Steve, I often felt I was drowning in a sea of meaninglessness. The mythic city held no fond memories for me and seemed so overwhelming and impersonal that I felt I would never form normal ties of affection with anyone. I'd be doomed to permanent alienation. The emotional weightlessness often made me sick at heart and physically ill, as if I were suffering a terrible case of vertigo. In a sense, I was, of course.

Isolated in a tenth-floor apartment on Staten Island while I worked on my doctoral dissertation, lacking a meaningful framework in which to imagine my life in New York, I was lost in an excess of empty space.

Many diarists have described how essential the role of their journal is amidst changing shores and selves. Anaïs Nin regarded the psychic trauma of her early uprooting from Barcelona as the origin of her lifelong passion for the diary. During a lecture she gave in 1973, she said, "When I came to America I couldn't speak the language, and I had no friends. . . . The diary became not only a companion, so that I wouldn't be lost in a foreign country with a language I couldn't speak, but also a source of contact with myself." Over time, Nin says, she realized that her journal took on a larger role in her life. "It became the diary of an adventurer," she wrote. "It made me look at my life, at sorrowful moments, at moments of great disintegrating experiences, and constantly reminded me that it was an adventure, that it was a tale." For Nin, the diary served to unify the tale, to reintegrate the shattered fragments of her experience.

Gwendolyn Bennett, a poet and artist of the Harlem Renaissance, kept a journal while living on an art scholarship in Paris at the age of twenty-three. Her diary helped ease the loneliness she felt in a new country whose language she didn't speak. On June 26, 1925, she wrote, "Could I mark this day I would put a black ring around it as one of the saddest days I have ever spent. I moved today to my new hotel. For two days now it has rained—the people tell me that this is typical Paris weather. A cold rain that eats into the very marrow of the bone and I am alone." Gwendolyn's suffering reached its peak on July 4, when she recorded in her journal: "A homesickness more poignant and aching than anything I can ever imagine held me in its grip. All day long I did not see or speak to a single one of my compatriots nor did I even hear a word of English spoken."

Twenty-five years earlier, Paula Modersohn-Becker, a young German artist, had quite a different experience when she went to Paris in order to immerse herself in its art. On January 1, 1900, she confided to her diary, "I am in Paris [and] feel a new world stirring within me." For Paula, her diary and letters make clear, Paris represented the possibility of breaking away from the rigid feminine role she was expected to adopt and of taking herself seriously as an artist. In a letter written several weeks after her arrival, her tone is exuberant:

> The air, when one walks across the bridges over the Seine! There seems to be a shimmering and mixing of subtle gray, yellow, and silver tones which completely shroud the branches of the trees. And the beautiful buildings are set off with a wonderful depth against this atmosphere. The gardens of the Luxembourg at twilight—oh, just twilight here! . . . And the street life! Every moment there is something new to see.

Paula's subsequent stays in Paris were in part an escape from the duties of domesticity that threatened to engulf her in Worpswede, the little rural village and artists' colony where she lived with Otto Modersohn, her artist husband. It also opened the door to the artistic innovation frowned upon by the more traditional members of their circle. Paula knew that she was coming into her own. Her fourth and final visit, in 1906, marked a trial separation from her husband. On February 24, she wrote, "I have left Otto Modersohn and I am standing beween my old and my new life. What will it be like? And what will I be like in my new life? Now it is all about to happen." In May she wrote jubilantly to her sister, "I am going to become something—I'm living the most intensely happy period of my life."

But perhaps the most riveting account I have come across of the attempt to reinvent oneself in a new country and language is Eva Hoffman's beautiful memoir, *Lost in Translation*. Leaving their beloved Warsaw in 1959 after a resurgence of anti-Semitism, the fourteen-year-old Eva, her parents, and younger sister crossed the Atlantic by ship, arriving first in Halifax, then continuing on by train to Vancouver. There, without language or memories, Eva was sick with nostalgia. "It was here that I fell out of the net of meaning into the weightlessness of chaos," Hoffman recalls. When her friend gave her a diary with lock and key for her birthday, Eva had wondered,

> If I am indeed to write something entirely for myself, in what language do I write? Several times, I open the diary and close it again. I can't

decide. Writing in Polish at this point would be a little like resorting to Latin or ancient Greek—an eccentric thing to do in a diary. . . . I finally choose English. If I'm to write about the present, I have to write in the language of the present, even if it's not the language of the self.

Her diary offered Eva the promise of continuity, a chance "to update what might have been my other self." It also provided a means of entry into the new world. "I learn English through writing, and, in turn, writing gives me a written self," she discovered.

For many years, Eva Hoffman felt herself caught between "two stories and two vocabularies," two different "diagram[s] of the psyche," until eventually she achieved an integration wherein "each language modifies the other, crossbreeds with it, fertilizes it." Near the end of her account, she notes:

> I'm writing a story in my journal, and I'm searching for a true voice. I make my way through layers of acquired voices, silly voices, sententious voices, voices that are too cool and too overheated. Then they all quiet down, and I reach what I'm searching for: silence. I hold still to steady myself in it. This is the white blank center, the level ground that was there before Babel was built, that is always there before the Babel of our multiple selves is constructed. From this white plenitude, a voice begins to emerge: it's an even voice, and it's capable of saying things straight, without exaggeration or triviality. . . . We all need to find this place in order to know that we exist not only within culture but also outside it.

Hoffman's attempt to find a voice that, rising from silence, rings authentic at the boundary of two cultures and languages offers a wonderful description of the journal writing journey. Our task, too, is to work our way down through the many voices we have internalized over time to our "voiceless ground" in order to arrive at a voice that is uniquely our own. This is the challenge and the promise that journal writing holds out to us.

Even a temporary dislocation can be disquieting. The poet L. L. Zeiger spent a month in an artists' colony during the summer of 1977, and found that the "unique combination of intense privacy and intense interaction with strangers" caused her to begin keeping a journal for the first time in her life. At the beginning of her stay, especially, the journal was her lifeline. An early entry reads, "In many ways, I am quite isolated here—and not always by choice. . . . What must I seem like to them? Gray-haired, clearly older, but wailing like some self-deprecating waif in the midst of all this creativity. . . . The problem: I have no one to ally myself with, no one to talk to, but this journal." In the course of recording her wicked observations of those around her, this diarist muses, "How must I appear in everyone else's journal? Glad I can't see!"

Whenever we step into a new environment, we are forced—and free—to reinvent ourselves. The journal remembers who we have been, as it witnesses who we are becoming. What are the geographical markers of meaning in your life? What significance, literal and symbolic, does place hold for you? Where is your home?

A Mirror of the Changing Self

Self-Image and Aging

During my early twenties, as I've said already, I experienced a significant weight loss over a period of several years. The transition from ugly duckling to beautiful swan was, as I'd anticipated, an earth-shaking one. But I was not prepared for the intense ambivalence I felt about becoming suddenly visible in a society that sees young women primarily as sex objects. After a plump and self-hating adolescence, I certainly wanted to be thought attractive and sexy. But it hadn't occurred to me that the men whose attentions I had craved would see me as only that, as though my I.Q. had plummeted along with my weight. My confusion and mixed feelings are evident in the prolific journals I wrote during that time, whose entries give ample proof of my shaky self-image. Who and what I had been until then, who I wanted to be, and who I thought men thought I was, were all at odds with one another. One minute I believed the world was my oyster. The next, I walked unthinkingly to the size eighteen rack to buy a skirt. I had no clear sense of my body's size or boundaries—the perfect foil for all projections. Obviously, measuring up to the feminine ideal was not going to resolve all of my insecurities once and for all, as I'd hoped. If anything, things just got more complicated. Through it all, my journal provided one safe place, one source of stability in my tenuous world, mirroring the changes while reminding me that I was qualitatively more than my current weight and body size.

And of course there is one kind of change that none of us escapes —aging. For women, it carries clear-cut value judgments that cannot help but affect our self-image. Here is the British novelist Antonia White, for example, in a revealing journal entry. "The feeling of physical inadequacy, of being ugly almost to repulsiveness, comes up often so strongly. I try to fight it rationally, tell myself that I am no more repulsive physically than most women of my age," she wrote at the age of thirty-six! Our double standard is deeply entrenched. Gray hair and wrinkles may symbolize a certain weathered wisdom and the charm of worldly experience in men of a certain age, but they never call virility into question. For graying women in our society, sexual attractiveness itself is at stake (there is no female equivalent of "virility"). Paul Newman may well be sexy at seventy, and Robert Redford at sixty, but an enlightened male interviewer recently asked Susan Sarandon in all seriousness whether she thought she would ever play a sexy role again. She was forty-seven years old. Gloria Steinem, told that she didn't look forty, offered the now-famous response, "This is what forty looks like." The fact that public figures are challenging cultural myths about "older women" augurs well for all of us. Here is an entry from Sheila Gelbman's journal that shows the difficult journey toward self-acceptance so many of us experience.

Today I danced to African music. It was not a need to dance that drove me but a knowledge that, once dancing, it brings much pleasure and makes me feel happier to be alive. I see now how my desire to exercise daily came from fear of not being as attractive and also more deeply a desire to keep myself from getting older creating in essence a state of struggle against the natural rhythm of life and decay. . . . I am no longer a teenager, I am a woman whose breasts have suckled two children, whose heart has buried one of them in cold earth, whose thighs know the pleasure of a woman's gifts, both in receiving and giving, whose hair is painted silver with the struggle of relationship, whose brown eyes have wept deeply till there were no more waters in the body. I am forty-three and have the right to grow older . . . to be loved with extra flesh and silver hair, varicosed veins and colorless face.

If we buy into our culture's obsession with eternal youth, taut and streamlined bodies, and ever-flawless skin, the best we can hope for is a fleeting moment in the spotlight, before time and weather take their toll. But if we can escape the tyranny of false images, who knows what power might be ours? Women writers are just beginning to give us stories about their lives as older women, and what they are telling us is much more complex and interesting than any of the old stereo-types suggest. We know that older women have been made invisible in society. What we haven't understood is that this very invisibility can bring with it a new freedom to observe and to act. We sacrifice our status as objects of the male gaze and, in return, become subjects of our own lives. Writers like Carolyn Heilbrun and Germaine Greer claim that it is only as a woman painstakingly puts aside the external expectations that have determined her life that she comes into her own, becomes fully herself. Very often this happens during her fifties, coinciding with menopause. In "Serenity and Power," the stunning final chapter of The Change, Greer says,

> Only when a woman ceases the fretful struggle to be beautiful can she turn her gaze outward, find the beautiful and feed upon it. She can at last transcend the body that was what other people principally valued her for, and be set free both from their expectations and her own capitulation to them. It is quite impossible to explain to younger women that this new invisibility, like calm and indifference, is a desir-able condition.

Our task, then, as we grow older, is to reclaim our lives for ourselves. Over and over again, women are getting reacquainted, in their diaries, with their buried selfhood and power. Journal writing brings us back to something essential and timeless within us, something that sur-passes our changing age, shape, and size.

Caretaking

Self-image, at any age, has much to do with how we see ourselves in relation to those we love the most: parents, husband or partner, children, close friends. Since our sense of self is forged largely in community, it's not surprising that self-image is threatened when things don't go well. Melissa Gayle West describes her painful battle with the internal voices that were constantly telling her she didn't measure up as a mother to her little girl. Dialoguing with them in her diary, gradually she gains an understanding of what is happening.

July 25, 1990. Who is this Good Mother inside my head? Who is she? At first she was not separate from me. I carried her not just in my head but upon my back, my back so tired from her great burden of guilt; but this, I thought, this is what mothering is about. To feel so tired. To feel so guilty. To feel so inadequate. . . . Bit by bit I understand that this Good Mother voice inside my head represents everything I have heard or read about mothering, from parents, culture, religion.

Once Melissa was able to sort this out, she began to feel "more awake, more alive," and the voices lost their power to destroy her confidence.

At the far end of motherhood lies the experience of relinquishing one's children into the world, yet another variation on the theme of letting go. The lengthy journal excerpt that follows shows Dolores LaFata's experience of just this.

February 8, 1994. I awake early—4 A.M. It is the morning of the day that my son will leave to enter the Army. It is a cold winter's day. Outside the snow is swirling. . . . Suddenly I am roused from my reverie as I sense him standing next to me. . . . He tells me that he is feeling somewhat apprehensive, he hopes that he has made the right choice, entering the Army. I tell him that it is natural to feel nervous before undertaking any new endeavor. Part of me wants to say, don't go, for I am also about to take the next step into a new chapter of my life and I am also anxious: my children are leaving home—my son to the Army, my daughter is getting married in July, my other daughter has been talking about getting her own apartment. I have been a mother for almost 26 years now and, very shortly, I will be retired from "active duty." There are so many things I want to say to him. I want to tell him: if they have war, don't go. Instead, I say—be careful. . . . As he walks down the front steps to the waiting car, I am thinking of those first tentative steps he took at age one, and the first time he rode on the school bus, and the first time he crossed the street, etc. They were all rehearsals for this day. The car pulls away and he is gone. The image of him leaving freezes in my mind as his breath was frozen on the early morning air. It is only 5 A.M. now—soon a new day will begin.

Both mother and son are at crossroads in their lives; for both, a new day is dawning. Unfortunately, there is little support for a woman who, having spent the better part of her life in active duty as wife and mother, now searches for herself. For Dolores, her journal is a cherished companion along the way.

The contemporary artist Anne Truitt decided to keep a journal during a time in her life when, despite having achieved a certain amount of recognition for her work, she felt she had lost part of herself along the way. In the final section of *Daybook*, she explores the relationship between the mother and artist in herself, and comes to terms with her changing role in the lives of her three grown children. In September 1978, she wrote,

> A change is taking place—took place, I am beginning to believe—in that moment when I recognized in myself a new "I" who respected my grandson. I feel her as I write. She stands clear in a new dimension. She sees that the artist has already claimed the territory granted her by the departure of the children. With an objectivity untainted by pity, she observes the mother crouching over the family hearth and notices signs that the old habits of motherhood are beginning to pall; she foresees a time when they will become vestigial.

And yet, Anne's realization that the mother's loss is the artist's gain does not preclude a visceral sorrow over the end of active motherhood, a feeling "akin to a wasting illness" that drains her vitality. "Some unnameable loss seems to have occurred to my body itself," she writes. "Am I, in that gesture of placing my hand on my breast to soothe myself back to sleep, substituting my own body for the lost bodies of my babies?"

Käthe Kollwitz's journal also reflects a sense of bodily loss as her sons became independent and maternal ties began to loosen. In April of 1910, she wrote,

> I am gradually approaching the period in my life when work comes first. When both the boys went away for Easter, I hardly did anything but work. Worked, slept, ate and went for short walks. But above all I worked. And yet I wonder whether the "blessing" is not missing from such work. No longer diverted by other emotions, I work the way a cow grazes. . . . Yet formerly, in my so wretchedly limited working time, I was more productive because I was more sensual; I lived as a human being must live, passionately interested in everything.

Kollwitz's journal shows us the full spectrum of motherhood, for less than a decade later, she has become her mother's caretaker. "Dear Mother," she wrote. "She is often sick. Then she is downcast, says her head feels so confused. She does not know what to do or where she belongs. And it is so moving when she gravely and dignifiedly takes my hand and gives me heartfelt thanks because we keep her with us. Then I feel such love for her that I could make any sacrifice for her sake."

Elaine Marcus Starkman's fictionalized "journal of caretaking" expresses a similar tenderness—mixed with the frustration, sorrow, and anger she experienced during the time she cared for her aging mother-in-law. At first, Starkman celebrates having "the transmitter of our heritage and culture" living with the family, pleased that her teenaged children show such interest in their grandmother's stories. But before long, the novelty has worn off and the daily demands of caretaking drive her to the limits of her patience. In August 1987, she reflects, "Drove home the twenty miles from Berkeley like a mad woman. Imagined Ma lying dead on the floor. . . . Came back to a mess, breakfast dishes strewn about, clothes, everywhere, the stereo blasting. . . . First the kids, now the parents." But, although caring for her aging and rapidly deteriorating mother-in-law reminds her that she, too, is no longer young, Starkman also experiences precisely those liberations of middle age described by Germaine Greer. "Not everything about aging is bad," she notes, on New Year's Day, 1989.

"To be oneself at last. Free of the opinions of others. To live as one wants. A centeredness, an inner direction. A lessening of both disappointment and expectation. . . . To accept that there is a natural end to all things."

As she records poems and dreams, anger and insight in her journal, she undergoes enormous changes. Her children leave home and get married; her mother-in-law enters a nursing home and her own parents become frail; she turns fifty, has a story accepted for publication, and awaits the birth of a grandchild. Through it all, the diary is where she is able to draw together the many fragments of her life into one whole. In May 1991, she writes, "Gaining inner peace is what counts now. How to get it, how to hold onto it. My writing seems more important than ever." Another entry shows her moving in the desired direction: "today I have room / for all selves / they nestle / without jostling / those who love me / or each other / today black flowers grow wild / in my garden." This is a beautiful journal, full of tenderness and anguish, of sorrow for what has been lost, and gratitude for what nevertheless has been given.

The nurturing we do may indeed take many forms throughout our lives. What caretaking roles are you leaving behind at this time in your life? Which ones are you entering into? Why not explore their significance for your life in your journal?

Changing Professional Hats

In a society where we define ourselves primarily by what we do to earn a living, a change of occupation can well precipitate an identity crisis. Vocation is an important component of our self-image. For women especially, with our recent entry into the public and professional domains, careers carry important connotations, offering us what men long have taken for granted: an identity outside the home, a voice in public affairs, financial independence, a sense of accomplishment, and the possibility of self-actualization.

Indeed, Mary Catherine Bateson believes that as shifting professional identities increasingly become the norm, we will have to rethink our ideas about what constitutes an accomplished career. She observes,

> I have had to retool so often I estimate I have had five careers. This does not produce the kind of résumé that we regard as reflecting a successful life, but it is true of more and more people, starting from the beginning again and again. Zigzag people. Learning to transfer experience from one cycle to the next. . . . Learning is the new continuity for individuals.

For Bateson herself, as evident in the epigraph to this chapter, writing has provided the thread of continuity among various careers and lives. Keeping a diary provides a wonderful opportunity to contemplate a career change, to imagine ourselves in other professional roles and capacities, to reinvent ourselves again.

Lives in Crisis

Sometimes we are challenged by crises that seem to shake the very ground we walk on, so far-reaching are their ramifications. Each of us holds certain basic beliefs about the meaning of life, for example, but not all of us will undergo spiritual crisis and rebirth. All of us will die, but some of us will experience periods of chronic illness and our own dying. Many changes come to us unbidden. When this happens, the journal can sustain and comfort us, as the diarists on the following pages have found.

Chronic Illness

The much-loved diarist May Sarton wrote her *Endgame: Journal of the Seventy-Ninth Year* under a cloud of ill health and pain. Warned by her doctor halfway through the year not to expect any significant improvement, she was forced to reconsider her reasons for continuing to write. "I began to think about . . . how much one needs a reason for living," she tells us.

> Without grandchildren, for instance, there is nobody really whom I live for, although I have many dear friends. But what I should live for is to continue my work till the very end. There are, after all, numbers of people who face chronic illness, illness which can't be cured, and perhaps they will be glad to find somebody who can talk a little about it.

Sarton's case was unusual in that she always wrote her journals for her readership. What isn't unusual is that keeping a journal can give life meaning when little else seems to matter. She concludes the entry, "So this is the beginning of a new journal—the journal of a woman who now knows she will never get well." But by the end of the year she has drawn strength from the process and resolves to continue into her eightieth year, "because I need to sum up and, in a way, discover what is going on around me and inside me."

Elaine Shelly, one of the diarists in *Life Notes*, kept a journal during a lengthy period of ill health in which she was finally diagnosed as having Epstein-Barr virus. In October 1989 she wrote in her journal, "One of my biggest problems with being ill is dealing with my self-image. I feel guilty for not working. I feel embarrassed that I'm not tough enough to just take a few days off and run back to work." Six months later, a tentative diagnosis of multiple sclerosis was offered and, for the next year and a half, Elaine lived with great uncertainty concerning every area of her life: her prognosis, her physical and mental capacities, her job and medical benefits. The following September she wrote in her journal, "I think I finally understand what risky living is. It is choosing to take the journey of reclaiming my humanity. Writing and having a chronic illness has facilitated this process. They help me and force me to break down the walls that stifle my own humanity. It is a risky, revolutionary journey to take."

For a woman with chronic illness, the journal may provide a place where she is more than the sum total of her symptoms. It offers a means of keeping her humanity alive. Where restricted circumstances make normal social interaction difficult, companionship with one's self is more important than ever. For Alice James, afflicted with various physical and nervous ailments, journal writing promised both an emotional outlet and a balm for loneliness. She began the diary on May 31, 1889, with the following entry.

> I think that if I get into the habit of writing a bit about what happens, or rather doesn't happen, I may lose a little of the sense of loneliness and desolation which abides with me. My circumstances allowing of nothing but the ejaculation of one-syllabled reflections, a written monologue by that most interesting being, *myself*, may have its yet to be discovered consolations. I shall at least have it all my own way and it may bring relief as an outlet to that geyser of emotions, sensations, speculations and reflections which ferments perpetually within my poor old carcass for its sins; so here goes, my first Journal!

Alice continued writing as long as she could, then dictated her final corrections to her companion, Katherine Loring, just hours before her death in March 1892. She's not the only diarist who wrote up until the moment of her death, but she was unique for the obvious interest she took in her own dying process, as we see in the following quote. "This long slow dying is no doubt instructive, but it is disappointingly free from excitements," she wrote on February 2, 1892, a month before she died. She continued,

> One sloughs off the activities one by one, and never knows that they're gone, until one suddenly finds that the months have slipped away and the sofa will never more be laid upon, the morning paper read, or the loss of the new book regretted; one revolves with equal content within the narrowing circle until the vanishing point is reached, I suppose.

Crisis of the Soul

At some point in our lives, many of us undergo a crisis of the soul. The familiar lens through which we view the world alters; our old convictions no longer ring true; our usual certainties dissolve. This may take the form of an emotional crisis, a radical break with religion, or a transcendent experience. It may also come to us as a "dark night of the soul," where we experience a sense of loss and desolation, somber agitation, anguished internal conflict. We don't know which way to turn. What is common to all such experiences—whether they happen instantaneously or over time—is that long-held beliefs and assumptions about our purpose in life become transparent. We begin to get glimpses of something that may have been trying to break through for quite some time. We may have a sense that the world is splitting open and nothing will ever be the same: we feel different, the world looks different, and life takes on a new meaning. And, if we believe that any microcosmic change is reflected in the macrocosm, then the world itself is changed in the process.

For many women today, this comes as an experience of the divine Feminine. This is the dynamic pattern that guides Marion Woodman's co-authors in *Leaving My Father's House*. One of the three, Mary Hamilton, describes her anguish following the stillbirth of her firstborn child in 1976. After her son's death, Mary writes,

> I fear if the unconscious grief in me surfaces I will explode and the agony will kill me. I am afraid of the darkness of grief and yet I am driven to understand it. . . . Life is a living hell. I am driven to do anything to ease both the gnawing ache in my gut and the bizarre anguish in my head. . . . Every afternoon I discipline myself to record my feelings and insights in my journal. I am compelled to bring them to consciousness. I write and I write, trying to find meaning in my suffering. My journal is my lifeline.

As she writes, Mary Hamilton finds herself disintegrating into many pieces: "My self divides into three feminine voices, three different complexes that take over my pen as I write in my journal." There is "Good Mary," or society's idealized woman; Eve or "Bad Mary," who represents the repressed instinctual side; and "Medicine Woman," who speaks feminine wisdom and can help to heal the rift between Good Mary and Eve. Following Medicine Woman's prompting, Mary dialogues with these voices and, the following summer, gives birth to a little girl. "For the next two years I work daily with journal writing and dialoguing with dream symbols," she writes. The process of

healing and transformation continues for fourteen years and thousands of journal pages. With time, Medicine Woman evolves into
"Nellie," whose wisdom is to " 'Love humanity as your own family.' "

Gabriele Rico, too, describes a descent into the vortex of long-
buried anguish. Told by her doctor that she would need surgery for
bowel cancer, Rico left her three adolescent daughters in the care of
her husband and spent a month alone in an isolated mountain cottage,
hoping to complete her book. Instead, she experienced "an un-
planned explosion into grief." Her terror is palpable as Rico describes
her most deeply repressed memory: the child's forced visit to the
grave of her mother, who had been blown up by a bomb in front of
her seven-year-old daughter, two months earlier.

> . . . The name engraved on polished stone:
> No. Stop. No. Don't go!
> Child's mind slams shut. Body speaks:
> Heart pumps waves of liquid, looking for an exit,
> through legs, trunk, arms, neck—explodes.
> Child's eyes burrow into a flowered apron,
> throat swallows and swallows and swallows.
> Control.
> We walk, wordless, in the lying May sun.

For many years, the unwept tears poisoned Gabriele's body and, although she doesn't say it in so many words, she intimates that they
finally culminated in her bowel cancer. The recovery of that traumatic
key memory from her abandoned childhood plunges her into an
unprecedented experience of grief. At last she is able to weep. "A
third of a century later, something big gives way," she writes. "Hot
tears spread like live flames, sear the throat, catch for a split-second,
then explode. I cried, and could not stop. I cried, it seemed, almost
without stopping, for four weeks. Words began to flood onto the
paper brought for a different purpose." Through staying with the
process and writing in her journal, no matter how painful, Rico
turned this crisis—"total, terrifying, ultimately, life-saving"—into a
pathway to transformation. "It was the beginning of letting go of
incapacitating fear to face life's uncertainties instead of trying rigidly
to control them," she recalls.

Journal writing can accompany you, no matter where your crisis leads. It can help you to express and understand your evolving place in the universe, as Hannah Hinchman found during her own life crisis at age thirty. "When my little cat died, I hit bottom, and from there I must have known a last-ditch effort was required to survive," she recalls. "I launched into entries that take on the very heart and structure of my life, harrowing and merciless, some of them. But the journal was the ideal listener. It stood aside and allowed many selves to speak without getting confused, impatient or judgmental." The same is true in my own journal.

The Journal as Lifeline

In extreme circumstances, the journal may become a lifeline. There are instances where the process of journal writing has sustained the writer beyond her anticipated life span, where she lived on precisely in order to finish saying what she had to say. Where all other possibilities for creative action cease, the diarist's commitment to bear witness may allow her to create a world beyond the antiseptic hospital room or the four bare walls of a prison cell. Joyce Mary Horner, a retired English professor, began to write a journal after entering a nursing home in 1974, temporarily, she thought. She was to spend the rest of her life there, and continued writing throughout those six years as a way of keeping her mind stimulated and her spirits up. Her published journal reveals a woman intensely engaged with the world around her. In spite of her increasing physical limitations, Joyce never lost her capacity to empathize with the overworked staff and those patients worse off than herself. If it is possible to grow old with true grace, she shows us how it is done. Her journal reveals the daily ups and downs, the small joys and disappointments that loomed large in her restricted circumstances. In June 1976, she wrote,

> This morning after hearing Elizabeth was coming out for a picnic and then getting the Academic Overture on the radio, I felt extraordinarily alive, while yesterday I felt shut in impenetrable gloom, changing only to a kind of desperation when I spilled a glass of milk over everything.

I almost cried over the spilt milk—it was too much. A climax of absurdity and littleness.

Writing under more dire circumstances, Etty Hillesum regarded her journal both as practice for the book she planned to write when the war was over, and as a means of bearing witness to the rare, holy acts of love and courage she saw in that dark period. "Later, when I have survived it all, I shall write stories about these times that will be like faint brush strokes against the great wordless background of God, Life, Death, Suffering and Eternity," she wrote in July of 1942. "And I shall wield this slender fountain pen as if it were a hammer and my words will have to be so many hammer-strokes with which to beat out the story of our fate." Although Etty did not live to write her book, thirty-nine years after her death her journals were published and, a year later, translated into English. Within a few years, they had been translated into more than ten languages.

Then there is Martha Martin who, stranded alone and pregnant on a shore in Alaska, kept a diary throughout the winter with the hope that if she died, her husband would at least know what had become of her. She begins, "I can hardly write, but I must. For two reasons. First I am afraid I may never live to tell my story, and second, I must do something to keep my sanity." Martha Martin did not die. She set her own broken arm and leg, killed an otter for food, skinned it in order to wrap the baby in its fur, secured wood for burning, prepared for the baby's birth, and delivered it herself. She also carried on writing until she and the baby were rescued by Indians the following spring. By then she hardly wanted to leave! More than anything, her journal offers glimpses of a woman's dawning awareness of her own tremendous physical and emotional resources.

And what of Sylvia Plath, who exhorted herself to keep faith with life by writing, convinced that this was the only thing that really counted? In December 1958, with the help of her therapist, Plath arrived at an important insight. "I felt if I didn't write nobody would accept me as a human being," she reflected. "Writing, then, was a substitute for myself: if you don't love me, love my writing and love me for my writing. It is also much more: a way of ordering and reordering the chaos of experience." A month later she noted, "If I can only write a page, half a page, here every day and keep myself counting blessings and working slowly to come into a better life." Tragically, her writing could not save Sylvia Plath, in the long run. She committed suicide several years later.

In *Witness to the Fire*, Linda Schierse Leonard relates the story of the British writer Jean Rhys, who, in 1914, began to write a journal in a time of despair after the end of a tumultuous marriage. After Rhys bought colorful pens and notebooks to cheer up her drab room, Leonard tells us,

> Every day and long into the night she recorded her feelings of lost love and rejection in those exercise books, which became her diary. After more than a week of this constant writing, she felt the worst of the heavy blackness lifting. From then on she wrote whenever her intense feelings began to overwhelm her—her creativity became a source to transform the hopelessness of her addiction.

Instinctively, Rhys knew that the key to coming to terms with her anguish lay in writing. "All I can force myself to do is to write, to write," she observed. "I must trust that out of that will come the pattern, the clue that can be followed." Throughout her long life, a life full of alcoholism and the never-ending quest to recapture a lost and perfect love, writing is what kept her going. Even when human ties fail us, the journal is patient.

Forever Changing, Forever the Same

Like the diarist herself, the journal evolves over time. What begins as a five-year diary with lock and key may change into something quite different. In the summer of 1937, after two and a half decades of passionate journal writing, Anaïs Nin noted, "The diary was once a disease. I do not take it up for the same reason now. Before it was because I was lonely, or because I did not know how to communicate with others. . . . Now it is to write not for solace but for the pleasure of describing others, out of abundance." Nin's diary was to change form many times throughout its long life. "All through life it changed roles, it became various things," she said in a lecture in 1973. "It was a writer's notebook, it was a storage place for dreams, it was a sketch-book of everybody around me."

In the final chapter of her book, titled "Journal Jottings," the theologian Nelle Morton, too, traced her journal's evolving function over many years, noting,

> My faithful journal, which has changed form and face many times since the '30s, has carried all sorts of miscellany—quotations, dreams, joys, angers, pains, failures, stories of experiences, happenings, reviews, poetry, and all of these interacting with one another. Isolated seeds of ideas in time sprouted and grew into questions and resources that have shaped my living. . . . The germ of the idea had been there many years.

The writer Gail Godwin summons the difference between a first date and a long marriage to describe her own changing relationship with her journal. "When I began my diary, at age thirteen, I traversed that naked space between my mind and my little book's pages as hesitantly as a virgin approaching a man who may or may not prove trustworthy," she remembers. "Now, two-and-a-half decades later, my diary and I have an old marriage. The space between us is gone." Gail describes the gradual evolution of her diary from a sounding board for adolescent woes to something very different. She notes, "As I became less trapped in my universe of moods and recognized my likeness to other people and other things in the universe-at-large, my entries began to include more space. Now there are animals and flowers and sunsets in my diary . . . I complain less and describe more."

Like Gail Godwin, I've found my journal evolving over the years, an ever-broadening spiral of experiences and interests. In July 1977, after a two-month holiday in Europe, I wrote, "Sometimes I wonder how much longer I will be keeping a detailed journal. For a week or so now, I have had the thought that the journal has served most of its cathartic purposes in my life and that I will probably be writing much less often in it, in the future." Not surprisingly, I did not write less frequently after that. But the journal's role gradually changed. It stopped being mainly a narcissistic pool in which I found reflected an ever-fairer self, and began to take on a more diverse, more interesting focus. The relentless self-preoccupation of my early twenties diffused into a broader awareness and inclusion of other areas of life. During my thirties, my journal came to include a far greater reflective dimension. There I thought out loud about friendship, about my writing, my dreams, about life in general. It is still my story, of course. But now it encompasses the world.

Like our lives, the journal has its own ebb and flow, its own high points and valleys. What doesn't change with time is its capacity to ground us amidst the never-ending fluctuations of life, and to bear witness. Through its many incarnations, our journal remains, as Etty Hillesum found, a place to return to and—"a continuum which is really one's life."

7

Dreams and Other Exceptional Experiences

I have never ceased to marvel at the admirable work brought about in the transaction between consciousness and the unconscious. The unconscious going into the deepest strata of life to find riches which were all mine, depositing them on the one bank of my sleep; and consciousness of the other bank, inspecting the find from afar, evaluating it, leaving it behind to be presented in my reality, a truth easy to understand, simple, clear, but which had not appeared to me before, not until I had been ready to accept it.

MARIE CARDINAL, *The Words to Say It*

The world of our dreams is vivid, boundless, and multidimensional. In it, our unspoken fears and desires are articulated in symbolic language that reveals their full passion and intensity. At once highly individual and deeply social, dreams bring together symbolism of the most personal kind with issues that lie at the heart of our cultural unconscious. For, as Jung has shown, dreams are not just individual. They have a transpersonal dimension as well.

Indigenous cultures have long regarded dreams as bearing sacred truth and have looked to them for guidance in their waking lives, basing life and death decisions on wisdom gleaned. Anaïs Nin, one of the great champions of dreams among modern diarists, said, "In antique cultures the dream was a part of life itself, influenced it. Everyone was engaged in unraveling the mysterious dreams which were an indication of a psychic life." Yet many people today live their entire lives never paying more than fleeting attention to their dreams. Fearful of what might surface from the depths of their mysterious nocturnal world, they suppress or "forget" them, preferring Holly-wood's celluloid images to their own highly personalized and poten-tially healing dream gifts.

On television not long ago I saw a fascinating discussion of "virtual reality," in which, by means of special three-dimensional glasses, viewers could move around inside a computer-generated environment of their choice. The experience was so convincing that one experi-menter had difficulty reorienting himself to the real world afterward. It is ironic that we already hold within us another level of reality— more compelling, mysterious, and beautiful than anything a computer could generate on our behalf! The difference between virtual reality and the dream, of course, is that the former can be controlled. No suppressed fear will manifest itself, no unacknowledged grief surface. The ego carries on undaunted, the master of its environment. Rather than authentic soul wisdom, virtual reality provides the viewer with a computerized "near-life" experience.

The label "dreamer" is used nowadays as a gentle reprimand to someone who builds castles in the air and is out of touch with the "real" world. This could only happen in a society like ours, where the realm of the imagination and the arts is given far less importance than business, science, and technology. But what happens to our souls in such an environment? What becomes of "the nameless softness that makes human beings human," to use Christa Wolf's words? Dis-counting our dreams, how do we begin to understand our own wordless yearnings, our suffering, and our visions? Where do creativ-ity, empathy, and lovingkindness fit into a society blindly obsessed with accumulation, expansion, and mastery?

For our dreams are no less than windows into our innermost being. With varying degrees of subtlety, they reveal our most troubling concerns, our secret anxieties and desires. On the most obvious level, they symbolically express our veiled emotions. Many people report having classic anxiety dreams, for example. They may find themselves suddenly naked in a crowd, losing their teeth, walking into an exam unprepared, or falling off a cliff. Dreams about missed connections and accidents frequently precede travel. Before leaving on my open-ended trip to Europe in July 1979, I had several such dreams, culminating in a particularly vivid one where the driver and I were the sole survivors of a bus crash, trying desperately to get out the door before the bus burst into flames. Our psyches try in advance to anticipate potential problems, rehearsing the worst-case scenario in symbolic expression of our very real fears.

But dreams also have a social dimension. We are embedded in our culture's history, inescapably drawn into the "social neurosis" of our time, as the psychiatrist Trigant Burrow observed, earlier in this century. According to Jung, too, "Each period has its bias, its particular prejudice and its psychic ailment. An epoch is like an individual; it has its own limitations of conscious outlook." The psychiatrist Montague Ullman, who has devoted many years to developing dream-sharing groups, claims that "just as the dreams are carriers of the potential for personal change, they are also carriers of the potential for social change to the extent that social factors become visible in our dreams." Our dreams, Ullman says, "reveal the content of our social unconscious, that is, what we allow ourselves to remain unconscious of with regard to what is going on in society." Dreams always work toward healing—of our individual selves, of the society around us, of the human species as a whole. In 1984, Christa Wolf recounted one dramatic example of how urgent social concerns are manifested in dream material. "What dreams women tell me they are having!" she noted.

One young woman who was expecting her second child dreamed that she had already given birth, that an atomic war had begun, and that all people, including her children, were suffering from burns and radiation sickness and were doomed to die. Since she had no other way to rescue her children from their torment, she killed them with a hammer. Then along with her husband she searched for a means they could use to kill themselves, too. But there were no longer even any tall buildings left standing, for them to jump off.

Wolf relates this dream to show that while women everywhere have hoped that entering the public realm would empower us, our dreams reflect our sense of impotence when it comes to changing things at the deeper levels. This realization was especially poignant for women in a socialist society like that of the former German Democratic Republic, which claimed to have achieved full equality for women. It's no coincidence, either, that this dream occurred at the height of the Cold War in the early eighties, symbolizing as it does the threat of nuclear annihilation experienced by countless numbers on both sides of the Iron Curtain during those years.

For Jung and many others, dreams also put us in touch with the transpersonal level of existence. In his words, "The dream is a little hidden door in the innermost and most secret recesses of the psyche, opening into that cosmic night which was psyche long before there was any ego consciousness, and which will remain psyche no matter how far our ego consciousness may extend." In short, dreams tap the collective unconscious, that bedrock layer of being at which we are all connected, echoing a communality we have all but lost in our waking lives. According to the Jungian analyst Janet Dallett, those who do hear that echo do not have an easy time. "Our culture has no niche for people who descend to the place of the big dream," she says. She explains,

> Unless they happen to be artists, they have no place to take their gifts, and they risk being thought crazy if they speak of what they see. If they do not speak of it, they may in fact go crazy from carrying alone a burden of symbolic material that belongs to the culture as a whole, material that could heal our social wounds if we received and understood it.

Since dreams do indeed reveal our cultural shadow, it is not surprising that many women and men today are dreaming about a long-denied feminine presence attempting to break into consciousness. According to Marion Woodman, dreams of a dark goddess abound among her analysands. "Usually she is black or oriental or simply dark," Woodman tells us.

She may appear as a proud gypsy, a dancer in a tavern, a sacred prostitute, a Mary Magdalene. Always she is outside the collective value system of the dreamer's conscious world, and while she may be wounded or disfigured, she carries immense potential for new life. Hers is the energy that can unite the opposites—the whore and the idealized virgin—because she contains both. . . . The human body becomes a vessel for human love when one surrenders to the Black Goddess in whom spirit and instinct meet.

Dreams may provide valuable insight and guidance for our personal lives, as well. The writer Amy Tan recalls a dream from her mid-twenties in which she flew through the air with rented twenty-five-cent wings that were none too secure. She reflects, "I realized there were many things in my life that I was not allowing myself to do because I lacked the confidence. I needed the props. I could see all the props that I'd been using and they were just like those twenty-five-cent wings. I could see how ridiculous it was." The Japanese-Canadian writer Joy Kogawa also describes the insight and direction her dreams provided at a critical moment in her life. "In 1964 I was in a crisis of ideals in my life," she writes.

The problems of evil seemed to me to be so enormous, so impossible. I felt there would be answers in the dream world. I woke up night after night with a pen beside me, and it was just like a volcano: the dreams, the images were so suggestive; they were more than suggestive, they were almost directive and instructive. . . . I kept that up for years, and the discipline of it was in simply insisting on remembering and then playing with it, not giving up on it, and trying to find out what the meaning of it might be.

And for the Jungian analyst Sheila Moon, it was a dream that finally led her to begin writing. She recalls,

The first dream I had in this small hotel overlooking the lake was that I was with Mrs. Jung and she said to me, "Begin writing, and do a little bit every day." So I wrote some every day, sitting by the lake in the sun, watching children play in the daisy-filled grass. I was writing my own active imagination, letting it flow from me wherever it wanted to go. Before I was finished with it, long months after I had reached home and returned to work, it was more than 400 handwritten pages.

Although Sheila wrote without thought of publication, she sent her writing to a publisher on the advice of a friend, and it was published. Thus began her writing vocation—the result of a dream message from Emma Jung, her beloved analyst in earlier years.

Several years ago, after a number of requests, I began to think of offering a coed journal workshop. During that time I had a dream about three middle-aged men breaking into a houseful of women preparing for a party. Here is that dream, in full.

I am in "*the big old house*" which has appeared so often in my dreams. It is always the same house and has a musty odour that I hate. The *living and dining rooms* are large, shabby, dark, dusty and *unused. Large, clunky furniture*, that isn't at all attractive. (I have dreamed of this house about ten times, I'm sure, and don't know what it means. My psyche? New York?) I am dusting a large china cabinet and putting my *little green depression glass plates* in it (do I plan to stay a while?) and someone else, Nellie [my sister] and Maria C. [a workshop participant] is helping me put the room in order for an upcoming party tonight. I don't think there are any men here. These rooms have not been dusted since we moved in, four years in October (just like this house), so there are cobwebs and some spiders running around. I'm humming the song, "*From a Distance . . .* you look like my friend."

The telephone rings and I go into the kitchen—the one room that I *do* like—to answer. Janet W. [an English friend] is cooking and washing dishes and passes the phone to me. A quiet voice asks for Marlene.

"Speaking," I respond.

"Are you still interested in selling your house?" she asks. "I heard it is being divided and sold, and I'm interested."

I'm surprised. "Who told you that?"

She replies, "*Mr. Derkson, the owner.*"

"I pay rent to Mike M., who is the landlord and owner, as far as I know," I tell her.

Outside on the stair landing at the back door, I notice some activity, and assume it is people starting to arrive for the party. Suddenly there are *three menacing middle-aged men with guns in the kitchen.* One of them holds Janet against the wall with his gun in her ribs, in a cruel, nasty way.

A gang robbery, is my first thought. Then I don't know what to do with the telephone receiver which is still in my hand. Should I hang up? I don't want to startle them because they might shoot me. My knees turn to jelly. This could be it, I think. *They may kill us all.* This might not even be a robbery, although I'd gladly give them whatever I have: $200 in my wallet, and whatever else they want.

I awaken in fright.

What does it mean?

Day residue and associations: Three men in the living room. Steve invited Jason and Manabu over last night. The room felt utterly different than it had just the night before, during the women's journal workshop. The words of the song, "From a Distance," expressing the hope of global peace and understanding and an end to war, are important. The theme of being violated and invaded by men is central in my dreams. Steve has commented on it, too. Why three men, middle-aged? My first association was to the "three wise men"; now I'm also thinking "Father, Son, and Holy Ghost." When I entered the living room last night, Steve laughingly said, "Now the group is complete. Jung's fourth, missing feminine element is here." Is this an archetypal dream? Did the three men in the dream want to be invited to the party? To my workshop? Were they angry that I hadn't included them? They wanted to take something from us; were they out to destroy us? Do they represent my fear of patriarchal vengeance, literally "the wrath of God," of the Trinity, on the work I'm doing with women in the workshop? Since every element in the dream represents a part of myself, do they represent my own animus, too?

October 29, 1994. As I'm typing this dream into the computer, it occurs to me that the woman's telephone enquiry about dividing and selling the house refers to the workshop. Perhaps I'd be "selling out" by opening it to men, when I've always seen my task as providing a safe place for women. And I've been puzzling about the significance of "Mr. Derkson." It's a common Mennonite name; it too echoes the threat of traditional male-dominated religion.

February 23, 1995. Is the significance of the song the hope of reconciling feminine and masculine in this culture and in myself, in a way
that clearly hasn't been possible up to this point?

On a conscious level I was willing to open the workshop to men,
but it seems clear that my unconscious perceived this as a grave threat.
Since my whole purpose was to create an environment in which
women could hear one another into speech without potential male
interference, this isn't surprising. In the dream, as in the workshop
itself, I felt a powerful sense of responsibility for the other women's
safety. Clearly, I could have done—could still do—much more work
with this dream.

Journal writing creates a conversation between the conscious and
unconscious parts of our psyches. The dream's images and metaphors
become intelligible through exploration and amplification in the
diary, often with fascinating results. Not long ago, *Writers Dreaming*
appeared, a collection of interviews with writers in the United States
about the role of their dreams in their fiction. Bharati Mukherjee, one
of those interviewed, says that the endings to her stories often come
to her in dreams. The first time it happened, she was finishing a novel
about a traditional Indian wife in New York who simply can't adjust
to her new surroundings and seems destined to commit suicide in
order to end her unhappiness. Mukherjee explains,

> But instead, in my dream, she decided to kill her husband. The first
> thing I said to my husband as he woke up was "I got it! The guy's
> going to die!" Therefore I wrote the novel in which the wife, in a
> misguided but very self-assertive act that was very important to me
> personally, actually does murder her husband while he's having his
> breakfast. And, so, the poor husband bleeds into his Wheaties.

While the author thought she knew how the story should end, her
unconscious was taking her in a very different direction. Since dreams
and the creative imagination alike are fed by the unconscious, it makes
sense that the ending of her novel would come to her by way of a
dream. Many writers draw characters, images, even entire scenes from
their dream journals. The novelist Anne Rice began her second vam-

pire novel after a particularly gripping dream, for example, and Anaïs Nin based whole novels on dreams she'd had. Other writers simply record dreams in their journals in order to see what their unconscious is up to. Antonia White kept track of hers for more than fifty years, both in and out of analysis. "Dreams . . . always prod me since they usually mean something is boiling up," she wrote. "They seem to say that I am missing something through over-anxiety or the temptation to take a line which is not my true one."

Working with Dreams

Sometimes I sit down to record a dream with no sense of what it means or whether it's really worth bothering with. While writing, without fail, I find myself remembering more than I thought I did. The dream's inner logic begins to reveal itself to me and often synchronicities (Jung's term for meaningful coincidences) become apparent.

Some years ago I wrote down a dream about one of my earliest best friends. Despite having been out of touch for more than a decade, I had dreamed of her at least half a dozen times in as many months, but on this occasion, I woke up in tears. Annemarie was born three weeks after I was, into a home just down the street from ours. Until the time we started school, we fought. She pinched me, and I pulled her hair. Then we became inseparable. In eighth grade, she took me out on the school soccer field during lunch hour and told me that her father had taken a job thirty miles away. I cried bitterly. We swore to stay best friends and to write, telephone, and visit each other as often as we could. From time to time I spent weekends with her and her older sister, Molly, and the three of us shared tips on how to attract boys. At university in Vancouver, Annemarie and I both lived near the ocean, in apartments four blocks apart. We met regularly for lunch between classes, wept on each other's shoulders when love went wrong, and remained close. Until we were twenty-five. Then something happened. I don't think that either of us understood why, but we parted ways just after she finished law school and soon dropped all contact. As I dated my journal entry on the morning of October

25, 1990, I realized with a sudden shock that it was her birthday. It had been more than a decade since I'd seen her or been in touch, much less sent a birthday card, but obviously my subconscious had not forgotten.

The emotional content of the dream was not especially vivid. As the tears dropped into my journal, I knew that the dream was about the loss of those passionate early bonds that are fierce and pure, with nothing calculated about them. At a time when I felt desolate without a close-knit circle of friends, Annemarie stood, it seemed, for all I had loved and let go of over time: everything I'd tossed out, let slip casually through my fingers, or lost through no choice of my own. This dream provided an occasion to mourn all of these losses. It was the last one in the series. If dreams are "the royal road to the unconscious," as Freud suggested, working with them in our journals can help light the way. At first we see only dimly, but soon we begin to glimpse what stretches before us—the breadth and depth and richness of what has been cloaked in darkness. The disproportionate emotion that accompanied my dream about Annemarie was the clue that something else needed to be brought to conscious awareness. Once I understood what that was, the dreams stopped.

Dreams also inform us of how our unconscious has registered the day's events—often very differently from our conscious selves. This is where journal writing is so essential. It brings the two experiences into dialogue with each other. As we write, the dream opens itself to us. It may yield its meaning only gradually, through free association, quiet reflection, dialogue with symbols. At other times its meaning may come to us so forcefully as to jolt us. When I hit on something true and important, my body recognizes it before my mind does. A current passes through me, and my nerve endings tingle with its authenticity from scalp to toes.

Classical psychoanalysis and its offshoots have always placed great significance on dreams. For Freud, they were the key component of the psychoanalytic process. In Jung's autobiography, *Memories, Dreams, Reflections*, he drew substantially from the dreams he recorded in six small leather-bound volumes that he called the "Black Book." Dreamwork is often a significant dimension of modern psychotherapy as well. Clients may be asked to keep a journal of their emotions and dreams to complement their other therapeutic work. Marion Woodman will even refuse a potential client who isn't prepared to spend an hour a day on "soulwork," including careful work in a dream journal.

Traditionally, the analyst has regarded her- or himself as the expert, with the final say about how the dream is to be interpreted. Sometimes this has left the dreamer frustrated, as in the following journal excerpt. After Mary Elsie Robertson received a Freudian reading of a dream from her analyst, she reflected, "I felt cheated by this interpretation. It seemed to me this dream had more to say about my life situation than his interpretation would indicate. A dream like that is like a poem which can be read on several levels. On one level, he may be right. And yet this isn't a level that is helpful to me." While her analyst may have been satisfied with his work here, the dreamer experienced his interpretation as reductive and off the mark. No healing can have taken place.

More recently, authority has been shifting to the dreamer herself. The therapist creates the temenos, or sacred space, in which the dream is given attention and asks probing questions in an effort to help the dreamer understand its symbolism. However, she will not project her own interpretation as the truth. In or out of therapy, if we work with dream images through writing, painting, dancing, singing, or other forms of creative expression, says Marion Woodman, we allow "the healing process to transform what would otherwise be dead images into life energy."

Remembering

Psychologists and sleep researchers tell us that everyone dreams. Whether or not we remember our dreams is another matter. There is more than one theory concerning why some people don't remember their nocturnal adventures. They don't get enough sleep and awaken in a stupor. They don't want to remember because they aren't ready to face what they might uncover. They do have limited recall but volun-

tarily suppress it. Marion Woodman offers the most convincing expla-
nation I have yet seen. Of her clients who claim they don't dream she
says,

> The fact is they do dream, but when the alarm clock rapes them out of
> the underworld, they have no conscious container strong enough to
> hold the images that are creating new life. However, if they try, they
> catch an image each night. They write it down in their journal, or
> paint it along with their associations. Gradually the unconscious begins
> to trust that the ego does care and gradually complete dreams follow.
> Nuns, prostitutes, pirates, murderers, gypsies—an astonishing cast of
> characters begins to appear in the bourgeois living room. Allowing
> these complexes to talk, move, dance, sing, and draw is the beginning
> of releasing repressed energy from opaque, unconscious matter.

Attentiveness, curiosity, and desire heighten recall. If you patiently
keep reminding your unconscious that you want a dream, you will
begin to remember. You can assist the process by preparing the stage.
Place pen and paper beside your bed, along with a night-light. Jot
down a sentence or two about the overriding mood, and the most
prominent impression or event of the day. This will help you to
consider "day residue," those elements from the preceding day that
appear in altered form in your dream, in working with the dream
afterward. You might also wish to read something evocative—one of
the many books on dreaming, for example, for ten or fifteen minutes
before turning out the light. Then affirm to your unconscious that
you are ready to receive a dream. If you awaken during the night,
write down anything you remember, no matter how fuzzy. Describe
it in as much detail as possible, and see where that leads you. An
emotion may lead to an image that, in turn, may lead to an entire
dream scene. Some dreamworkers even advocate speaking your dream
into a tape recorder. That way you have not only the content, but your
vocal inflections as well.

While preparing my first workshop on journal writing and dreams,
every night before going to sleep I read several pages of the relevant
chapter in The New Diary. That week I had more dreams than at any

other time in my life, even without asking for them! On the first day of the workshop, one woman claimed that she never dreamed or, at least, never remembered her dreams. I distributed some printed pages about dreams and suggested she read them before going to bed that night. The next day she returned, tired but pleased with herself. She told the group that after reading the article and requesting a dream the night before, she found herself waking up every hour or so with one. The fifth time this happened, out of exhaustion she finally quit. Sometimes, too, women bring dreams to the workshop, saying, "I don't really want to work with this. I already know what it means." Yet if they dialogue with a symbol or explore their associations further, without fail they are amazed at what they uncover.

Another factor in remembering may be the kind of sleep you get. If you drop into bed in utter exhaustion and get up five hours later to the screech of an alarm clock, the chances of remembering anything of your dreams are minimal. Though such a routine may be a practical necessity most of the time, perhaps you can give yourself a weekend when you can wake up on your own and linger in bed, allowing the dream images to float into consciousness. Some dreamworkers advocate moving as little as possible upon awakening. Once the images surface, you'll have to reach for your notebook and pen, but until then, keep your eyes closed, don't change position, and tune in.

What if it's a nightmare you finally remember? Who wants to recall a dream of being publicly humiliated or tortured, or worse, perhaps, of being the torturer? If you frequently have frightening or violent dreams, it doesn't necessarily mean you have a secret desire to murder your mate or yourself. Your unconscious, in its own inimitable way, is working out fundamental issues in your life by attempting to restore balance. Maybe it's trying to compensate for your doggedly pleasant and good-natured waking persona by giving expression to the part of you that thinks, "The hell with everybody else; I just want to do what I want!" One diarist I know has had many violent dreams over the years about every conceivable kind of violation, in which she has been both perpetrator and victim. In her day-to-day dealings with people, she strives always to maintain a calm equilibrium and to suppress any hint of frustration, let alone anger. Perhaps the violent dream imagery represents her repressed "negative" emotions, demanding their due over time. Whatever transpires in your dreams, however, you can safely assume that your unconscious is always working for healing.

If you don't remember your dreams straightaway, don't give up. Persevere. I've had workshop participants whose dreams began to emerge only after they had been paying attention for several weeks. Yours will, too. It's just a matter of desire, patience, and time.

Keeping Track

When you remember a dream, write it down right away and be sure to date it. What you lose is not retrievable. The writer Amy Tan says, "I remember my dreams every morning, but if I don't write them down . . . they retreat and the door closes and I don't remember them anymore." Even if all you remember is an image, an emotion, or a single scene, write quickly in the present tense and don't stop. Allow the dream to unfold before your eyes again. Keep going even if there are parts that you don't remember clearly or if you've lost part of a scene. Don't worry about grammar or organization, just stay with the dream. You are on a treasure hunt.

In the middle of a busy day, a sudden memory of a dream from the night before may flash before your inner eye. You'll have to decide whether it is significant enough to take time to record. If you decide to write it down on a scrap of paper, tuck it into your journal that night so it doesn't get tossed out by mistake. I have worked with dreams that are three years old, and I've heard of people finding new levels of meaning in a dream image a decade old. Sometimes a dream doesn't even make sense until years later. Because the unconscious does not recognize linear time, past, present, and future are simultaneously available to it. Marion Woodman, for example, said recently, "I'm just beginning to understand dreams I had twenty years ago, and I still don't know what they're fully about." Dreams can even be precognitive. Anne Rice dreamed that her daughter was very ill with a blood disease even before the little girl was diagnosed as having leukemia. This kind of experience is far more common than you might think. Cases of this sort have been reported down through the centuries, and volumes have been devoted to their study.

There are practical matters to consider, too. Will you write your dreams in your regular journal or designate a special notebook for them? Some people keep only a dream journal; others record their dreams separately, keeping track of recurring themes and motifs over time. Still others (like me) prefer to have dreams and other entries side by side in the same volume, in order to see how waking and sleeping reality intersect and illuminate each other. Rereading the journal later, you will be able to see how the concerns of the previous day are transmuted by your unconscious into an elaborately meta-phorical, beautifully poetic rendition of your experience. The writer Burghild Nina Holzer observes, "When you have everything in one journal, you can see how the fragments fit together. A dream might be a reaction to a previous event, or it might be signaling something ahead of time." In contrast, Holzer claims, "If one separates things out into different notebooks, it is harder to see the larger structure of one's life process, as it slowly evolves over many entries." Try using a different color of ink for dreams, or mark the first line of each dream entry with a yellow highlighter pen as you go. Devise your own system of easy location. You can even give each dream a title and compile a list of titles over time. Find out what works best for you.

Interpreting

Once we have the dream in the journal, how do we begin to decode its symbolic language? Karen Signell, a Jungian analyst who has worked extensively with women's dreams, claims, "Learning interpretation techniques is not the key to understanding dreams. You gain a general sense of how to approach dreams by experiencing many dreams, by learning how to cultivate your imagination and gaining confidence in your own intuition." Many of us may feel that we don't have the tools necessary to make sense of our own dreams, to enter their symbolic realm and bring back the riches at their core. But among dreamwork-ers like Karen Signell, there is a growing belief that symbols are highly personal, and that each person must learn to decipher her own. What is certain is that the more attention you pay to them, the more you'll remember, and the more exciting the whole process will become. A dream is a message from the hidden recesses of our bodies to our waking minds; it tells us something we don't already know. Karen Signell describes the world of dreams as "an unexplored wilderness where there are no clear guideposts."

Don't overlook the possibility of humor, either. The unconscious often communicates through a play on words, as in the following dream that my friend Gabi Rahaman recorded while struggling through the final stages of completing her dissertation.

> *April* 1993. Dreamt of having given birth to a strong, big, healthy baby girl which looked much older than a new-born child. Then the baby vanished and I was conscious of having misplaced it somehow. While still searching for the baby I suddenly found it again, or rather, I saw that it was sewn into a bag—beautifully embroidered—which covered it from head to toe. The embroidery was reminiscent of a Russian doll; the colour was blue, the background creamy-white. I sensed that the baby was perfectly happy in the bag, indeed, I felt it was in its rightful place. On waking up I couldn't make sense of this dream at all but several days later it suddenly hit me that this dream is a literal one, namely, it (the thesis) is "in the bag." The sudden force of this realization was almost physical.

All dreamworkers, regardless of orientation, would likely agree that your "day residue" is central to the dream's importance. The unconscious uses fresh material from the events of the preceding day to work through issues of long-standing importance to your life. What follows is an entry from my journal in which the experience of the day just past and concerns central to me at the time are woven together in a dream that held great significance for me. Along with the dream itself, I've included the day residue and other associations that became clear to me since.

> *August* 3/93. Dream fragment from last night: A dream within a dream. An older woman wades out into waist-high water to drown herself. She is a Holocaust survivor. A fireman or policeman goes in to bring

her back and she comes out without much of a struggle. Then she says, "The only thing that makes life worth living is . . ."—but I don't hear the end of the sentence. Other voices add responses. "The only thing worth living for is the light through the poppies." Another voice adds "the sound of water," and another, "stones." There are other responses which are, at the same time, lines of poetry that I am writing. So, I am writing it all and it feels like a gift to me. I awaken, in the dream, and try to remember more of it so that I can write it down, and feel—still in my dream—that as always, it's escaping me. But I weep tears of joy and feel it is wonderful.

Then I do wake up.

Now that I think of it, those lines have the quality of the beginning of Virginia Woolf's The Waves, where each of the characters utters short, beautiful statements. All of the images of things which people found worth living for were earthbound things—tangible delights. I told Steve about my dream this morning. He agrees it has an archetypal feel to it. I wonder whether it is telling me anything about my own book.

It's the image of the light through the poppies that left the strongest impression on me. Why poppies? Aren't poppies related to the production of opium, and to forgetfulness? Shining light on them may illuminate the subconscious and memory. That's what I was reading about in Anaïs Nin's Diary yesterday, at length. Perhaps the old woman felt if she was going to live on, she would have to come to terms with her own repressed memories, her own unconscious. My other association to poppies is the famous lines, "In Flander's Fields the poppies grow, Between the crosses, row on row." Again there is the association of death and forgetfulness, and the light has to shine through them, illuminate them. Perhaps the old woman couldn't go on living unless she made peace with her horrific past.

Day residue from yesterday: In the news—Demianiuk is to be released, after all, despite the torture he almost certainly perpetrated in the concentration camps. The Bosnian refugee interviewed on the Mac-Neil Lehrer News Hour described his own experience in a Serbian concentration camp.

Poppies are red: Passionate and colourful. The opposite of black and death. Their center is black, however. The colours of life and death. Before Christian times, black was the colour of fertility and the earth. Another earth-reference. Does the light shining through the poppies symbolize spirit illuminating matter, the integration of masculine and feminine?

October 30, 1993. Amazing. I had completely forgotten the fact that Virginia Woolf committed suicide by walking into the water! At least in part because she couldn't bear the thought of the Nazis arriving in London and seizing Leonard, who was Jewish.

October 15, 1994. I read just a few days ago that when an impersonal voice speaks in a dream, it is an archetype manifesting. In this dream, the lines seemed to come from disembodied voices, speaking poetry. What seems clearer to me now is that it's a dream about the possibility of reconciling life and death, for one thing. I know this dream was a gift, one I am still trying to understand more fully.

What about joining a dream group? There are small groups that meet for the sole purpose of working on their dreams together. Montague Ullman claims, "The time is ripe for resurrecting a tradition found in primitive societies, namely, the existence of an everyday working relationship between dream life and culture." Interestingly, Ullman has found that 90 percent of the participants in his dream-sharing groups are women. Group members work together, making each dream their own because, according to Ullman, "The collective imagination of the group can produce a richer array of metaphorical possibilities relating to the dream imagery than a single individual can." In our present state of estrangement from ourselves and one another, he suggests, this communal dreamwork not only answers our need for self-revelation and intimacy, but allows us to see through our own self-deceptions.

Other kinds of dream groups exist as well. Check for groups, workshops, and seminars in your area, since the offerings continue to expand. And persevere. In my experience, Marion Woodman and Karen Signell are right: The longer you work with your dreams, the more you'll come to understand their poetic language, and the richer your insights will be. Read books about dreams and dreamwork, and sample what various approaches have to offer. Attend a dream workshop. Discuss your dreams with your partner or close friend.

With time, dreamwork may well become a most rewarding aspect of your journal writing journey.

Dreamwork in the Journal

In *Wisdom of the Heart: Working with Women's Dreams*, the Jungian dreamworker Karen Signell says, "Looking at a dream is like looking at a poem, a treasured picture, an impressionist or surrealist painting. You have to look at it in your own way, let it move you, see what it stirs up in you. I found that, when I worked with these dreams, the more times I looked at them, came back to them, the more I could see." Many different modes of dreamwork lend themselves to journal writing. In my workshops, I distribute a handout summarizing various approaches and suggest that participants experiment with these. You may wish to try out some of the following suggestions for working with dreams you have recorded in your diary.

• *Underline or highlight key elements, images, or scenes.* Not long ago I had the following dream:

August 4, 1994. I am in the back of a pickup truck with Karen and several other workshop members. Sandra is driving. We are in England, in the countryside south of London. Suddenly we see a group of women sitting outside on the rolling green hills—brightly dressed in long "old-fashioned" clothes—sitting on what seems like a stone bench. A minute later, another such group appears. Then I realize—these are gypsies and we are in their territory. Then there are many of them, all out in the green open: laughing, talking to each other, walking and running, clearly having a good time. It looks like all women; I don't see men. The pickup stops, and we get out. There are some items for sale and Sandra buys a lovely little girl's dress that they made. The pattern is ethnic batik and it is beautiful. Karen has a baby girl. I wonder if they'll be friendly—they may feel we're invading their space. Are we welcome? Am I welcome? One of them can't speak English (they all speak Romany), so she calls another older woman who does. We have to go back to the pickup and continue but I desperately want to spend more time here—or to come back.

After I had recorded this dream and underlined the elements italicized here, I wrote down my associations:

> What stays with me is the free and adventuresome spirit of the women, the beauty of their clean multicoloured clothes, and my own desire to be part of it. All the women had long, clean, dark hair. There was something untamed, spontaneous, joyful about them. I wondered what they did for shelter at night, and how they could be warm enough sitting out there in their beautiful dresses, but they didn't seem worried. These women were making crafts to sell, and being in nature, daughters of the Earth Mother. They were speaking their own language. (There's my long-standing fascination with gypsies, although the only ones I've seen lived in squalor. These were poor, but clean and beautiful.) What is the importance of the little girl's dress and Karen's baby girl?
>
> Day residue: Steve, Ernie and I talked yesterday afternoon about a feminine mode of being in the world. We all felt that male and female modes must be integrated in order to reach a state of wholeness. I had dinner with Margery last night, and we talked about living with women rather than men (not necessarily in a lesbian relationship) and about sensuality and sexuality. I've been working on my chapter on journal writing and healing. What, exactly, is "healing," and what do women need to be healed of? I reread Anne Frank's Diary yesterday. How she yearned to be out in nature—sky, stars, sun, open breeze. That was all-important to her.
>
> I know this is an important dream, but I don't yet know exactly why. Exuberance. Wildness. Colour. Spontaneity. Laughter. Dance. A child. Nature. Community. Everything I yearn to have more of. Why a pickup truck? And why was I in the back of it, being driven, half asleep and trying to keep warm? A man's vehicle. But also connected to the land; usually farmers have pickup trucks. Why did we have to continue on our way instead of staying there? Goal-oriented movement? And why didn't I just say, "I want to stay here, pick me up on the way back." Fear?
>
> I saw and wanted it: the proximity to nature, the colours, the motion, the vibrancy, the groups of women so at ease, so at home with each other. The men were not conspicuously absent. They were just irrelevant, out of the picture. It seems clear that it's a dream about the feminine. And in the dream, the women are speaking a "different

language." Since both Karen and Sandra were in my last workshop series, perhaps it's also telling me something about the workshop. But what? That we are heading "in the wrong direction." That we are too blindly following old, engrained patterns? In what way? I thought I'd been cherishing and nurturing community and sisterhood, creativity and spontaneity in the workshop all along. But maybe we are too domesticated a species. Perhaps the dream is trying to tell me that we need to get more deeply in touch with the wildness in ourselves. If so, how can we do this?

Clearly, the imagery in this short dream scene has rich meaning for me. Now that I have it safely in my journal, I can go back and continue to unravel its message. Each time I reread it, additional nuances of meaning reveal themselves to me. One obvious approach would be to dialogue with each significant element of the dream.

• *Become each part of the dream.* In Gestalt dreamwork, every aspect of the dream has significance and reveals some aspect of your own psyche. What follows is an excerpt from the journal of Karen Laszlo. Her dream contains a frequent motif of hers: a fish that flies and a parrot that swims. After relating the dream, Karen became the parrot and the ocean, two of the significant dream elements.

I am swimming in the ocean of peace, calm, when a dread comes over me and I am quickly afraid. But afraid of what? Sharks . . . and within that instant of realization I see a fin. I knew it would be a shark. I am in a panic. The water becomes a deep blue green. I think to myself: "If I float motionless the shark will not bother me. I will be a clam and the shark will go away." As the fin draws nearer, I am thinking "soon I will see it" and with that I do see, but what I see is a vividly colored parrot swimming on its side under the water, and what I mistook for a fin was a wing sticking up out of the water. I am instantly pleased, at once relaxed and thankful—in awe that this parrot is swimming play- fully around me. Everything becomes very "comforting," very natural, very matter-of-fact.

I am the parrot. Is it connected with my "swimming in the air" dreams? It must be—here is its counterpart—a bird flying in the sea. Am I comfortable out of my element? Am I adaptable to others? I can breathe under the water in dreams, much the same as I easily swim through air—comfortably, effortlessly . . . I am the ocean. I am all-consuming. A protective quenching of all that comes to me. I can be kind and cruel. I am safety. I am peace. I am the real world that holds all the answers. I am the least asked-about and perhaps the least thought- or cared-about. I am where dreams belong. Floating, buoyant, deep, intrusive in a soothing way; to rock and mother you and to hold you up where your world is heavy. I am a fire sign—I feel most comfortable in water.

• *Dialogue with the dream's components.* Ask each dream element what it holds for you, what it wants to tell you. Let the dream voices speak. In the process of a long-anticipated separation from her husband, Dorald Patsos had the following dream:

I am in the lobby of an apartment house and I cannot find the key to an apartment I have sublet. . . . I go to what looks like a concierge desk and ask for help. The person behind the desk is unhelpful and keeps asking me who I am and why I don't have the key. I am embarrassed and he recognizes this and begins to kid me, making me more embarrassed and agitated. I leave the lobby and then return but now it looks like the entrance to the Clark Street subway station. I go up in the elevator and worry that I may have dropped the key down the elevator shaft. Once again I try to gain entry to the apartment but I still don't have the key. It is very important to me to get into this apartment and I am now overwhelmed because of the missing key and again people keep asking me who I am. I go out into the street and begin looking in the gutter and the sewer for the key. There is muddy water in the gutter. I check my pockets again to see if it is on my key ring.

Here are excerpts of Dorald's dialogue with the main elements of her dream:

Key, what are you doing in my dream? I am the means to home. I am a way to get in—I am a clue, assistance to gaining entry to something you want very much.

Key, what are you? Why won't the door open without you? Why is everything locked up? Must I keep myself locked in once I get inside or if I find the key can I come and go?

Humiliation and embarrassment do you have anything to do with the paintings from my room? Do you have anything to do with fear or reluctance? You are so afraid of being wrong and being ridiculed that we are at the edge of everything you do. Everyone misplaces keys, has paintings (dreams), makes mistakes, has desires and wants. There is nothing to be afraid of. Maybe people were laughing at you because they thought you were silly to be so upset—maybe they thought you should calm down.

Sewer, what are you? Will I lose my key in you? Will my "home" be lost? I am that part of you that could keep you from doing what you want. I am the dark, murky water that could destroy your dreams or poison your desire. I could strip you of the way home.

Water, what do you mean? Are you a cleansing symbol of rebirth or are you the water from the sewer that will destroy my dream? I can be both. I show you that nothing good can come without a price. There are two sides to me: The good and the bad. I can quench your desire for freedom. I can clean the key or I can swallow it and you will never find it or it will rust and be covered in dirt. . . .

Key, are you me?

The themes of independence, risk, security, and identity become clearer as Dorald dialogues with her dream. Significantly, the Clark Street subway station is the stop for her therapist's office, a reminder that there is support for her journey toward a new identity.

• *Focus on a single image or symbol from the dream and flow write about it.* And keep in mind that it may be the most puzzling or incongruous element of the dream that is charged with the most energy. Here is an excerpt from Robin Garber-Kabalkin's journal about a dream in which she was dancing at the edge of a ravine, fearless and exultant. In her waking life, Robin told us, she hadn't danced in many years.

Dancing on the Ledge above the Ravine—Where I was always afraid to go. I am the ravine. I have always been here, waiting for this woman to confront me. So many others have scaled my inner walls—some fearlessly, others on a personal mission, overcoming their fear. But she

—she has always stood at the rear, allowing everyone else to push past her, knowing that I was here, waiting for her, knowing that I was her supreme test, which of course, I'm not. Ignoring me, acting as if I really didn't exist, her night terrors reminded her of my existence— the journey of her days brought her ever closer to my gaping, threatening . . . Who am I? What do I represent? Even she does not know. But she can guess. And all her guesses reveal her insecurity, her sense of not belonging, her doubts about who she is.

Today she has travelled all the way to my outer rim. It is an act of extreme courage for a coward such as she. And most remarkable of all, she is dancing—dancing on the edge above a canyon—with as much abandon as she can muster—not a lot by any standards, but an admirable show for her. I will not interrupt her. She is whirling now, but soon her rapturous bubble must burst. For having danced once upon the ledge is not enough. She must return again and again, dancing each time to exorcise another demon. And each journey will have its own pain, its own fear. And each dance will be its own victory. And each time, I will be here, ready to echo her own delighted applause.

At the dangerous edge of the ravine the dreamer dances her own healing. Another workshop participant repeatedly dreamed about being a passenger in a bus. At first, she was puzzled about the dream's symbolism; then she began to understand it as a reflection of her situation at that time. Although she saw herself as having taken charge of her life in the midst of a traumatizing divorce from her psychotic husband, in actuality she hadn't been "in the driver's seat" at all. Someone else had been driving the bus, and she was just a helpless passenger.

• *Alter your perspective in your dreamwork.* If the content of your dream is too threatening, if the thought of reliving a nightmare in the present tense is too alarming, record the dream in the third person, as if it belonged to someone else. This will give you enough distance to get it all down on paper, where you can look at it from the more dispassionate perspective of your waking ego.

• *Note what common themes emerge as you keep track over time.* You might jot down simple descriptive titles on the last page of your journal, and when it's full, reread them to see if there is a common thread. Years ago, while completing the requirements for my doctorate, I had a series of dreams of finding myself at high altitudes, suffering from vertigo. In the dream I did not know how to get safely down. I suspect it was my unconscious trying to prepare me to come down to earth after spending five years in the rarefied spheres of academic discourse. Paying attention to recurring themes will provide you with additional insights over time.

Exceptional Human Experiences

Finally, there are transcendent experiences that have the capacity to alter our lives in dramatic and unforeseen ways. These have been studied and defined by my friend Rhea White, a psi scholar and writer, as "exceptional human experiences" (EHEs). Ranging from near-death and out-of-body experiences to moments of mystical union with nature or another human being, these encompass any moment or event that transforms our lives in some significant and lasting way. Often, although not necessarily, they contain an element of the paranormal. There may be precognitive knowledge or the uncanny sense of déjà vu, an experience of telepathy or a clairvoyant vision. An EHE may entail a series of synchronistic occurrences or a dramatic conversion of some kind. But it can also be a book that changes your life in unaccountable ways, a dream that provides crucial insight or guidance, or a conversation that has far-reaching consequences. These experiences are spontaneously generated. They come unbidden, often at times of inner turmoil and crisis, and usually have a giftlike quality. Always, they leave inspiration and a sense of rebirth in their wake. Our previous understanding of the meaning of our lives and our connection to those around us is expanded and transformed. Sometimes it can take years for their full implications to become clear.

Rhea White's own story is a powerful example of the lifelong impact of such an experience. In the midst of a severe snowstorm in March of 1952, a coal truck skidded into her car. Rhea recalls that she left her body, rose up in space, and thought, "This is what it's like to die." At the same time, she felt "the 'everlasting' arms holding me

. . . filled with the absolute conviction that 'nothing that ever lived could possibly die.' " Rhea suffered eleven fractures in the accident and spent many days in the hospital under heavy sedation. She remembers, "When I was alone and awake, I could sense this singing stillness. It was what I had felt when I was up in space. I felt deep peace and a kind of poised expectancy. And I could feel myself healing, feel my bones knitting . . . somehow I could consciously *feel* it in my bone cells." This event drastically changed the whole direction of Rhea's life. Until that time, she had been headed toward a career in professional golf, but after her near-death experience, she felt an intense need to understand what had happened to her and turned for answers to books on philosophy, mysticism, religion, psychology, and parapsychology.

What can journal writing add to such a transformative moment? As with dreams, it can illuminate the nature and meaning of the experience. Although Rhea had begun writing a diary several years earlier, after her accident it became an important focus of her many questions and insights. Writing on a near-daily basis, she pondered the significance of her dreams and other exceptional experiences, and of the books she was reading. More than forty years later, this experience is still casting new light on Rhea's life, as we can see in the following recent journal entry. After awakening at 3:30 one morning with a "eureka" insight, she wrote, "This morning, I feel that same surety of a solid road beneath my feet that I had back on campus after the accident. I was on the road of meaning and I knew it. Now, blessedly, I know it again after all these years." Several days later, on the anniversary of her near-death experience, she reflected in her journal, "Once again I feel I am turning a corner—having a major insight. And I felt the heart of that great peaceful Silence the accident introduced me to." So convinced is Rhea of the transformative potential of these experiences—particularly the importance of writing about them—that she is currently preparing a book on how to write one's EHE autobiography.

Many other diarists, too, have described inexplicable moments that altered their lives in profound ways. Burghild Nina Holzer tells us that over years of keeping a diary, "I had come to realize that the writing process often produced altered states of consciousness in me that were very much like mystical visions. . . . Without any conscious attempt, my journal had become a record of the sequence in which some mysterious process manifested itself in my writing and in my life." Holzer describes a time in her life when, filled with chronic physical pain of unknown origin, she lived alone out in the country, with her journal as her only companion. As she explored the countryside around her, she began to have intimations of a greater wholeness in the universe. "Something began to come together," she writes.

> Something about inner and outer. One image with another image. Little by little my pain became less. The dreams kept coming, even by day, even out on my walks. First I didn't know what to call these dreams that came in the middle of the day. First I called them poems, but later I simply called them visions, and by then I knew it didn't matter whether they came at night or by day. They were part of the same map . . . the journal had taken me to a place of health where no doctor could have.

Loran Hurnscot (pseudonym) underwent a long period of spiritual crisis and suicidal despair after breaking with the esoteric teachings of P. D. Ouspensky. She was on the very brink of killing herself; then, on October 4, 1941, she wrote in her diary,

> Suddenly I was swept out of myself—knowing, knowing, knowing. Feeling the love of God burning through creation, and an ecstasy of bliss pouring through my spirit and down into every nerve. I'm ashamed to put it down in these halting words. For it was ecstasy— that indissoluble mingling of fire and light that the mystics know. There was a scalding sun in my breast . . . and the bliss of heaven filled me.

And Rebecca Cox Jackson (1795–1871), a free black woman who founded a black Shaker sisterhood in Philadelphia, kept journals of her spiritual visions after her religious conversion at the age of thirty-five. Entry after entry describes visitations from angels and other beings bearing spiritual lessons and insight. Here is an excerpt from her diary of March 1843.

In the morning I found myself under great power of God. An angel came in the room, and I found my body under strange feeling. I thought I was dying. I was seized with a trembling within and without my body, and I was then carried away. The earth trembled and a great storm came from the south. The house that I was in began to shake, and the people all ran out. I stood still. . . . And then I was all alone, and my vision ended, and I was very happy.

Despite their differing forms, these experiences were clearly life altering, in each instance imbuing the diarist with a sense of meaning and an expanded sense of her life's purpose. In every case, journal writing was the channel for expressing this meaning.

Jung claimed that his life's work was inspired by a series of dreams and paranormal experiences he had in his late thirties. "To-day I can say that I have never lost touch with my initial experiences," he wrote in his autobiography during the 1950s. "All my works, all my creative activity, has come from those initial fantasies and dreams which began in 1912, almost fifty years ago. Everything that I accomplished in later life was already contained in them, although at first only in the form of emotions and images." Parapsychologists and others who study such experiences offer intriguing explanations for their existence. Montague Ullman believes they are a manifestation of our deep need for communion, "a kind of deeply hidden connective tissue available when other connective strategies fail." How welcome is this promise of healing, of wholeness, in our time of fragmentation.

8

"This Drama of the Process"

Journal Writing and Creativity

How to make art as though it came from a single breath, the breath of life, the breath of joy, the breath of love.

ETHEL SCHWABACHER, *Hungry for Light: The Journal of Ethel Schwabacher*

How I should like . . . to write a sentence again! How delightful to feel it form & curve under my fingers!

VIRGINIA WOOLF, *The Diary*, Volume Four, 1931–1935

On January 17, 1936, the artist Emily Carr wrote in her journal,

Over and over one must ask oneself the question, "What do I want to express? What is the thought behind the saying? What is my ideal, what my objective? . . . The subject means little. The arrangement, the design, colour, shape, depth, light, space, mood, movement, balance, not one or all of these fills the bill. There is something additional, a breath that draws your breath into its breathing, a heartbeat that pounds on yours, a recognition of the oneness of all things.

The diaries of countless writers and artists, such as Virginia Woolf and Sylvia Ashton-Warner, Emily Carr and Anne Truitt, reveal another dimension of journal writing. They show us the diary as a fertile ground of creative process. Journal writing can provide a unique channel of creativity for all of us, whether or not we are artists by profession. It invites the free play of imagination, intuition, and desire, demanding only—and nothing less than—authentic expression.

"Healing and creativity are two sides of the same coin," Gabriele Rico tells us. "Underlying both is the idea of wholeness. The urge to survive and the urge to create are interconnected." In 1982, May Sarton observed in her journal, "Whatever the wounds that have to heal, the moment of creation assures that all is well, that one is still in tune with the universe, that the inner chaos can be probed and distilled into order and beauty." Creative people in all fields describe a state of heightened awareness in which all boundaries fall away and they experience communion with their work and the world at large. In the moment of creation they are, indeed, whole.

"The Realm of the Mothers"

"The creative process has feminine quality," Jung tells us, "and the creative work arises from unconscious depths, we might say, from the realm of the mothers." Creativity isn't something possessed by only a handful of such geniuses as the Brontë sisters, Sylvia Plath, and Frida Kahlo. We are creative every day of our lives, in myriad ways. And while we may readily recognize the creative process when it leads to a painting or a novel, it more often takes the form of planning a meeting or a menu, resolving a problem at home or work, juggling our time to the greatest benefit, or simply looking at something familiar with new eyes.

Etty Hillesum saw creativity as inherent in every aspect of conscious living. As her outer circumstances grew more bleak, she felt the demands of her life growing simpler. Everything false and superfluous was stripped away; only the essential remained. In April 1942, four months before she entered Westerbork transit camp, which was the last stop before Auschwitz, she wrote, "All that matters now is the 'deep inner serenity for the sake of creation.' Though whether I shall ever 'create' is something I can't really tell. But I do believe that it is possible to create, even without ever writing a word or painting a picture, by simply moulding one's inner life."

But of course, Etty Hillesum did write. And for her, as for most diarists, psychic life and journal writing were interwoven in a fluid process of reciprocal influence, each shaping and shaped by the other. Molding the inner life became one with writing in the diary. For creativity consists precisely of bringing out of ourselves what is uniquely and specifically our own. Stephen Nachmanovitch tells us, "As our playing, writing, speaking, drawing, or dancing unfolds, the inner, unconscious logic of our being begins to show through and mold the material. This rich, deep patterning is the original nature that impresses itself like a seal upon everything we do or are." And upon everything we write. In our diaries, that rich, deep patterning reveals itself time and time again in unpredictable ways. When we sit down with a blank page and pen in hand, some urge to express ourselves is manifested, and we can never foresee what will take place. The moment of creation is always a surprise.

Keeping a journal is itself a creative process. Since we don't start out with any preconceived plan, we may begin in one place and end up somewhere very different. And it's precisely this freedom from external constraints that opens the door to inspiration. Nachmanovitch offers musical improvisation as one example of the creative process. Here, memory (the past), intention (future), and intuition (present) are fused in the moment of creation, unique and non-repeatable. All of us need, Nachmanovitch claims, "some channel of flow from heart to reality and a way of recording it," a "totally judgment-free, discrimination-free pouring out of heart." This is what the diary offers. Here, too, everything comes together in the moment of writing: memory, aspiration, and the fullness of the moment.

It is hardly astonishing, then, that many writers keep journals. The free flow of the diary offers a balance to the careful crafting necessary in their other work. Sue Grafton, a mystery writer, notes,

> I'm finding now that some of the freest writing I do is in the journal because psychologically that feels like playtime. Once I get into the chapter itself it starts feeling too earnest. I think, this is a solemn piece of writing here and I had better not make a mistake, and so I start

getting tense. In the journal I can write down exactly what I'm thinking. Often it's quite lovely writing and I just lift it from one document
to the next.

And here is Virginia Woolf after a hard day's work, in November
1939: "Oh how gladly I reach for this free page for a 10 minutes
scamper after copying & re-copying, digging in those old extract
books for quotes all the morning!" For her, too, the diary was a joy
and a relief from the perfectionist standards she set for her "serious"
writing. "How glad I am to escape to my free page," her next entry
begins.

Because women have not always been free to make art, we often
create with consciousness of our gender. "Now I am a woman again
—as I always am when I write," Woolf wrote in her diary, upset at
being treated as an aging woman in her late forties. And Katherine
Mansfield (Woolf's friend and sometime rival) reflected, "Life and
work are two things indivisible. It's only by being true to life that I
can be true to art." The mystery of the creative process is the central
theme of her journal. For Anaïs Nin, too, creativity infused every
aspect of daily life. Informed by her psychoanalyst, Otto Rank, that
men are the creators because, unlike women, they don't fear cutting
the umbilical cord, Nin turned this around. "Not wanting to be
separated from human life became the basis of my art," she wrote in
1972. And, from my own journal:

June 1994. I am observing my own way of working on this book—Chapter Two, at the
moment. I begin at the point that I left off the day before but before I know it, I'm
somewhere else. In the past I'd have thought this was a disorganized and fragmented way
to work because at the end of the day it's difficult to say, "This is what I've done today."
Now, however, I wonder if it isn't just an organic way of working that goes naturally with
the fact that this book isn't out to make an earth-shaking argument or to prove a point.
It does seem to be a spirallic way of working—in keeping with the nature of the material
—moving ahead, circling back to old territory, detouring along the way. I'm always
working on the entire book at once, with a particular emphasis on one chapter. My bodily
sense at the end of a day's work is that the whole thing has somehow shifted a little, not
that I have written or edited X number of pages. It is anything but a linear way of
working. As I get closer to completion I will have to check for loose ends, consistency, and
follow-through. Now, however, I have the luxury of leaping from here to there as

glimmers and inklings surface. This seems to be in the spirit of journal writing but I have yet to see if it makes for a clear, coherent, readable book.

"The Gentle Vibration in Things"

Creative women in many fields use journal writing as an outlet for their work. Judith Malina, co-founder of The Living Theatre, kept a diary of its early years, recounting its dramatic ups and downs and her many passionate involvements of that time. The notebooks of the great dancer Martha Graham show her brilliant choreographer's mind at work, alternating hurried reflections about the symbolism of her work with concrete stage directions. The New Zealand writer Sylvia Ashton-Warner used her diary to explore the philosophy of "organic teaching," which evolved through her work with Maori children. Sylvia experimented with a pedagogy that radically reversed the conventional wisdom, noting, "To bring them to do what I want them to do they come near me, I draw them near me, in body and in spirit. They don't know it but I do. They become part of me like a lover." In her diary, she described progress made in her work with her young charges. By far the majority of published journals indeed are those of women writers, who capture fleeting images, snippets of conversations, ideas for stories, and lines of poetry in their diaries. Many have commented on the significance of the diary for their other creative work. Gail Godwin, for one, says,

> I write fiction because I need to organize the clutter of too many details into some meaning, because I enjoy turning something promising into something marvelous; I keep a diary because it keeps my mind fresh and open. Once the details of being me are safely stored away every night, I can get on with what isn't just me. . . . I had to keep a diary for many years before I could begin writing fiction.

Perhaps the most voluminous diaries by women writers published to date are those of Virginia Woolf and Anaïs Nin. Unlikely companions though they are, the many volumes of their two journals illuminate every step of the writing process—from excitement over the original flicker of an idea to dismay at the uncomprehending or downright nasty responses of clueless critics. A Writer's Diary was assembled and edited by Leonard Woolf, from Virginia's manuscript diary after her death, in order to cast light on her "intentions, objects, and methods as a writer" and show "the extraordinary energy, persistence, and concentration with which she devoted herself to the art of writing." This, it certainly does, offering fascinating insights into Virginia Woolf's creative process and the planning, crafting, and revising necessary to render the finished work of art. It also reflects the moments of self-doubt and despair she experienced in the throes of creation. Anaïs Nin's earlier volumes reveal her belief that diary and fiction are inimical to each other. In 1936, she noted, "Conflict with diary-writing. While I write in the diary I cannot write a book." But by 1974 she had managed to reconcile the two: "I found I could do both, one was feeding the other. . . . Writing fiction made me write the diary better, writing the diary made me write fiction from more spontaneous sources." Antonia White's published diary revolves around the telling question she asked herself in November of 1939 that was to haunt her throughout her life: "Do I or do I not seriously want to write?" She did, it appears, but the process never ceased to fill her with self-doubt and anxiety.

Artist and writer alike may use the journal to explore their thoughts on a work in progress, to grapple with a conceptual issue, and to record the moments of jubilation and despair that inevitably accompany the creative journey. For Katherine Mansfield, the journal provided a place to ponder and articulate what it was she sought most in life—" 'a mystery, a radiance, an afterglow.' " Paula Modersohn-Becker contemplated in her diary what she hoped to capture in her painting: "I feel and sense with ever greater vividness that intimacy is the soul of all great art," she wrote in February 1903. Then,

I have to learn to express the gentle vibration in things. The curl in them. I have to find expression for it in drawing too. . . . The strange waiting that hovers over opaque things (skin, Otto's brow, fabric, flowers), which I have to strive to achieve in its great simple beauty. Strive for the greatest simplicity by means of the most intimate observation. This is greatness.

And what of women in music? The diary of Clara Schumann (1819–1896) reveals the self-doubt of a talented performer and composer who denigrated her own creativity for years before finally coming to terms with it. Despite receiving encouragement from both her father and her husband, Robert, Clara Schumann judged her own work inferior and, in November 1839, confided to her journal, "I once thought that I possessed creative talent, but I have given up this idea; a woman must not desire to compose—not one has been able to do it, and why should I expect to? It would be arrogance." Yet Clara continued to create music and, less than a decade later, confessed to her diary, "There is nothing greater than the joy of composing something oneself and then listening to it." After her husband's early death in 1856, Clara went on to support her eight children by giving concert tours. When her friend, the composer Johannes Brahms, advised her to stop, she held her own beautifully, informing him, "The present moment, when my powers are at their greatest and when I am most successful, is hardly the time at which, as you advise, to withdraw into private life."

In spite of her own spirited initiative and enormous creative ability, however, Clara continued to see her primary vocation as the dissemination of Robert's work. Almost three decades later, her diary shows her still grieving for her lost love, as she prepared his letters for publication. "These letters awaken my longing more than words can say, and my heart's wounds bleed afresh," she wrote. "What have I possessed and lost! And yet how long have I gone on living and working. Where does one . . . find the strength? I found it in my children and in art—they have sustained me by their love and art too has never played me false."

Through journal writing, then, artists of every stripe have found inspiration for their creative work. In their diaries, they've played with ideas, experimented with artistic techniques, and jotted down flashes of inspiration. Virginia Woolf was only the most famous one, with her frequent reflections on the writing process. In one oft-quoted passage, she observed, "The advantage of the method is that it sweeps up accidentally several stray matters which I should exclude if I hesitated, but which are the diamonds of the dustheap." Here she was referring to the promising nuggets of truth and beauty retrospectively found amidst the lengthier diary proceedings. Written in haste before the inner critic could censor them, these turn out to be the hidden jewels in her diary.

You don't have to be a professional artist or writer to use the diary as a springboard for invention. Keeping a journal will almost certainly reveal unsuspected aspects of your own creative potential. Through capturing ideas and inspiration otherwise lost, your diary, too, may become a sourcebook for other kinds of writing, a creative notebook in which you embark on many new projects. With time you will cultivate a sensitivity to your own buried treasure.

"Deep Old Desk, Capacious Hold-all"

In a journal entry in 1919 that has since become famous, Virginia Woolf reflected,

> What sort of diary should I like mine to be? Something loose knit, & yet not slovenly, so elastic that it will embrace any thing, solemn, slight or beautiful that comes into my mind. I should like it to resemble some deep old desk, or capacious hold-all, in which one flings a mass of odds & ends without looking them through.

She was asking for a lot, but after all, she *was* Virginia Woolf! Over time, the journal will become a rich source of inspiration for your other creative work. Whether you are a diarist with a novel inside you or a university student writing weekly essays, a freelance writer on the lookout for fresh material or a poet in search of the perfect metaphor, the diary can become an invaluable writerly aid and companion. Judith Minty has used her journal as a sourcebook, choosing material in order to "expand on it, let some image/feeling grow to assume its own body in a poem or prose piece." And Tristine Rainer describes how *The New Diary* gradually evolved out of her own journal:

> Over a seven-year period I made entries about my own process and about my reflections on other diaries, without considering to what use I might later put them. And I asked myself questions about journal

writing, to which at first I didn't have answers. Gradually I began to see the answers to those questions evolving on the pages of my journals. The concept for this book developed organically and effortlessly out of my personal diary.

Then there is the remarkable story of the French-Algerian writer Marie Cardinal. For years Cardinal endured chronic mysterious vaginal bleeding of no organic origin. Then she found a psychoanalyst in whose care she slowly came to understand the unspeakable trauma that lay at the heart of her psychosomatic illness: her mother's repeated attempts to abort her, and the subsequent emotional neglect she'd suffered as a small child. Bringing that horror to conscious awareness restored her to life—and to creativity. Near the end of her seven-year analysis, to her own wonderment, Cardinal began writing a journal. "At night and very early in the morning, I wrote," she says.

When the notebook was full, I began another. During the day I hid them under my mattress. When I shut myself into my room in the evening I retrieved them with the joy that might have been reserved for a handsome new lover. It happened simply, easily. I didn't think I was writing, even. With pencil and paper, I let my mind wander.

In contrast to the structured nature of her analysis, Cardinal observes, the notebooks contained "the elements of my life which were arranged according to my fancy: going where I pleased, living out moments I had only imagined. . . . I was conscious of being more free than I had been." As it became clear to her that this writing was "the most important thing I have ever done in my life," Marie Cardinal resolved to tell her story, and those notebooks became the basis for her autobiographical novel, *The Words to Say It.*

The longer you have been keeping a diary, the greater its potential riches. Not only is there more to draw from but, over time, you have a record of process and change. Since time has a way of altering perspectives and reordering priorities, something that you wrote casually a few years ago may, upon rereading, strike you as a brilliant starting point for a story or an essay. With time and practice, you can train your eye to detect your own "diamonds in the dustheap."

The Greek-Canadian writer Smaro Kamboureli wrote a long prose poem about the immigrant experience, using entries from three journals that offered different versions of her personal history. Weaving together actual and invented journal passages in her fiction, Kamboureli believes she has found a more authentic way to convey her experience. "I made up a lot of entries to create a narrative that would make my immigrant experience more accessible," she explained in an interview in 1986. Gail Scott, another contemporary Canadian writer, not only kept a diary herself while writing her novel *Heroine*, but also had her protagonist write one. Scott explains that her protagonist has "a series of masks [and] a very perturbed relationship to reality, whatever reality is. I like to think there's a movement through the novel out of hysteria towards something else, which happens, actually, through the writing in her diary."

But again, you don't have to be a professional writer to do this. Mary Anne has published several short personal essays, which began as workshop exercises, in the women's column of a New York newspaper. In one, she described her pride, as a single mother, over her son's graduation from high school; in another, the poignant experience of seeing her daughter off to college. In the women's literature classes I teach, students routinely keep class journals in which they can relate their life experience to the material covered in class. Often, a journal entry may evolve into a full-length essay, as happened with the following excerpt from Janet Fraka Casiano's journal.

Hagar Shipley is making me melancholy (happy/sad). Margaret Laurence has done in *The Stone Angel* what Carolyn Heilbrun is describing and lamenting the lack of in *Writing a Woman's Life*. She has written a story from a woman's perspective and its reality is very close to home. (This is an experiment at typing a journal entry and it's not working. I'm too critical and keep going back and revising. This is not coming out free flowing! But I'm getting out what I think is an outline for a paper on the unspoken in *The Stone Angel*, so I guess it's okay.) Not only does she share Hagar Shipley's physical struggles, Margaret Laurence reveals Hagar's rambling thoughts, indecisive moments and fear of her appearance to others. This similarity to my own aging and that of my mother, reminding me of our bickering and unsaid words—the story could be ours.

For me, too, the journal continues to provide inspiration and material for creative projects of all kinds. In its pages, I find ideas for workshops and articles, titles for as-yet-unwritten books, and, beyond that, ideas for songs, for quilts and other sewing projects, for travel that might combine business and pleasure, for menus and recipes, for Christmas and birthday gifts. Like many other longtime journal writers, I suspect there's a novel in there, maybe even two or three! If you want to begin a writing project and need inspiration, why not sit down with an old journal and start reading. What you find will surprise you, and no doubt you'll end up with at least one or two splendid ideas for the story or article you want to write. And, having seen what your journal holds, you won't let those momentary flashes of genius escape you in the future. You'll jot them down immediately.

For Christa Wolf, the diary serves to heighten perception of the writer's ear and eye, and works as "a means to remain active, to resist the temptation to drift into mere consumption." In the course of daily life, she observes, "I sometimes note down short monologues by people in stores, at the hairdressers or in the trolley. How do they talk? What do they talk about? What's important to them?" Directly or not, these conversations work their way into her fiction. What stories, essays, or poems are buried in your journal? What drama is there to be discovered, enhanced, and shaped? What stray thought or flight of fancy might prove to be the seed of your creative realization? Perhaps one of your dreams might provide the outline for a short story.

Once you discover the wealth of material your journal contains, you may want to go a step further and consciously cultivate it as a creative notebook. There you can jot down ideas for writing and other kinds of creative projects. When I visited the National Yugoslavian Costume Museum in 1979, I was so thrilled by the beautiful Slavic dress and embroidery that I sat down on the floor and attempted to sketch some of the designs in my journal. Several months later, back in Vancouver, I made some gypsy skirts based on those sketches.

Other writers, too, have reflected on the diary's value as a creative notebook. Erica Jong recommends that aspiring poets keep track of ideas, lines of poetry, and dreams that might become poems. And Linda Pastan tells us, "As a poet, I work with small scraps too: images, ideas salvaged from notebooks, lines from old failed poems, phrases jotted down while driving a car or riding on a train." The poet Yvonne Moore Hardenbrook says, "I write something every day even if it is just a line. I've learned to write down thoughts as they come, no matter where I am. I keep note pads all over the house. Periodically I gather up all the pieces of paper, copy off the lines and drop the typed pages in my 'idea' folder." Alix Kates Shulman organizes her ideas and material in special notebooks. She explains, "Into my regular writer's journal go story ideas, overheard bits of conversation, compelling words, notes from my readings—anything that stimulates my writer's imagination and I am afraid I may forget if I don't record." After losing a suitcase in the Los Angeles airport, which contained a notebook with five years' worth of notes for her next novel, she now carries her journal onto the plane with her!

Like these writers, you might include bits of dialogue you hear in passing, evocative phrases and sentences from the newspaper, questions that haunt you, written or visual character sketches, plot outlines, ideas for articles, and titles for future works. Your creative projects may also include pottery designs, landscape gardening, or plans for your dream house. What about including inspiring quotes from other writers' work? Sara Ruddick says that she began to keep a journal while reading Virginia Woolf's diaries—"its subject a mix of Woolf and me." She explains, "I walked for hours, watching people watching each other and themselves; following Woolf, I imagined their inner life. In Woolfian rhythms, I heard the city's voices, personal conversations, and impersonal markers—subways, traffic, clocks. . . . I was discovering my eyes and ears."

For Fanny Burney, who kept a journal for seventy-two years, her journal writing was frequently the only mode of creative expression possible. Employed as a Keeper of the Robes in the Court of George III in 1786, she worked eighteen-hour days, with no more than two waking hours for herself. These precious hours, Judy Simons tells us, were spent writing, "an activity she grasped like a life line." In October 1788, Burney wrote, " 'In mere desperation for employment, I have just begun a tragedy. . . . Had not this composition fit seized me, societyless, and bookless, and viewless as I am, I know not how I could have whiled away my being; but my tragedy goes on, and fills up all vacancies.' " Even in extreme circumstances, Fanny Burney used every spare moment to write, making what she could of an intolerable situation.

In a fascinating twist on how the journal may be used as a creative notebook, Dorothy Wordsworth (1771–1855) kept a notebook for her brother, William, who drew liberally from it for his poetry. Dorothy thus became her beloved brother's surrogate journal keeper, registering his every mood. Meanwhile, tragically, her own creative energy was repressed, resulting in various psychosomatic illnesses. In April 1802, sister and brother went for a walk, Dorothy's decription of which was to become the core of one of William's most famous poems. In her journal she wrote,

> We saw a few daffodils close to the water side. We fancied that the lake had floated the seeds ashore . . . there were more and yet more and at last under the boughs of the trees, we saw that there was a long belt of them along the shore, about the breadth of a country turnpike road. I never saw daffodils so beautiful they grew among the mossy stones about and about them, some rested their heads upon these stones as on a pillow for weariness and the rest tossed and reeled and danced and seemed as if they verily laughed with the wind that blew upon them over the lake.

Two years later William wrote "I wandered lonely as a cloud." In the poem, interestingly, he wandered alone!

The much-loved Mexican artist Frida Kahlo kept a journal for the last decade of her life, often using it as an artist's sketchbook. Her biographer informs us, "The drawings in the journal are done in bright colored inks, pencils, and crayon. . . . They often have the look of having been made in a trance or by someone drugged. Color bursts wildly out of outlines, lines hurtle or meander as if she were doodling. . . . The starting point for many images was a drop of ink." Frida herself wrote, in a characteristically enigmatic entry, "Who would say that spots live and help one live?! Ink, blood smell. I do not know what ink I would use that would want to leave its track in such forms. . . . Inked worlds—land free and mine."

How can your journal serve as a creative notebook? What ideas are

escaping you for lack of being recorded? Perhaps it's time to start a
creative projects journal, as Tristine Rainer calls it, or an idea folder,
like Yvonne Hardenbrook's. Make it a repository of ideas, lines of
poetry and prose, images, sketches, plot ideas and story outlines,
notes of your reading, observations of the world around you, stray
thoughts and impulses, and anything else that takes your fancy. Over
time it will become your treasure chest.

"Loosening the Ligaments"

Rereading her diary on Easter Sunday, 1919, Virginia Woolf was both-
ered by its "rough & random style" but conceded that "it has a
slapdash & vigour, & sometimes hits an unexpected bulls eye." Then
she added, "But what is more to the point is my belief that the habit
of writing thus for my own eye only is good practise. It loosens
the ligaments." Katherine Mansfield noted in her journal, " 'It's very
strange, but the mere act of writing anything is a help. It seems to speed
one on one's way.' " English professor Deborah E. McDowell keeps a
journal for similar reasons. She explains,

> Because this is writing done solely for myself, with no concern for
> sound, sense, or the approval of others, I think of it as freer writing. In
> my journal entries I am able to close my mind and ears to that bloated,
> overfed superego, that disgusting internal critic and censor who finds
> everything I write for "scholarly" and "professional" audiences want-
> ing and "unfinished" in some respect.

Your journal can provide a protected space for writing practice.
Whether you are "rehearsing" a writing assignment or an important
letter, a short story or a newspaper column, writing in your journal
will get your creative juices flowing and allow your thoughts and
feelings to spill onto the page, unimpeded by the fear of premature
criticism. The author Patricia Hampl says that this kind of writing
practice is an integral part of her workday. "I usually begin the day by
writing, swiftly, what I see out the window," she writes. "It's the
keyboard, arpeggios, scales, limbering." The analogy to musical scales

is apt. Just as piano exercises keep the fingers supple and limber, writing practice, in Natalie Goldberg's words, is "a warmup for anything else you might want to write . . . the most primitive, essential beginning of writing." She adds, "The trust you learn in your own voice can be directed then into a business letter, a novel, a Ph.D. dissertation, a play, a memoir. But it is something you must come back to again and again." Anaïs Nin, who had no shortage of vivid metaphors for the diary's role in her life, also testified to the importance of having a protected environment in which to practice writing: "Secrecy is the very element which created this stalactite cave, this world of truth," she wrote in November 1941. "As I grow further away from feminine reflection and nearer to art, to objectivity, I do not want to lose this drama of the process, from the first blurred reflections of emotional waters to the lucidities of the poet and analyst."

Writer's Block

At one time or another, anyone who writes suffers from writer's block. At those times, the journal is often our best friend. Given the way we work—high expectations breed anxiety—it's not surprising that when the pressure to produce is lifted, we find we can write again. Around about the time I began working on this book, I came across several passages in Nachmanovitch's Free Play that seemed so relevant that I immediately wrote them out and placed them above my desk. "When you are stuck," he advises, "meditate, free associate, do automatic writing, talk to yourself and answer yourself. Play with the blocks. Stay in the temenos of the workplace. Relax, surrender to the bafflement; don't leave the temenos, and the solutions will come. Persevere gently." My usual reaction to feeling blocked is to get frustrated and berate myself for wasting time, and then to get up in disgust and do something "useful." But the passage that has proven most comforting at times when I'm sure the muse has deserted me once and for all is Nachmanovitch's following gentle reminder:

> The work[wo]manlike attitude is inherently nondualistic—we are one with our work. If I act out of a separation of subject and object—I, the

subject, working on it, the object—then my work is something other than myself; I will want to finish it quickly and get on with my life. . . . But if art and life are one, we feel free to work through each sentence, each note, each color, as though we had infinite amounts of time and energy.

Yes, indeed. Sometimes this has meant spending an hour with my journal in prime working time during a morning when I had great hopes of "getting ahead" with this book—trusting that this is not mere self-indulgence but an integral part of the process. At other times, it has meant sitting before the computer as, over and over again, it went into screen-saver mode while I daydreamed. If that doesn't help, I return to the journal, conveniently nearby, and try to write my way to the heart of the block. What is the problem and where do I feel it? It turns out, not surprisingly, that it's almost always some kind of unrealistic expectation of what I ought to accomplish that day. Gloria Naylor, too, says she keeps journals "to help me sometimes when I'm stuck in a piece of work. I will write out what it is I want to say and why I'm not saying it [and] I've come to terms with a lot of demons that way." During a creative block of longer duration, journal writing may be a way of keeping one's writing arm oiled and ready, should inspiration come.

Occasionally a writer may even begin a journal specifically to overcome her own resistance. In September 1944, the English novelist Barbara Pym wrote, "Once before, after Christmas 1942, I started a diary because I was unhappy and it helped to write things down. Now I start because I have had . . . the fear that I shall never, never write that novel or do anything at all worth doing." As for Antonia White, despite periodic doubts about the value of her journal, she continued to write it for more than half a century, filling forty notebooks and binders. Although she didn't count her journal notebooks as "real work," in October 1935 she reflected, "How fast, how comparatively painlessly I write to-night. . . . I have sat here for only one hour and a quarter and how many sheets are covered—over ten pages —over 1200 words. If I could do as much each day to my book, I would have the body there to work on in a few weeks." The contrast between her sense of ease in the diary and trepidation about writing fiction couldn't be more sharply drawn.

First Drafts

Your journal provides a safe and efficient place to compose a first draft —of a letter or an essay, a short story or a professional memo. Safe from premature exposure to curious eyes, your writing can find its natural shape and flow. Along the way, you can enjoy the luxury of digressing to follow an image that intrigues you or a metaphor that has punch. Even if you decide not to use what you write, your journal contains the record of what you felt, thought, and imagined that day. Several years ago, I decided to end an unsatisfactory friendship by means of a letter. I wrote three pages in my journal without pausing, with the thought of revising it later where necessary, then realized the draft said exactly what I wanted to say. The only change I made was to take off a redundant P.S. Then I copied it out and sent it off. What began as a first draft proved to be the finished product. By pouring myself into my journal I had given myself the freedom for this.

Here is an excerpt from the class journal of Linda Hatter, a student in my women's literature class, which became the basis of her term paper.

> In all the books I've been reading, one theme pops up over and over —language. Is it a "male" language and therefore one that will never allow women to express themselves fully? . . . Toni Morrison's *Beloved* for the most part uses existing language, and is in no way hurt by it. There are certain alterations that she makes: "rememory" and "disremember." . . . So I guess Morrison is, in a way, rewriting the language —or just making us re-define the words we have.

Anaïs Nin often used lengthy passages from her diary for her fiction. In *Volume Four*, she describes the following dramatic experience of how the two came together at a time when she'd reached an impasse in her fiction.

A snowstorm. I was working on *This Hunger*, when my typewriter broke down. I went out into the snow with it, to get it repaired. When I came back, I did not feel like writing the continuation of Djuna's life at the orphan asylum and her hunger. I felt like writing about snow. I wrote every image, every sensation, every fantasy I had experienced during my walk. The snowstorm had thrown me back into the past, into my innocent adolescence, surrounded by desires, at sixteen, intimidated, tense. . . . They all fused: snow, the frost of fear, the ice of virginity, purity, innocence, and always the sudden danger of melting. I wrote myself out. And when I was finished, I realized I had described Djuna's adolescence, and the adolescent contractions of other adolescents. I had written thirty-eight pages on the snow in women and men, on Djuna and the asylum, her hunger.

"Among Dark and Silence"

The artist's path is often a lonely one. In September 1974, the sculptor Anne Truitt reflected in her journal, "The essential struggle is private and bears no relation to anyone else's. It is of necessity a solitary and lonely endeavor to explore one's own sensibility, to discover how it works and to implement honestly its manifestations." The writer and activist bell hooks, too, confided to her diary, in 1979, "Writing is a lonely process. Writing little poems and stories, however 'great' in the anonymity of closed-in rooms . . . can never be as fulfilling as touching another person, holding them close."

You work alone, long quiet hours behind a closed door, often with the sense that nothing much is coming of your writing or art. The work demands no less than everything you can give. Even when it's complete, there is no guarantee of an audience. You try to get your book into print, your paintings into a show. More solitary work, often rife with heart-wrenching disappointment along the way. So much depends on timing and luck. Amid all the uncertainty and isolation of the artistic journey, the journal can serve as a loyal companion. Over and over again, Emily Carr described her longing for a community of kindred spirits. "Why, why, why must I always stand alone in my work, away from other artists, away from seeing other worthwhile work?" she implored her diary in November 1933. "How completely alone I've had to face the world, no boosters, no artist's backing, no relatives interested, no bother taken by papers to advertise, just me and an empty flat and the pictures." And her diary. Even Sylvia Ashton-Warner, with a loving husband, three young children, and a doting lover, occasionally felt the tug of isolation. "Is it really loneliness for my own kind that makes me enter this diary?" she asked herself on November 19, 1943. "Individual experience cannot but be lonely." When no interested friend is available, the journal provides us with a means of discussing our work with ourselves. It offers companionship and a chance to dialogue with the Muse, transforming the raw ache of loneliness into the welcome balm of solitude so necessary to every artist's existence.

It also provides a forum for self-exhortation, a medium of support and encouragement. While traveling this long and often lonely road, we need to give ourselves a little affirmation, just as we would to a friend. " 'It is time I started a new journal,' " Katherine Mansfield wrote, in an uncommonly self-tolerant mood. " 'Come, my unseen, my unknown, let us talk together. . . . I must try and write simply, fully, freely from my heart. Quietly caring nothing for success or failure but just going on.' " Emily Carr, too, often reminded herself of the true sources of inspiration for her art.

So, artist, you too from the deeps of your soul, down among dark and silence, let your roots creep forth, gaining strength. Drive them in deep, take firm hold of the beloved Earth Mother. Push, push towards the light. Draw deeply from the good nourishment of the earth but rise into the glory of the light and air and sunshine. Rejoice in your own soil, the place that nurtured you when a helpless seed. Fill it with glory—be glad.

Her journal reads like a compendium of hard-earned wisdom. "Do not try to do extraordinary things but do ordinary things with intensity," she instructed herself. And how nice to meet her in a rare moment of satisfaction with the way work has gone. "I painted well today, working on the summer sketches, reliving them—loving them," she wrote on September 23, 1936. "I think I have gone further this year, have lifted a little. I see things a little more as a whole, a little more complete."

Käthe Kollwitz, near fifty, found herself "overcome by a terrible depression" that focused on her perceived limitations as an artist. On March 31, 1916, she wrote in her diary, "Gradually I am realizing the extent to which I already belong among the old fogies, and my future lies behind me. Now I am looked upon more or less kindly as a dignitary." Despite feeling that her best days might already be over, Kollwitz resolved to "return, without illusions, to what there is in me and go on working very quietly. Go on with my work to its end." By the following July she could write, with obvious quiet satisfaction, "From so many sides I am being told that my work has value, and I have accomplished something, wielded influence. This echo of one's life work is *very* good; it is satisfying and produces a feeling of gratitude. And of self-assurance as well." Etty Hillesum, too, counseled calm and simplicity for herself. "Sometimes I have a fleeting urge to express this or that in elegant words, but I kill the urge straightaway, find all that now much too contrived," she wrote in April 1942. "It will all balance out in the end. Have patience. Slowly, steadily, patiently."

But the journal may also reveal the artist in a sterner mode, admonishing herself to be more productive, to waste less time and daydream less. After a three-week hiatus in her writing, Sylvia Ashton-Warner had harsh words for her writing self.

All this writing what I'm *going to do,* in living as well as working, the time alone that is squandered, the *time* I spend in the entrancing world of fantasy, fattening my soul on the stolen prizes of what I want to happen. Unless I economize on my dreaming and put the savings into my thinking, what I want to happen will not happen.

Continuing in this self-critical mode, her next entry reads, "Today I lay on the bed and groaned aloud because when I read the words I had written they had no meaning for me . . . and I couldn't do anything but groan about it." But by the following day Sylvia was writing again and found that "the words this time had meaning."

Work in Progress

"Of what should I write here except my writing?" Virginia Woolf asked her diary in October 1924. The fact that she did is what makes her diary so fascinating. Journal writing may illuminate the artist's evolving conception of her work in progress. For readers, such diaries provide intriguing insights into the genesis of works of art. Woolf, for one, frequently elaborated on her creative strategies in the diary, reflecting in detail on her current work. While composing *Mrs. Dalloway* in the summer of 1923, she wrote, "I should say a good deal about The Hours [later renamed], & my discovery: how I dig out beautiful caves behind my characters; I think that gives exactly what I want; humanity, humour, depth. The idea is that the caves shall connect, & each comes to daylight at the present moment." Several months later, she noted, "I think the design is more remarkable than in any of my books," and then, once more, we learn something of her inventive strategy: "It took me a year's groping to discover what I call my tunnelling process, by which I tell the past by instalments, as I have need of it. This is my prime discovery so far." For Etty Hillesum, the diary served in large part as a confidante for her passionate desire to write, a desire not dimmed by the unlikelihood of its ever happening. Even when she knew that her departure for the Westerbork camp was imminent, Etty observed, "I still suffer from the same old complaint. I cannot stop searching for the great redeeming formula. For the one word that sums up everything within me, the overflowing and rich sense of life."

For the visual artist, journal writing provides a complementary medium of expression. In her autobiography, *Growing Pains*, Emily Carr described her habit of asking herself, each time she was about to begin a new sketch, " 'What attracted you to this particular subject?' " and " 'What is its core, the thing you are trying to express?' " The diary was key here. She tells us,

Clearly, and in as few words as possible, I had answered these questions from myself to myself, wording them in my little note book, presenting essentials only, discarding everything of minor importance. I had found this method very helpful. This saying in words as well as in colour and form gave me double approach. I knew nothing about the rules of writing.

Under strict doctor's orders to discontinue her solitary sketching journeys into the rain forest after she suffered a heart attack, Emily, ever resourceful, decided, "One approach is apparently cut off, I'll try the other. I'll 'word' those things which during my painting life have touched me deeply." Thus began her second artistic career, this time as a writer. Georgia O'Keeffe, too, used her journal to think out loud about her art. " 'At the moment I am very annoyed,' " she wrote. " 'I have the shapes—on yellow scratch paper—in my mind for over a year—and I cannot see the color for them—I've drawn them again—and again—it is from something I have heard again and again till I hear it in the wind—but I cannot get the color for it—only shapes. None of this makes any sense but no matter.' " For Anne Truitt, artistic work is akin to giving birth. "When I conceive a new sculpture, there is a magical period in which we seem to fall in love with one another," she wrote in her journal. "Its life is its own. I receive it. And after the sculpture stands free, finished, I have the feeling of 'oh, it was you,' akin to the feeling with which I always recognized my babies when I first saw them, having made their acquaintance before their birth."

Knowing that even the most accomplished writers and artists have moments of uncertainty, even hopelessness, sustained me in the writing of this book. How well I can identify with Carr's terse summation "Did good work this morning. Did poor work this afternoon."

July 1992. I wonder if it would be helpful to write this book "to someone"—that is to have my projected reader in mind as I write, instead of writing for a vast, anonymous readership. I want to write with a dear friend in mind. Perhaps that will help me to create an intimacy, a living relationship between the reader and my book. It may also allow me to fashion an appropriate style and tone, and to infuse the book with warmth, to preserve its loving impulse. The vast and anonymous readership does not exist, in any case, except in the abstract. What does exist is the individual woman reader, looking for encouragement and inspiration, just as I always do when I read.

November 1994. Writing this book is like being on a long, extended treasure hunt, never knowing in advance quite what I'll find. I'm journeying in and among so many lives, so many stories, so many similar and diverse experiences. So much joy and sorrow, exultation *and grief. I'm living many lifetimes in one. Even when I'm tired, stuck, or discouraged, I'm still exhilarated—and always in such good company!*

Dealing with Critical Response

"Its the curse of a writers life to want praise so much, & be so cast down by blame, or indifference," Virginia Woolf reflected, feeling that her novel *The Voyage Out* had been slighted. "The only sensible course is to remember that writing is after all what one does best; that any other work would seem to me a waste of life; that on the whole I get infinite pleasure from it; that I make one hundred pounds a year; & that some people like what I write." The diary has afforded many writers and artists a safe place to vent frustration over scathing and unjust reviews, and to air feelings of despondency and the futility of persevering with their work. Here is Antonia White, for example, in August 1952.

> The reception of *The Sugar House* has been the coldest and most hostile I have ever had. Only 4 good reviews; the rest ranging from tepid to real downright sneering and hatred. In some cases, most in fact, the point of the book has been completely missed and the contradictions are farcical. . . . I feel so crushed and depressed. . . . I felt I ought to stop any further attempt at serious writing.

And yet, the very act of venting her despair was therapeutic and enabled Antonia to go on writing. May Sarton, too, expressed her anguish in the pages of her journal. Here is her reaction to a review of her novel, *Kinds of Love*, in the early 1970s.

> The darkness again. An annihilating review in the Sunday *Times*. I must have had a premonition, as I felt terribly low in my mind all weekend. Now it is the old struggle to survive, the feeling that I have created twenty-four "children" and every one has been strangled by lack of serious critical attention. . . . What a lonely business it is . . . from the long hours of uncertainty, anxiety, and terrible effort while writing such a long book, to the wild hopes . . . and the inevitable disaster at the end.

"For women, the journal has been one of the few places in which they could be writers and women, without paradox," Cinthia Gannett tells us. We see this clearly in the journal entries quoted throughout this chapter. Indeed, many women writers and artists claim that it's while they're engaged with their art that they are most themselves. Seventeen-year-old Marie Bashkirtseff, having just discovered her talent for painting, wrote with obvious relish, "In the studio all distinctions disappear. One has neither name nor family; one is no longer the daughter of one's mother, one is one's-self—and the individual—and one has before one art, and nothing else. One feels so happy, so free, so proud!" Sylvia Ashton-Warner, heading off to her little writing hut, mused, "My personality changes. Off fall the wife, the mother, the lover, the teacher, and the violent artist takes over. I am I alone. I belong to no one but myself. I mate with no one but the spirit. I own no land, have no kin, no friend or enemy. I have no road but this one."

No friend but the journal, that is.

9

❧

Writing for Your Life

Further Suggestions for the Journey

You need only claim the events of your life to make yourself yours. When you truly possess all you have been and done, which may take some time, you are fierce with reality.

FLORIDA SCOTT-MAXWELL, *The Measure of My Days*

Keeping More Than One Journal

One of the questions I'm often asked is "Do you put everything into one journal, or keep separate journals for dreams, and creative ideas, and so on?" Ideally I prefer to have one all-inclusive journal. But since my main volume is always a large bound book, I carry small supplementary diaries in various handbags. If I write on the road, I cross-reference it in my "main" journal and refer back to it later if necessary. A simple note—"See pocket journal" and the date—tells me where that entry is. In addition to the "ideas" notebook I described in the previous chapter, over the years I've kept journals of poetry, sewing projects, and psychotherapy; various travel diaries; and, when I was studying voice in England, a small notebook of my teacher's suggestions regarding vocal technique.

You'll want to experiment to see what kind of arrangement serves you best. One workshop member has two or three journals going at any given time, and simply writes in the one that most appeals to her that day. Recently she had a linen-covered spiral-edged book, a larger yellow notepad, and a small pocket diary that accompanied her at all times. Another diarist commented, "I have four journals: one for bad feelings, one for 'everyday,' one for dreams, one that is a yearly recap." Marguerite began keeping a diary on a large wall calendar, hoping to understand the pattern of her severe asthmatic attacks. She devised an elaborate system for color coding her symptoms and, by the end of the month, the page resembled a piece of modern art. Eventually she expanded it into a bound book. At some point, you, too, may want to keep more than one journal at a time. If you like to doodle or draw, why not get an artist's sketch pad to supplement your written journal. One disadvantage of keeping several journals simultaneously is that if you want to go back and reread entries from a certain period of your life, you'll be flipping through more than one book. But that may be a small price to pay.

Some diarists keep separate notebooks of the most private aspects of their lives. The writer Barbara Godard describes what happens to emotionally volatile material in her journal.

> Great white spaces in this diary when I should confront intense moments of shock and mourning and avoid them by not writing. But these are displaced, coming out in my other diary, in that dream diary I keep, trace of anxiety and pain, which is ordered by the unconscious and its disruptive rhythms.

Indeed, the most common supplementary journal is the dream journal. Many people begin their diaries this way. My sole reservation here is that recording your dreams separately doesn't give you immediate information about what else was going on in your life at that time. Understanding that link is essential.

When the diarist intends to publish her diary, she may keep a second, private journal for unchecked emotional outpouring. Burghild Nina Holzer tells us, in the opening pages of *A Walk Between Heaven and Earth*, "This is not my private journal even though it contains many entries about my personal life. During the time of this writing quest I also kept a private journal." Ethel Schwabacher, too, kept public and private journals, from 1978 until her death in 1984. The former was typewritten, the latter, a handwritten notebook. In Schwabacher's published journal, her daughter, Brenda S. Webster, one of the book's editors, offers glimpses of what the private volumes contained without resorting to quotation, which would have violated her mother's wishes. She tells us,

> Whereas the public journal shows a mature artist at the height of her powers as writer and journalist, in control of her chosen medium of language and concerned with questions of general human and artistic importance, the private notebook shows a confused, ill, and angry old woman, terrified by her diminishing ability to control her own life.

Of course, like the editors of the published journal, I, too, would have respected Ethel Schwabacher's wishes for privacy, but I can't help wondering how differently our understanding of her would evolve if entries from the private diary were included alongside the others. What a complex and multifaceted portrait that would provide.

Toward the end of her life, Schwabacher actually did begin to include personal material in her public journal. Five years before she died, at the age of eighty-four, she asked herself, "Shall I allow the personal to enter this journal? Or shall I imagine that great art was done entirely influenced by other great art and knowledge of the past? No, I feel that it was as well the outcome of extremely intimate experiences, enjoyed or suffered by the painter." Even so, the worst of her emotional suffering remained confined to private pages. The editors inform us, "At a point when the public journal abstractly discusses ambiguity in art, the private jottings ask in anguish (referring to the arthritis) 'Does the pain cause the fury or the fury cause the pain?' " Ethel Schwabacher was able to turn her anguish into art. "Out of all the clash, turmoil, and suffering recorded in the private notebook, she makes in the public journal a beautiful mosaic," the editors conclude.

Some diarists prefer to keep a separate notebook for purely cathartic writing. In her beautiful published diary about recovering from breast cancer, Deena Metzger relates, "I paste Barbara's letter into my journal. This is not the only book. There is another black book for wailing and howling and dreaming. This book is for talk." In addition to her primary journal, Antonia White kept three special diaries, including one of her three-year psychoanalysis, beginning in 1935. The other two concerned romantic involvements: one with a man in 1937, another with a woman, ten years later. White wrote explicit sexual passages in French.

Kate Tomibe (pseudonym) kept five journals simultaneously, during her confinement to an internment camp for Japanese Americans in 1943. Here she explains the journals' purposes.

> In my five-year diary I will briefly record my daily activities with little or no comment. Then I have a book in which I write book reviews and outlines of textbooks. In my other journal I will write essays which will later be translated into Japanese if time permits. In this day-by-day record I will augment the recording of my activities by impressions of people and events. However, I will omit any activity which hasn't much significance, and also keep out petty emotions such as jealousy and wanting someone who doesn't care, etc. . . . I don't think I'll have much use for my book of "Personal Memoirs" because I'm past the adolescent puppy love, crush-a-week stage. However, I'll keep it to write in if I have any petty emotions which should be excluded from this journal.

If you have been experimenting in your diary, perhaps you have tried out different modalities of writing. Elaine Marcus Starkman drastically changed her style of journal writing after twenty-five years. "After all these years, I have a room of my own and a new method of journaling," she noted.

> With my left-handed scribbling I could never write in those beautiful hardbacks one buys in good stationery stores, but I no longer have dozens of faded spiral notebooks lying around either. I've begun to keep my journal on the computer. Late at night I fumble into my room, turn off the lights, flip the switch, close my eyes, pound away, and wait for surprises.

Accomplished typists in particular may find, along with Elaine, that fingers flying across the keyboard are better able to keep pace with mental processes than when they are pushing a pen across paper. Another advantage to computer journal writing is that you can track down old entries instantly with a click of the mouse. But I confess that I'm too much a paper fetishist to contemplate it myself. I love the physicality of journal writing—the look and feel of paper and pen, the finality of the handwritten word that cannot be deleted or erased. And the process of selecting beautiful new bound books provides far too much aesthetic pleasure for me to give them up in exchange for merely functional hard drives and floppy disks.

Writing on the Road

Sometimes people who don't regularly write journals keep travel diaries, recording sights, experiences, and impressions of places they visit. There are even special travel diaries on the market, complete with headings such as "places visited," "sights seen," and "miles traveled," for those who want a concise factual summary of their trip. My journal has been my most cherished travel companion over the years, especially when I've journeyed alone. For each journey, I began a corresponding diary, using its pages to make the transition from my sedentary life-at-home to a footloose and transient lifestyle. There I described how I felt about what I saw and experienced. This added a rich layer of meaning to my time on the road. The diary also kept me company in my hotel room at night when I was too exhausted or too nervous to go out alone. When everything around me was unfamiliar and mysterious and even my dreams echoed this strangeness, my journal reminded me who I was.

Travel means discontinuity. The very nature of an extended trip is that you find yourself in continually changing surroundings and situations. And each time you move on, you are forced to reinvent yourself anew; in fact, this is one of the attractions of the open road. Many of us, especially during our twenties, travel as much to rediscover ourselves as to experience a different culture. Christina Baldwin has gone so far as to say, "My real journey had very little to do with traveling Europe, and a whole lot to do with traveling my own mind." Precisely. In 1979, I spent a long afternoon conversing in a café, next to the train station in Bologna, with a philosophically inclined Sicilian fruit exporter who spoke fluent English and German. We spoke openly about our lives, the way strangers often do when they know they are not likely to meet again. He told me about his wife and new daughter, and asked me about the purpose of my open-ended travels in Europe and the Middle East. And before he helped me find my train, he told me it seemed to him the inner journey I was on was more significant than what I would see and experience externally. He was right, of course. I had gradually abandoned my religious upbringing in the years before this journey but still identified strongly with my European background. Now I'd come to see the continent whose cultural and intellectual heritage I claimed, and to rethink my identity. Rereading my journal of that trip, it's clear that I was far more concerned with my inner life than with the castles and cathedrals of Europe. Similarly, in *Journey to Wholeness*, Barbara Marie Brewster writes about rereading past journals, "I began to see my travel journals of long ago as a log of external experiences which paralleled the expanding interior awareness of the young woman named Barbara. As she had negotiated her outward journey, so too, the inner person had felt, perceived, developed, feared and triumphed."

Introducing her published travel diary, the African-American writer Eleanor Smith describes the seventeen volumes that chronicle her odyssey to various corners of the world. "This collection ranges from a special Trip Book to a writing pad and they come in all sizes and shapes," she says. Rereading them, Smith discovered more than she was looking for; she reflects,

These journals share my thoughts and experiences about the scenery, culture, customs, and people of the countries in which I have traveled and serve as a memory source for the things I have learned. However, after fourteen years of journal writing I find they have an added dimension I had not anticipated. I am able to look back over my experiences and realize how I have changed and grown and to see the things that have remained so much a part of my life.

Journal writing while traveling, especially when you are moving from one place to the next at a rapid tempo, is a way of reflecting upon your daily encounters in all of their freshness and immediacy. Here you can preserve those unique and unforeseen moments that always and only occur when we are free of our usual ballast. Coming back to an old travel diary years later, you'll be amazed by the vivid rush of memories that engulfs you. I had hours of pleasure, not long ago, rereading the journal I wrote during those months in Europe and the Middle East. People, places, and incidents that I hadn't thought of in ten years came back to me in full color, evoking other memories not even in the journal. The exact spot where I sat in a café, the dynamics of a stimulating conversation, what I ate for dinner on a specific evening, the landscape during a particular train trip—all returned in a rich flood of memory.

While flying, diarists often describe a sense of being "high above it all"—betwixt and between, no longer "here" and not yet "there." When Anaïs Nin was forced to leave Paris for New York in the winter of 1939 because of the war, she was heartbroken at first. As the train carried her farther and farther away from her beloved city, she wrote, "It seems as if I will never tear myself away from France. Each mile of the journey, each landscape, each little station, each face, causes a painful separation. I carry with me only two briefcases filled with recent diaries." Yet, on boarding the hydroplane that would transport her from Portugal to the Azores, then on to Bermuda and finally to New York, she reflected, "Strange that when we finally fly, the separation from the past seems easier to achieve. Height and distance from the earth seem to stabilize the spirit, to liberate it from its sorrows. We enter the consciousness of the cosmos." Her feelings, not surprisingly, were to fluctuate many times in the course of that journey, but she clung to the diary as the one stable factor in a life headed beyond her control. Many years later, flying from New York to San Francisco, Nin observed, "I always like to write by the cold, clear light of airplane cloudscapes. It is a special light, not golden as I imagine the light of Greece, not blue like the light of snowy mountains. It is intensely white, sharp. But if I see everything clearly in this light it is not because of the light itself but the altitude and separation from those I love."

An empty bound book has become my favorite gift for a friend who is going on an extended trip or is changing residence. In moments of disorientation, culture shock, or just plain nostalgia for something familiar, a journal is a loyal and comforting presence. It reminds us of who we are. A friend who had dreamed of going to Italy last summer had to travel south to Florida instead, in order to settle affairs for her frail and difficult elderly aunt. The night before she left, I gave her a bound book with a Carl Larsson painting of a woman tending an enormous bouquet of azaleas on its cover. Although my friend wouldn't get to Italy as she had hoped, there was nothing to prevent her imagination from taking off in quiet hours of journal writing between caretaking tasks.

Gloria Bowles began writing a diary during her junior year at a college in Paris in 1961. She has been writing ever since. On a return visit in June 1986, she reflected on the experience of journal writing while abroad.

> I am having a magnificent time, walking, looking in Paris. . . . Walking, walking, stopping at the Alésia for a café crème, hot and delicious. . . . Reading in the evenings, presently Duras in French; and being *dreamy*. It's the dreamy side that does not get expressed much at home because "la vie quotidienne" [daily life] intervenes always. Not surprising that people can write when they are abroad . . . I like this dreamy, less productive side.

Time, leisure, and freedom from external constraints allowed Bowles to enter realms of the imagination not accessible during her usual life at home. In fact, this experience gave her food for thought about that life, as we see in the next entry, written on the flight home. "I do not want to leave. The liberty one feels on vacation, a total involvement in one's surroundings. The beauty of Paris, which is so transporting. Do I live as though I were *unfree*?" Again, the diarist's perspective shifts, away from her usual responsibilities and routine. The results of such reflection can be liberating. Here is Michelle Herman, writing in the Blue Ridge mountains in the summer of 1978.

> I woke up this morning to the sun filtering through the mesh in the tent's flap door. And I was delirious. Drunk on sunlight and absurdly fresh air. . . . Now, sitting at the campsite . . . writing in my notebook by the bright smoky golden light from the kerosene lamp, I keep thinking (uncharacteristically) that this past year has not been bad . . . writing in fits and starts but at least writing, managing to make a living, working out what I could. And now there's this, this extraordinary, beautiful, slow calm quiet world. . . . I'm *alive* and I *climbed a mountain for the first time in my life!*

The French feminist and social critic Flora Tristan kept diaries of her travels through Peru, England, and France between 1833 and her early death at forty-one in 1844. During her last long journey through France, she met with as many working men and women as she could, hoping to help them organize a national Workers' Union, in the wake of the Industrial Revolution. On Sunday, April 14, 1844, she reflected, "Truly it is a rugged business to be in the service of humanity. It is eleven o'clock at night; I have not had time to breathe for a single instant since seven o'clock this morning." Almost a century later, another noted social activist, Eslanda Goode Robeson, kept a detailed journal of her three-month trip to Africa in 1936. Throughout, she described and commented on what she observed, often noting parallels between black-white relations in various African countries and the southern United States. Her passionate involvement with all she encountered is clear.

> We are off Dakar, Senegal, West Africa. The air is very heavy, the sea gray and hot and calm, the sky lead colored. And it is a gray and heavy thought that between 1666 and 1800 more than five and a half million kidnaped Africans, my ancestors, began the dreadful journey across the Atlantic from this very stretch of coast, to be sold as slaves in the "new world." I say began the journey, because records show that more than half a million of them died en route. No wonder the sea and sky and the very air of this whole area seem sinister to me.

Eslanda's compassion and admiration for the people of Africa continued to grow, the longer she traveled and the more she experienced.

One of the most intriguing accounts I have come across is Marion

Milner's *Eternity's Sunrise*, a retrospective analysis of her own travel diaries. In "A First Visit to Greece," she explains that she had been too busy during the trip itself to write in her diary, but had set five days aside at the end to travel to Venice on her own, and write. As she began, the chronological account of each day's highlights seemed lifeless, but then,

> In the dark background of my thought, like a fitfully lit cave, there were gleams as if from a not entirely buried confusion of treasure. And then something happened. When I let go of the attempt to find words to describe those events which had seemed the most important, and simply faced the dark confusion, just sat and stared into this cave of memory, I began to notice my thoughts coming back again and again to certain objects, those trophies and keepsakes that one brings back from holidays.

These "small private moments that come nuzzling into my thoughts, asking for attention" Milner came to call "bead memories," representing moments of heightened perception in which the realms of thinking and feeling, imagination and reason were fused. These were the magnetic kernels of meaning at the heart of her travels.

I end this section by noting that it's never too early to begin keeping a travel diary. Here is an entry from the notebook of my six-year-old niece, Chelsea, describing the start of her family's summer camping holiday in 1994.

> We lefd Aug 13 5:19 am Saterday We had Lunch at a restaurant It was our frst day. There I bought a Post card. and we had Dinner. We went for a wlk. I gest woke up—The next morning Aug 14 '94 Sunday. I went for a bike ride and I got Lost then we talk for a while.

Keeping a Journal for Someone Else

What about people who write diaries on someone else's behalf? Perhaps the most common form of surrogate journal writing is that of mothers who keep diaries for their infants or young children. Karen

Laszlo keeps journals for both five-year-old Andy and two-year-old Aaron. In them, she describes details of the babies' progress during their earliest months, all of their "firsts," and her own experience of mothering them. What follows are excerpts from Andy's journal, begun before he was born.

7/20/88. We're about a month away from finally holding you! Your father and I are always thinking of you, imagining this and kidding about that! And your room is almost finished. The rocker finally took its place in the corner near your bookshelf and the little lamp your dad and I found in a flea market is repainted and looking grand.

11/18/88. It's been over 3 months since you were born, I still watch you sleep—I still sometimes can't believe you're my baby . . . so beautiful, so perfect, so sweet.

8/5/89. My Baby Boy is One! Dear Panda, I really can't believe that all those days have passed by already. I still try to peek at you every morning before you wake up and can't imagine my life without you. I hear all the sounds you create from little breaths to great big crashes when you throw a toy—I see you splash in the pool or try to take some steps—I smell that special baby smell or sprinkle you with powder—and I feel that soft smooshy face . . . and thank God for it all!

After her mother died suddenly, Dawn Bennett-Alexander, aged twenty, found herself with many unanswered questions. Years later, she decided to keep journals for her three daughters, so that in the event of her own premature death they would not have to go through the same thing. She began writing to her second daughter, Anne, when she was only three months pregnant with her, in 1979. Here is an excerpt from that diary.

I'm sure you'd like nothing better than to sit by a nice crackling fire at the age of thirty and read about what it was like when you were a day old, then five months, etc. Especially since time has a way of eroding the memories that seem so vivid while they're happening. Plus, this

way you have a contemporaneous account of what you were like, and
I'll bet it will come in handy when you have kids of your own.

Dawn included details of the pregnancy. "At three months, just as
with Jen, I have started to show somewhat," she wrote. "You've not
been hard on me so far. My first pregnancy was an absolute breeze. I
love being pregnant." Her daughters, Jenniffer, Anne, and Alexandra,
so enjoyed hearing entries about themselves that by the ages of fourteen, twelve, and five, they were all writing journals, too.

At forty-two, Ethel Robertson began keeping a diary in the form of
a letter to her future grandchild, with the clear intent of passing it on.
"I want to talk about myself and I want you to be interested. I may as
well be honest about it," she wrote on March 11, 1924. "You do
understand that you are not living soul yet, but as I assume that you
will materialize in due course and appear in the flesh, I shall try to
catch your attention. . . . Behold then—your grandmother!!"

In rare instances, someone may write a journal on behalf of someone else who cannot do so herself for political reasons. Between 1938
and 1941, the Russian writer Lydia Chukovskaya kept a diary of her
friendship with the great poet Anna Akhmatova. During those years it
was dangerous for anyone to keep a diary, all the more so for a famous
person. In the introduction to her published diary, Chukovskaya recalls
her earlier dilemma.

> In those days, Anna Andreevna lived under the spell of the torture
> chamber. . . . To write down our conversations—wouldn't that mean
> risking her life? Not to write anything about her? This would also be
> criminal. In my confusion I wrote sometimes more openly, sometimes
> more secretively, kept my notes at home, sometimes at a friend's,
> wherever I felt was safer. But invariably, whilst re-creating our talks
> with the greatest possible accuracy, I omitted or veiled their main
> content.

As time went on, Chukovskaya began to serve as Anna Akhmatova's
surrogate journal writer. She tells us, "Day by day, month by month,
my fragmentary notes became less and less a re-creation of my own
life, turning into episodes in the life of Anna Akhmatova." The balance

continued to shift and by 1940, Chukovskaya notes, "I had virtually ceased making notes about myself, whereas I wrote about Anna Andreevna more and more often." Why did Chukovskaya feel moved to do this? Because she recognized that something of monumental significance was happening to her country in that period—and to her beloved friend. "Before my very eyes," she wrote, "Akhmatova's fate —something greater even than her own person—was chiselling out of this famous and neglected, strong and helpless woman, a statue of grief, loneliness, pride, courage."

Rereading Old Journals

I leafed a little through my diary this morning. Thousands of memories flooded back. What a rich year it has been!
ETTY HILLESUM, *September 26, 1942*

On April 20, 1919, having just finished writing a long article, Virginia Woolf paused to read through her old diaries, "as one always does read one's own writing, with a kind of guilty intensity." Troubled by "the rough & random style of it," she nevertheless found "it has a slapdash & vigour, & sometimes hits an unexpected bulls eye." Since Leonard Woolf published *A Writer's Diary* in 1953, the eyes of thousands of readers have gratefully beheld Virginia's diaries, enjoying not only their "slapdash and vigour," but their wit, elegance, and biting commentary on the people around her.

Once you have been writing for a while, you'll likely find yourself flipping back through earlier volumes to see where life has brought you. If you have the least tendency toward self-criticism, you may find yourself silently (or loudly) passing judgment on your own past actions and attitudes. "I should have been able to do better than that," you may think, or, "I can't believe I really wrote this." Here are two things to remember. First, hindsight is always perfect. You did the best you could, based on what you knew then. Second, we aren't accustomed to seeing our own most intimate psychic workings, our own raw vulnerability laid bare on the page before us. This can be uncomfortable. We may instinctively want to deny, correct, cross out, erase, even destroy what we find. But the journal is invaluable precisely *because* it provides a reflection of our lives-in-progress, rather than an idealized image.

When I reread my own journals from the early seventies for the first time several years ago, I was shocked at how narcissistic and repetitive they were. I'd remembered writing much more about my life at university, about courses, professors, and friends, and my rapidly changing views on many things. What I found instead was an almost uninterrupted stream of reportage about how I was feeling about myself, who had or had not asked me out or paid me compliments, and so forth. Not only was I embarrassed rereading this, I was bored. No great literary gems here, not even particularly interesting reflections on my life. Still, having made the mistake once, years earlier, of destroying past diaries, I resisted the temptation to tear out the most offensive entries. That, too, was an important stage in my life.

> *August 16, 1981. I've been rereading old journals. I'm so glad I have them. Reading about my loves of the last year—I forgot that H. told me he loved me. I'm sure he doesn't remember that either. The journal seems to have different meanings for me at different times in my life: therapy, a record, description, and so on. I'm so glad I can always turn to it.*

Even if you periodically read bits and pieces of your journal, you may want to make a ritual of rereading each volume from cover to cover when it's full. In *The New Diary*, Tristine Rainer suggests leaving a few pages at the end for a reflective summing up of each volume's contents. Or, like many diarists, you might reread the year's writing on December 31, in order to sum up and take stock of what the year has meant. I often write a closing entry on the last day of the year, reflecting on its most significant moments and bidding the old year farewell. The next day I write an entry describing some of my hopes and dreams for the new one.

On the last eve of the year, George Eliot wrote in her journal, "The dear old year is gone with all its *Weben* and *Streben*. . . . So good-by,

dear 1857! May I be able to look back on 1858 with an equal consciousness of advancement in work and in heart." And Virginia Woolf
wrote, one New Year's Eve, "This is in fact the last day of 1932, but I
am so tired . . . that I am taking a morning off, & shall use it here, in
my lazy way, to sum up the whole of life. By that phrase . . . I only
mean, I wish I could deliver myself of a picture of all my friends,
thoughts, doings, projects at this moment." Antonia White regularly
took stock of her life at year end. On the second of January 1953, she
wrote, "Such a bore always writing about myself. But at the beginning
of a New Year, it's inevitable [to] try and cope with one's impossible
character." The following New Year's Eve, she reflected, "It certainly
has been an extraordinary year, full of changes and surprises," and
proceeded to itemize in detail what these were: "The most fantastic
. . . the nicest thing in 1953 . . . the most painful . . . the most upsetting . . . the most alarming . . . the luckiest . . . most comforting."

Some diarists routinely begin a new volume on the first of January,
even if they haven't filled their current one. Literally, as well as metaphorically, they close the book on one year and open a new one. In
practical terms, it makes the chronology of their lives more easily
accessible. Virginia Woolf did this, even apologizing to the diary
when, for reasons of economy, she had to continue writing in the old
one on occasion, and chiding herself when she felt she hadn't written
enough in the year just past. "Really it is a disgrace—the number of
blank pages in this book!" she wrote in December 1924. "The effect
of London on diaries is decidedly bad." Käthe Kollwitz, too, read her
old journals from time to time. Exactly one year after Virginia Woolf,
she reflected, "As I read I distinctly felt what a half-truth a diary
presents. Certainly there was truth behind what I wrote; but I set
down only one side of life, its hitches and harassments. I put the
diaries away with a feeling of relief that I am safely out of those
times."

You might write for years with no particular inclination to reread
past volumes, then suddenly, perhaps in your thirties or forties, find
yourself going back to them and searching for some important insights into your life. At any time of year, rereading old diaries can be
a means of taking stock of our lives, of looking at where we have

traveled and of rethinking where we are headed. In her essay entitled "Going Back Through My Journals: The Unsettled Self, 1961–1986," Gloria Bowles reflects,

> Newly aware that I was in the middle of my life, the journals held themselves out to me, a woman in her midforties wanting to go back and review her life, at least as that life was represented in her journals. It is odd. We write our journals but we seldom read them. One friend told me she threw her journals into the fire. Are we afraid of what we will find on these pages?

I think we *are*. At least to some degree. After I requested journal entries for this book from my friend Shira, she told me she felt dragged down into "old shit" as she leafed apprehensively through her old diaries. But difficult though it was, she slowly gained a reluctant admiration for how hard she had been working on her life issues over the years. That's a valuable thing to see about oneself, it seems to me.

Sometimes you may be comforted, even delighted, by what you find in an old journal. In 1934, Virginia Woolf noted, "I have spent the whole morning reading old diaries, & am now (10 to 1) much refreshed. This is by way of justifying these many written books. . . . The diary amuses me." For Antonia White, rereading past journals provided a uniquely honest reflection of herself that she valued greatly. In 1938, she wrote, "Somehow more truth and less distortion gets into these notebooks than into anything else. . . . They are like a photograph of myself to which I refer. . . . It is as if I kept my identity in these books."

The best discussion of reading old journals that I know of is Tristine Rainer's chapter "Rereading the Plot of Your Life." Tristine suggests that we question ourselves as we reread our diaries, and describes three main aspects of the writing on which to focus attention. "Word Indicators" include the use of "I," of questions, of words like "never," "always," and "should," meaningful slips of the pen, and superlatives like "best" and "worst." The second area of self-reflection, "Content of the Writing," refers to questions such as: Do we include full expression of our feelings? Are there major differences in the contents of past diaries? Is there a great emphasis on past and future at the expense of the present moment? Finally, "Trends and Patterns of Behavior" is my focus in the next section.

As you read through old journals, you may feel tempted to read something aloud to whoever happens to be in the room at that moment. Should you give in to temptation? Your journal is your inner sanctum and no one has the right to claim access to it. Not your husband, lover, best friend, mother, or child. Should you wish to share something, of course, that's a different matter. You may even allow someone close to you to read some pages of your journal. Anaïs Nin occasionally permitted close friends to read her journals and even to write in them, as a gesture of intimate friendship. We know, too, that Virginia Woolf and Katherine Mansfield considered reading each other's diaries, in the same spirit. In August 1920, Virginia confided to her diary, "We propose to write to each other—She will send me her diary. Shall we? Will she?" Did they? We don't know.

Promise your journal secrecy, at least for a time. Otherwise, there is bound to be the temptation, whether conscious or not, to censor your writing. And once you begin writing with a future reader in mind, you'll write differently. Gail Godwin says, "On several occasions I have actually read parts of my diary aloud to someone. But too much 'publicity' is destructive to a diary, because the diarist begins, unconsciously perhaps, to leave out, to tone down, to pep up, to falsify experience, and the raison d'être of the undertaking becomes buried beneath posings." During the three decades I've kept a diary, I have never shown it to anyone. So far, at least, it has been important for me to know that I am writing for myself alone. I know of no other way to write honestly.

Observing Patterns and Silences

Recurring Topics and Themes

Between the years of 1975 and 1979, my journals are almost obsessively concerned with three topics: my break with traditional Christianity, a major weight loss, and my burgeoning relationships with men. These preoccupations were the flashpoints for a dramatic identity crisis I was experiencing in that period of my life. Workshop member Mary Brady observed rather different concerns in her diary. In October 1994, she wrote, "In the past four years there have been recurring themes in my journals. The importance of my family, the value of time alone to fill my well, the camaraderie of my friends, the harnessing of time and, just recently, the significance of dream-catching."

Longtime diarist Gloria Bowles, too, detects recurring themes in her writing. "In rereading my journals I find patterns of experience I had never dreamed were there," she says. "When I read the old entries, it is as though I am looking at the life of someone I once knew." Who is it she finds there? "I see, first of all, a woman struggling to achieve independence and self-definition, 'the slow freeing of the self to its full capacity for action and creation,' as May Sarton so beautifully puts it." In an earlier entry, written in March of 1972, she had described some of the patterns evident in her journal: "Rereading my diaries. From Paris to Ann Arbor to San Francisco. Incredible confusion with men. Amazing, the repetition of experience. Work, men: how fit it all together?" Not surprisingly, the conflict between our need for independence and the pull toward commitment is a motif that surfaces time and time again in women's journals, past and present. Burghild Nina Holzer similarly observes that, after years of journal writing, she began to detect patterns. "I began to see that I was tracing something in the journal, that I was documenting something I was not conscious of," she notes. "I saw that certain themes had developed over weeks and months, and that random observations, thoughts, dreams, and sudden visionary images took place in a particular sequence." Her diary, says Holzer, is "a live web with definite patterns."

Emotional and Behavioral Patterns

As you read through old volumes, you may notice basic emotional and behavioral patterns as well. Some that I have observed in my own journals over the years include taking other people's rudeness and aggressiveness personally; wanting to assert my own beliefs in discussion, then agonizing over whether I spoke too boldly; and blocking out expressions of encouragement and appreciation, while never missing a word of criticism. The process of rereading past journals has told me more than I am eager to admit about lingering insecurities and holes in my self-esteem. But it has proven invaluable in my quest for self-awareness.

What are the dominant feelings described in your journals? Are there frequent passages of self-blame and guilt? Do you find anxiety, envy, fear, insecurity, bitterness, anger, self-rejection, or despair? Are there recurrent attempts at self-justification? Repeated references to physical ailments? How do your feelings affect your actions? When you are hurt, angry, or depressed, how do you tend to respond? Do you attempt to strike back when you feel injured? Engage in comfort-eating or drinking? What habitual patterns of self-defeating behavior can you detect as you reread past journals? And what about when you are happy? Do you downplay it? Do you hug your happiness tightly to your chest, afraid that it might escape you? Do you look for a friend with whom to celebrate?

Anne Morrow Lindbergh reread her old diaries with mixed emotions over what she found there. On July 3, 1935, she wrote,

> I read over my old diaries last night: last year at college, the summer before I was married. I have changed so little. All the faults just the same: self-centered, worrying about my sins; daydreaming, running away from the people I like best. And all the things I wanted to do—the writing—the same, only it has taken me about six years to get back there again.

At the same time, however, she experienced "a feeling of great confidence at recognizing myself—finding again the straight stick inside of me, that is I." Gloria Bowles says that even though journals proceed chronologically, they "double back upon themselves, establishing patterns." Rereading her own she notes, "It was a pleasure to find the writer always asserting herself but frightening to find destructive patterns of behavior." Barbara Marie Brewster discovered, upon rereading past journals, that "old" issues were continuing to make their presence felt. "I could see the old patterns, the ones that I was currently so conscious of needing to change," she wrote. "As a young woman I had written about wanting to fit in, wanting approval of others—and all the while I knew that what mattered was my own. Yet here I was 16 years later still learning that lesson." We all have issues that resurface over and over again in our journals throughout our lives. What are yours?

Avoidance and Censorship

What are the silences you have kept in your journal? Which of your thoughts and feelings routinely are left out? Kay Leigh Hagan suggests putting a "C" in the margin whenever you observe yourself censoring something. I use an asterisk. Pay attention to what you include and what you leave out. Make notes to yourself in the margin of your journal. Once you have done this for a while, you can review them. Are there many? Do they indicate a taboo area in your life? Are you ashamed to admit having certain emotions or thoughts, even to yourself? (I've occasionally found myself tempted to censor even my account of dreams.) Just as revealing as the topics we find ourselves returning to again and again are those never broached at all—the pregnant gaps in our journals. What inner constrictions render us mute concerning topics of great urgency in our lives? What is missing, and why? Marion Milner discovered, "The things I was prompted to keep silent about were nearly always the things I was ashamed of, which would have been far better aired and exposed to the cleansing winds of confession." By bringing them to the light of day, Milner found that she was able to reverse the effects of "blind thinking." Whether or not you decide to expose your own secrets to the "cleansing winds of confession," pay attention to what you don't write in your journal. This, too, will increase the range of what you know about yourself.

If you are having difficulty writing about a certain subject, try shifting from first to third person, as if you were describing someone else. If you know more than one language, you may find it easier to write in the nondominant one. This also offers built-in protection of your privacy. Some diarists even invent elaborate codes in which to confide their most intimate concerns. Harriet Blodgett tells us of Elizabeth Wynne, who, at the end of the eighteenth century, wrote her diary in a code by "transposing the last letter of each word to the beginning of the next one and incorporating some misleading capitals." Beatrix Potter, too, according to Blodgett, wrote in an elaborate code, fearing her parents would read her diary.

Sometimes we may indeed censor ourselves for fear of having our privacy invaded. Blodgett shows that young Emily Shore (1819–1839) confided to her diary,

> I cannot entirely divest myself of an uncomfortable notion that [it may] be read by some individual, and this notion has, even without my being often aware of it, cramped me, I am sure. . . . The vague fear I have above mentioned has grown into a sort of unconscious habit, instinctively limiting the extent of my confidence in ink and paper, so that the *secret chamber of the heart* . . . does not find in my pen a key to unlock it.

As Blodgett points out, Shore resolved to start a second journal: "into which I shall pour *all* the secret feelings of my heart; my sins, my weaknesses, my progress towards goodness . . . things known only to my conscience and my God." Exactly how she intended to ensure its confidentiality is not clear, however!

Writing Patterns

Finally, what patterns do you detect in your writing itself over time? What consistencies and fluctuations in motivation, style, form, and content? Do you procrastinate? Feel obliged to write every day? Have a tendency to write only when you feel blue, like Lou Nelson? "When life goes well, I do not find time to write," she observed in April 1976. "It is only when I am blocked by some sadness, or inspired by some relentlessness that I search out a pen or pencil and open my diary to a new page." And Gail Godwin confesses, "Sometimes I am delighted with the bursts of wild candor and arrogance in my journals, and I try to incorporate them in my public writing when I can."

She adds that these journal extracts show "patterns in my writing life, patterns I might not have perceived if I hadn't kept journals." Our goal in observing the patterns evident in our journals is, above all, to heighten awareness. This can lead to constructive change in our lives. Our diaries reflect more of our inner worlds than anything else we do. They have much to teach us.

Making Provisions for the Future

You have been keeping a journal for two, five, or twenty years, and there is a collection of past volumes in your bottom desk drawer, the corner of a closet, or locked away in a sealed chest. At some point you will want to think about what should happen to them and make provisions for the future. Simply destroying them may seem one obvious option. Rather than wonder what will become of your diaries with time or inflict that responsibility on someone else, why not just take care of the situation once and for all by getting rid of them? Don't do it. I did, and lived to regret it. Sometime during the early eighties I destroyed about five years' worth of my earliest diaries, written between ages eleven and sixteen. Rereading them one afternoon, I was filled with embarrassment over their adolescent sentimentality. On a sudden impulse, I tore them up and threw them into the garbage, along with all my creative writing efforts up to that time. It took several years before I comprehended what I'd done. Those pages represented my earliest attempts to understand myself and make sense of the world around me. Their loss is irretrievable.

Frances Rooney says she received a letter from an anonymous diarist who told her, " 'My sister wrote from Egypt that she had found my diaries, that they couldn't stay there where my mother might see them, and what did I want done with them. I told her to burn them. She did. I felt as if my first thirty years had been murdered.' " The East German writer Brigitte Reimann described a similar experience. On November 11, 1959, she wrote,

I just burned my diaries from the years 1947 to 1953—likely twenty volumes—and now my heart aches as if I had destroyed something living, some part of myself. The many hundreds of pages, covered with a childish scrawl, and later, an affectedly sweeping script . . . the many thousands of hours of my student woes, all those tiny and weighty experiences, day after day conscientiously recorded. . . . Why does it hurt like hell? . . . I have burned my childhood and youth, the memories that I don't want to be reminded of any longer. . . . I regret having thrown all of this into the oven.

Emily Carr, too, destroyed an early volume, after it was discovered and read by her sister. In her journal she recalled,

I used to write diaries when I was young but if I put anything down that was under the skin I was in terror that someone would read it and ridicule me, so I always burnt them up before long. Once my big sister found and read something I wrote at the midnight of a new year. . . . When she hurled my written thoughts at me I was angry and humbled and hurt . . . I burnt the diary and buried the thoughts and felt the world was a mean, sneaking place.

At least she continued to write. Many diarists have stopped, after similar experiences. And how interesting that they all burned their diaries. Perhaps they knew instinctively that reducing their journals' pages to ashes was the only way to neutralize their potent energy. Even Virginia Woolf momentarily entertained the thought as she contemplated what might become of her diaries: "Percy could burn the lot in one bonfire. He could burn them at the edge of the field where, so we think, we shall lie buried."

When I began working in earnest on this book in 1992, it finally became imperative that I have all of my journal volumes with me in New York. I carefully packed my first sixteen years' worth of diaries (1967–1983) into two sturdy suitcases, checked these aboard my United Airlines flight from Vancouver, and held my breath. It was more a groan than a sigh of relief that escaped me as both suitcases emerged onto the luggage belt, safe and intact. I won't tempt fate that way again. Next time I might not be so lucky.

But concern for the safety of our diary volumes is only half of the story. The other half is the question "What will become of them should anything happen to us?" Have you considered the future of your journals over time? Do you care whether or not anyone sees them? Are you secretly hoping someone might discover and decide to publish them? These are questions that every diarist, at one time or another, thinks about. A friend of mine has made detailed arrangements to have certain of her private journals destroyed in the event of her death. Others, she doesn't care about. Many people make half-hearted arrangements with friends to have their private writings destroyed in the event of their demise. Others, like myself, procrastinate, as we do with drawing up a will, superstitious somehow that making arrangements will precipitate the untimely need for them.

But avoiding the issue is no solution. In fact, it seems irresponsible to burden someone else—likely a grieving loved one—with the task of having to decide what to do with our most intimate outpourings. Virginia Woolf, too, gave thought to this issue. In March of 1926, she pondered, "What is to become of all these diaries, I asked myself yesterday. If I died, what would Leo make of them? . . . I daresay there is a little book in them: if the scraps & scratches were straightened out a little." That Leonard did not take his responsibility lightly is evident in Virginia's entry written a year later, as once again she asked, "What is the purpose of them? L. taking up a volume the other day said Lord save him if I died first & he had to read through these."

Several years ago I heard that a woman in the Midwest intended to open an archive for women's diaries and journals. If we were all to leave instructions that our journals be crated and shipped to her, she'd need a row of grain elevators just to store them all. Journals—like grain—prefer dry, cool environments, and I, for one, would certainly have no objection to such an arrangement. At least I'd know my journals were in good company! Unless you are convinced that your journal contains writing of superior quality and beauty, you aren't likely to ask someone else to go through and edit them for publication. I know I won't. Still, they are precious documents in their own right, and warrant more than an ignominious end as a pile of paper to be recycled or, worse, in the local landfill. If you have substantial amounts of writing to think about, perhaps you need to sit down soon and give the matter some serious consideration. I know I do.

Perhaps there is a friend to whom you can entrust them, with the hope that she (or he) might hear of an appropriate final resting place:

an archive or center for research on women's lives, or perhaps a scholar working on women's journals. Alternately, you may arrange to have certain volumes passed on to a trusted family member as a keepsake while other volumes are destroyed. Other possibilities may occur to you. Your journal volumes and mine are our most personal and revealing legacy. No matter what we finally decide, they deserve more than an accidental fate.

PART THREE

Sharing the Journey

10

───✦───

"My Lifetime Listens to Yours"

The Pleasure of Reading Journals

Lives do not serve as models; only stories do that. And it is a hard thing to make up stories to live by. We can only retell and live by the stories we have read and heard. We live our lives through texts.

CAROLYN G. HEILBRUN, Writing a Woman's Life

In her beautiful tribute to Käthe Kollwitz, Muriel Rukeyser wrote the following lines:

> Held between wars
> my lifetime
>   among wars, the big hands of the world of death
> my lifetime
> listens to yours.

Was Muriel Rukeyser responding to Kollwitz's art, sculpture, journal, or all three? We don't know. But there is no more fitting and beautiful metaphor for the process of reading women's journals than that of lifetimes, open and receptive to each other. For in reading someone else's diary, it isn't only our minds that engage with the words on the page before us; it's our hearts and souls as well. Our entire lives are called into play. A meeting of two lifetimes takes place.

On Reading Journals

What Carolyn Heilbrun claims above is true for me—I have lived my life through the stories I have read. Simone de Beauvoir's autobiography and Anaïs Nin's diaries were among the most important, instilling in me the belief that women could be creative in ways other than child-bearing. De Beauvoir's writing provided a model of woman's intellectual autonomy and of a relationship of equals between a woman and a man. Now I realize how hard she worked to sustain her lifelong alliance with Jean-Paul Sartre, and how much she suffered. But during my late teens and early twenties, her writing tantalized me with its promise of a life utterly different from the one I had been taught to expect, one that included independence, creative pursuits, and, astonishingly, a choice in the matters of marriage and motherhood.

What vivid memories I have of hours spent absorbed in reading journals. At eleven I discovered The Diary of Anne Frank, sharing—unbeknownst to me—with countless other young girls, that universal introduction to diaries. Hungrily I read, amazed that her feelings and thoughts were so much like mine, astonished that someone would publish these in a book. Almost three decades later, I still remember where I was when I read it and the guilty intensity with which I sped through the book, only to begin again when I came to the end. I felt as though I had seen into another's soul. A decade later, cozied into a corner of my favorite old sofa with a blanket, a mug of coffee, and Anaïs Nin's Diary, I marveled again that someone could portray her inner world so revealingly, engrossed in Nin's ability to convey the most subtle nuances of mood and emotion in words. And while my feelings about Nin's diaries have changed many times since then, the memory of that first shock of discovery and delight lingers.

I'm still reading. Along with many others, I'm inclined to look to published journals for some special kind of truth that we don't expect to find in fiction. And yet, some intriguing questions come to mind when we speak of "reading a journal." Doesn't the very idea challenge our usual assumptions that we write our diaries as intimate dialogues with our inner selves? Isn't privacy the defining characteristic of the personal journal?

What Is a Published Journal?

What, exactly, do we mean by a published journal? Do diaries constitute a literary genre and, if so, what are its characteristics? If, by journal, we mean a succession of dated entries intended for the writer's eyes alone, what do we make of Emily Carr's or May Sarton's, written with undisguised intent to publish? Does a diary necessarily have to focus on the writer's inner life? What of Amelia Stewart Knight, who described her family's exhausting trip westward in 1853, in a series of terse jottings—"Monday, August 29th—Traveled 10 miles last night and 12 today, and have camped about one o'clock on Road Creek. Weather very warm and dust bad"—with never a phrase describing how she felt about the many hardships they encountered? And what about fictional journals, such as *Ella Price's Journal* by Dorothy Bryant, Carol Shield's *The Stone Diaries*, or Jamie Fuller's *Diary of Emily Dickinson?*

What we refer to as a diary or journal may also call itself a daybook or notebook, log or chapbook. Common to all is the chronological succession of dated entries reflecting an ongoing process, yet how many variations there are! From Lee Pennock Huntington's journal of the seasons of country life to Anaïs Nin's intimate sexual revelations (so volatile that the uncensored manuscripts could not be published until after the deaths of everyone involved), and from Isabelle Eberhardt's diary of her travels across the Sahara clothed as a man at the turn of the century to Hannah Senesh's account of her work with the Palestinian-Jewish Resistance during World War Two, we have just a sample of the scope and variety of what is called a journal.

Published diaries fail, of course, to tell us anything about the tangible manuscript itself. What we get is its verbal content, mass-produced for widespread distribution. How much do we lose if we don't know what the original diary was written on, what the diarist's handwriting looked like, what she crossed out, wrote over, or replaced? Some diary scholars would say that we lose a great deal. Ideally, we'd have the original journal itself in our hands, noting all those details as well as possible enclosures, doodles, and changes in handwriting. Perhaps the diarist wrote partly in code, had her own idiosyncratic abbreviations or symbols, decorated and sketched in the margins. How much we might learn about her from clues like these! Some editors of journal anthologies have admitted feeling uneasy about reproducing original journal entries in standardized script and layout. No doubt something precious is lost in the process. And yet few of us have time and money to crisscross the continents in quest of diary manuscripts. What does it mean, then, to read a journal that presumably was written for the writer's eyes alone? Is a diary that has been condensed, edited, and otherwise altered still a diary? We think of journals as representing a slice of life; yet what we read isn't always —in fact, usually *is not*—identical to what was originally written. All kinds of questions arise about projected audience and self-censorship, and about the circumstances of publication.

Who Decides to Publish, and Why?

Who decided that a particular journal would be published, for example, and when? If it was the diarist herself, did she write hoping, like the late-nineteenth-century Russian diarist Marie Bashkirtseff, to see her journal in print one day? "If I do not die young I hope to live as a great artist," Marie proclaimed, "but if I die young, I intend to have my journal, which cannot fail to be interesting, published." Lest she be thought vain, she explained, "The record of a woman's life, written down day by day, without any attempt at concealment, as if no one in the world were ever to read it, yet with the purpose of being read, is always interesting; for I am certain that I shall be found sympathetic, and I write down everything." Another young diarist, Yvonne Blue, raged against an imaginary future editor, even while insisting that she wrote for herself alone. "The worst thing is the way they correct ungramatical phrases, and put down what they think you meant, and switch sentences around, and leave out the most interesting parts," she wrote indignantly.

> When I read a diary I want to know just the errors the author made, and the personal parts and so forth. It's not fair. They would leave out my pet parts and write a lot of junk in the front about me, and make me feel silly and sentimental and senseless. I don't want *anyone* to have fun out of what I sweated for, after I am dust and ashes.

Some diarists decide to go public with their writing only after much deliberation. Gloria Bowles, a writer and women's studies professor, says, "A dilemma arose when some people encouraged me to publish *The Unsettled Self*. . . . I had to ask myself: Would my journals be interesting to other women? Would they be *useful*? Even the feminist . . . thinks twice before releasing her private writing into the public sphere." After thinking twice, Bowles decided to go ahead and was drawn to conclude, "The publication of parts of my private journal may be my most radical political act." Toi Derricotte, too, claims she decided to make her diary public because she believed her experience as the only black person in a white neighborhood might have social importance. "Though the writing began strictly as a personal document, after several years, I came to think that the work probably had value for others too," she writes.

If the diarist *did* write with a future reader in mind, did she, like May Sarton, make a conscious decision to omit certain aspects of her life? In the final pages of *Encore: A Journal of the Eightieth Year*, Sarton offered illuminating insights into her own thinking on this score. "People often think that I give myself away in these journals written for publication," she says. "They do not realize apparently that large areas of my life are never mentioned. I have never gone deeply into a love affair. For that important side of my life, intimate relationships, deep friendships, readers have to go to the novels." At the same time, Sarton defends the journal consciously written for publication, which is, she claims, "a genre in its own right." Sarton believed that writing with a reader in mind had a beneficial effect on her diaries. "Knowing my journals would be read has provided a certain discipline for me," she tells us. "It has forced me to try to be honest with myself and thus with my readers, not to pretend that things are better than they are, but learn to evaluate without self-pity or self-glorification what has been happening to me."

Often diaries reveal the writer's ambivalence about whom she is writing for. In 1835, the Quaker diarist Deborah Norris Logan firmly declared, "This book is only to myself. I should not venture half the folly it contains if I were in the habit of showing it to others." Yet Logan repeatedly addressed "the readers (perhaps now unborn) who hereafter shall peruse these pages." And what about Virginia Woolf's tantalizing question "Do I ever write, even here, for my own eye? If not, for whose eye? An interesting question, rather." Beatrice Webb, too, reflected, "It would be curious to discover who it is to whom one writes in a diary." Whether the writer originally wrote her journal for her eyes alone or with thoughts of a wider readership, there are many interesting questions about its publication. Perhaps, like Anaïs Nin, she decided to publish only many years later. If so, what prompted her decision to go public and to what extent did she edit her journal entries? Was she merely correcting spelling and grammar, or did she edit the diary's contents as well? Sometimes the answers to these questions are provided in a foreword or even the journal itself; at other times, we are left guessing.

One key concern for diarists who decide to publish their writing is protecting other people's privacy. This is why published journals may contain only sketchy information about the writer's most intimate relationships, even where she might have preferred to include more. Anaïs Nin honored her husband Hugh Guiler's desire for privacy by leaving him out of her published diaries. Generally, her way of dealing with this issue was to show people her "diary portraits" of them before publication, lest they have any objection. Other writers have dealt with the issue by assigning a pseudonym to the people they wished to protect or simply by using initials, as May Sarton and Marion Milner have done.

Perhaps a diarist edits her journal with the aim of avoiding repetitiveness or of shortening it. While the resulting cuts may improve the text aesthetically, they may also obscure important facts about her inner emotional landscape. Margo Culley, a scholar of women's diaries and journals, goes so far as to claim that "it is precisely in what is repeated that we find the preoccupations, the obsessions, the 'meta-phors of self' of the diarist." Sometimes it's precisely the passages of greatest emotional intensity that the writer decides to cut. In the introduction to her third volume, Anne Morrow Lindbergh recalled the period of grief and despair following the kidnapping and murder of her infant son and, soon after, the death of her beloved sister, Elisabeth. "All this inner turmoil was, of course, hidden," she writes. "Between my face-to-the-world and the inner pits of despair, there was no bridge of expression." Then she notes, "The habit of writing almost daily in my diary . . . probably saved my sanity. If I could write out moods which could be admitted to no one, they became more manageable." Thirty years later, editing those diaries for publication, Anne chose to delete the most anguished entries of those years. She explains, "Many pages of these depressed diaries were destroyed long ago, and of what remained, I have cut still more. But some entries are still there, left in this volume. For after all, this is part of the story, as it is part of many people's hidden lives. . . . My depressions were the inner counterpart of the outer frustration of our lives."

Perhaps the diarist only wrote on one specific topic. During a period of crisis, Anne Truitt decided to keep a journal for one year in order to come to terms with the role that her artistic vocation had played in her life. She bought a brown notebook and began to write in bed every morning. She tells us, "The only limitation I set was to let the artist speak. My hope was that if I did this honestly I would discover how to see myself from a perspective that would render myself whole in my own eyes." Whether Truitt entertained thoughts of publishing as she wrote, however, and to what extent she edited her diary, we don't know.

What if someone other than the diarist herself decides to publish the journal? What authority do they have, and what is their relation-ship to the journal writer? Usually it's the diarist's literary executor, often her husband or partner, a close friend or family member. Emily Carr left adamant instructions for her friend and executor, Ira Dil-worth, concerning the editing of her diary for publication: minimally, that is. "I do know my mechanics are poor," she wrote. "I realize that when I read good literature, but I know lots of excellently written stuff says nothing. Is it better to say nothing politely or to say something

poorly?" Those who have read *Hundreds and Thousands* know that Emily
Carr managed to avoid that unhappy choice. Her diary is both substantial *and* eloquent. In Virginia Woolf's case, her husband and editor,
Leonard Woolf, admitted he believed it was "nearly always a mistake
to publish extracts from diaries or letters, particularly if the omissions
have to be made in order to protect the feelings or reputations of
the living. . . . At the best and even unexpurgated, diaries give a distorted or one-sided portrait of the writer." That did not stop him,
however.

Not surprisingly, the person to whom the diarist entrusts her writing is often not the most objective editor. In Katherine Mansfield's
case, her husband, John Middleton Murry, edited her surviving diaries
for publication (she had destroyed many of her early volumes). What
he felt obliged to alter were the frank details of her lesbian loves.
Interestingly, as Harriet Blodgett points out, rather than omit entries
entirely, he distorted them with ellipses and dashes, seemingly wanting to tell and not tell at the same time. In 1979, East Germany saw
the publication of a diary by a writer called Maxie Wander, which
culminated with a poignant account of her losing battle with cancer.
Fred Wander, the diarist's husband and a well-known writer himself,
had edited her journals and letters for publication two years after her
death, at the age of forty-four. In his introduction he explained that
he had deleted passages in which his wife had "lacerated herself with
despair." As I read, I wondered why he did that. Was he simply trying
to protect her, even after her death? Did he feel her despair meant he
had failed her in some way? Was he concerned with preserving a
certain image of her? Did he feel constrained by a cultural context in
which literature was supposed to be uplifting and to offer "positive
socialist role models"? To what extent and in what ways did his cuts
distort Maxie Wander's journal?

On an even darker note, there are the diaries of Sylvia Plath, one of
the most controversial cases in recent times. In his foreword to her
published journals, Ted Hughes, her husband and editor, explained
that he destroyed one of the last two volumes because he did not
want their children to have to read it; the other volume somehow
"disappeared." Since their marriage had ended six months before
Plath's death, it is reasonable to suggest that he would have figured

prominently in her journal, and that it wasn't only his children he was seeking to protect. Recently, Hughes's motives and actions were held up to severe scrutiny by Mary Lynn Broe, who says of the "strategically chopped-up" published journals, "No one who has worked in the archive with these mutilated pieces of paper could really believe that cuts were made . . . to provide a 'readable book.' " Broe asks pointed questions concerning the content of these cuts, among them "Why is 'concern for the children and family' so selectively a matter of cutting the negative portraits of Ted Hughes, the father, and not of the mother?" She for one believes that we have yet to learn the truth about those missing volumes, and suggests, "If I had to speculate, I'd say that the journals will be 'found,' at least in part."

In another intriguing case, Frida Kahlo's biographer Hayden Herrera tells us that a friend purchased a red leather journal (believed to have belonged to John Keats) for her in a rare-book store in New York. Frida wrote in it from 1944 until her death ten years later, when friends tore out substantial sections, leaving only 161 pages intact. Her biographer does not offer any suggestions about the friends' possible motivation.

But the difficulties involved in preparing a diary for publication don't arise only out of problematic personal relationships. Even the most well-intentioned editor is faced with a difficult task, as Jan G. Gaarlandt discovered in the process of editing Etty Hillesum's diaries, forty years after her death. He explains,

> I was convinced that I was about to publish one of the most important documents of our time. I nevertheless had the painful task of making a selection from the diaries. To publish a 400-page diary by an unknown woman was too much of a risk, even in the eyes of this most faithful admirer. I have tried to convey the contents of the exercise books as carefully as possible, taking out repetitions, and many quotations. No word has been added.

Finally, out of "eight exercise books closely written in a small hard-to-decipher hand," the editor managed to create the manuscript published as *An Interrupted Life*.

And yet, isn't there something suspect about probing so deeply into another woman's private life and psyche? Where a woman wrote her journal hoping to see it published, we read with impunity. But what about those instances where she wrote from a deep inner need to understand herself, describing her most intimate feelings and thoughts with never an inkling that her diary might one day be made public? When all is said and done, isn't there something voyeuristic about peering into the private chambers of another woman's soul for a good read?

It all depends on the degree of empathy the reader brings to the text, it seems to me. This is something I've been thinking about since the early 1980s, when I first came across the published German diaries of Maxie Wander, and of Brigitte Reimann, who died at the age of forty in 1973. Like Wander, Reimann described the anguish of her struggle with cancer and, like Wander, she died too young. As I sat in an outdoor café in Stuttgart on a beautiful July afternoon and read the dated entries of Maxie Wander's alternating wild hope and despair, I had an uncomfortable sense of reading as a divided subject. Half of me was there in the hospital with the diarist; the other half, basking in the warm sunlight, felt guilty with the knowledge that I had survived her. Several months later, reading Reimann's diaries and letters, that feeling came back. The word that best describes it is "uncanny." Reading journals, we enter into a powerful and immediate identification with the diarist's experience. Meanwhile, however, I knew the outcome of the writers' struggles in advance. This is where the experience of uncanniness came in. My privileged knowledge, as a reader of their lives, created an uneasy ambivalence between the part of me that identified with them and the part that objectified them. They died at the end, after all; I didn't.

I think this highlights something unique and universally true about the experience of reading journals. As we read, the present tense and first-person pronoun invite us to enter into and identify with the diarist's feelings and thoughts. We become immersed in her inner world, perhaps more so than while reading fiction. And yet, another part of us remains outside all the while. This more critical part is constantly in dialogue with the diarist, noting where our perspectives alternately converge and differ. An element of voyeurism creeps in, I believe, when we read with only the second, more critical part of ourselves—objectifying the writer's experience without entering into it.

These are a few of the reasons why journals make such fascinating reading. What is it, then, that many of us, passionate diarists ourselves, look for in other women's diaries? What do we hope to get from journals that we don't expect from fiction or other kinds of nonfiction?

The Pleasure of Reading Journals

"Women today read and write biographies to gain a perspective on their own lives," Mary Catherine Bateson claims. "Each reading provokes a dialogue of comparison and recognition, a process of memory and articulation that makes one's own experience available as a lens of empathy." This is even more true of reading and writing journals, it seems to me. For journals require something different of us as readers than other kinds of writing. Reading a diary, we enter the writer's inner realm. We witness her intimate musings, her unguarded thoughts and feelings, her perception of the world beyond her own psyche. Thus, we are asked to come with a generous and compassionate heart and a readiness to suspend judgment and share the diarist's experience of her life. In return, diaries offer us many rewards. Barbara Godard describes a feminist mode of reading quite different from our usual attempt to "master" the text. What she says is especially relevant to reading diaries. Godard explains,

> Instead of battling her way out of a structure constructed to enclose her, a feminist reader may enter into dialogue with a female writer. The reader may give up the struggle to control the text, abandon the power game entirely, in an effort to connect with the woman behind the text. Such empathetic reading is constructed on the intersubjective encounter with the heart and mind of another woman.

Both Mary Catherine Bateson and Barbara Godard speak of the dialogue that occurs between female readers and writers, of a discussion carried on between two lives. Reading journals invites the intimacy of personal conversation. We read, yearning for authentic and spontaneous self-disclosure and communion, fascinated with what gives meaning to other women's lives. In her diaries and essays, Anaïs Nin wrote beautifully about our hunger to make sensitive, tender human connections, to feel understood and cherished, to be seen and loved for who we are. Over and over she described her amazement that just when she thought she'd revealed herself more intimately than ever, countless women readers wrote to her, saying, "You were describing my experience also." Nin came to believe that the more we see of another person's innermost workings, the more we come to accept and love them.

One of the pleasures of reading journals is getting a powerful sense of the writer's personality. This is conveyed largely through the degree of self-disclosure evident in her diary, something that varies dramatically from writer to writer. Take, for example, the journals of two artists born in 1865: Emily Carr in Canada, Käthe Kollwitz in Germany. Both Carr and Kollwitz used the journal as a sounding board for their work, to lament their own inadequacies as artists, to record public response to their work.

Kollwitz, one of the artists banished in Hitler's campaign against "degenerate art" during the 1930s, explored her vocation with an emotional restraint that makes her anguish over her beloved younger son Peter's death all the more poignant. Mid-November 1914, two weeks after receiving the heartbreaking news that he had been killed in battle, she wrote, "Terrible loneliness. In Peter's diary of last year, always the feeling of aloneness and abandonment. We would gladly have died for the boys and yet—abandoned and each one alone. As alone as if in a vacuum. Where are you—where are you roaming? Why don't you come to me? I am more alone than you ever were." But for Kollwitz, this kind of self-disclosure was rare.

Emily Carr, in contrast, poured her heart extravagantly into her journal, recording all her emotional states, from irritation and despair to contentment and celebration. On July 30, 1933, she wrote, "Oh, today I am akin to the worm, the caterpillar and the grub! Where are the high places? I can't reach anything, even the low middle." Yet shortly thereafter, settled securely into the comfort of her old van during a painting expedition into the heart of Vancouver Island's rain forest, she noted, jubilantly, "Last night we slept like babies. Each creature has dropped into its own niche. . . . It's wonderful to watch the joy of the pups playing tag among the cedars. There is a delicious little breeze humming among the leaves without bluster or vulgarity. Today I love life, so do the four dogs, the monkey and the rat." Carr's many emotional fluctuations, true to life, were dramatic and often mysterious, even to herself. Reading her diaries, we get the sense of an impetuous and expansive, utterly unpretentious individual.

Other Stories, Other Lives

Diaries plunge us into the midst of women's unfolding stories, stories whose progression may be as mysterious to the diarist as they are to us. As the diarist writes her story from one day to the next, her diary becomes the narrative of a life-in-progress, offering us a possible "text" for our own. Realizing that someone else has thought as we do —has felt the same emotion, drawn the same conclusion—affirms the solidarity of shared experience and our own potential for growth and fulfillment. This mirroring process allows us to see our flaws in perspective, just as we see another woman's limitations in the broader context of her whole personality. Over the years, May Sarton often described remorse over her destructive anger in her journals. But rather than disenchanting us, her painful self-scrutiny arouses our empathy and makes her more vulnerable, more human. Gloria Steinem's account of her painful adolescence lets us see our own childhood wounds as only one brushstroke on the wider canvas of our lives. Since she has survived and come to terms with her traumatic past, perhaps we can, too. Witnessing how another woman responds to her own perceived weaknesses or to difficult outer circumstances may illuminate unseen possibilities for healing in our own lives.

As we read about other women's aspirations and accomplishments, we discover new stories of how to live, what to aspire to, what choices to explore, new possibilities of who and what we might become. In her early twenties, the writer and activist bell hooks was occupied with the issue of black female creativity and the conditions under which women make art. In July of 1979, she wrote, "I want to be fulfilled in life and art. But when I look around me, so many women seem really unhappy with the choices they have made. Sometimes, I do not see any women doing things differently in a way that works, that satisfies, and I need to see this for it to be real." This was a woman clearly longing for inspiration: "I know in my heart that it is important for women to see other women doing many things. It gives one a sense of infinite possibilities." And in the years since she wrote those lines, bell hooks herself has become one of the role models she was seeking.

Reading journals connects us intimately with other women's lives and stories. It requires us to put our own egos aside and identify with a different perspective. We share the writer's experience of the turning points and inevitable losses by which we all measure our lives: the ebb and flow of love, friendship, and family ties; the juggling of multiple obligations and desires; shades of sexuality and the passing of time; the fluctuations in self-confidence and self-loathing, optimism and despair, vitality and inertia familiar to us all.

But until recently, the most important seasons in our lives as women have rarely been represented in literature. And where they have, it has usually been by male authors attempting to portray experiences they've never had themselves. In their journals, women attempt to write the truth about what it is to be pregnant and give birth, to feel torn between the needs of others (mates, children, aging parents) and their own desires; what it is to come out as lesbians in a misogynistic, homophobic society; how it feels to be a woman of color in a white racist culture, unattractive in a society that idolizes beauty, old in a society that worships youth. "The passenger down the slope of age is in need of supports," Deborah Norris Logan wrote in 1833. Often, alas, her journal was her sole source. May Sarton, too, reflected, "Growing old is, of all things we experience, that which takes the most courage, and at a time when we have the least resources, especially with which to meet frustration." For Florida Scott-Maxwell, keeping a journal was a way of attempting to find answers to the questions that came to her in old age. "I found queries going round and round in my head and I began to jot them down in this note book," she informs us, in the opening pages of *The Measure of My Days.*

"I put down my sweeping opinions, prejudices, limitations, and just here the books fails me for it makes no comment. It is even my wailing wall, and when I play that grim, comforting game of noting how wrong everyone else is, my book is silent, and I listen to that stillness, and I learn."

Writing in the nursing home where she was to spend the last five years of her life, Joyce Mary Horner confided to her diary, "Today a very low point—weather, feelings inside, asthma, minor minimal disappointments." Still, Horner found cause for rejoicing: "another perfect summer day," a surprise visit from her partner, "eating out of doors in the company one loves," a reading group, listening to classical music on the radio, and above all, sitting outside "in the shade of warm days with a breeze stirring, sounds of wood thrush and occasional cardinal, very occasionally the smell of pine." And how nice to read Emily Carr's contented statement, camping out in the woods with her animals at the age of sixty-seven: "In a grey woollen gown under the scarlet blankets, with pillows at my back and hot bottle at my feet, I find the earth lovely," she wrote. "Autumn does not dismay me any more than does the early winter of my body. Some can be active to a great age but enjoy little. I have lived." Old age, too, is one of the seasons of our lives; yet little has been written about it.

And then there are the extraordinary experiences. In addition to illuminating what Christa Wolf called "the precious everyday," women's journals provide glimpses of situations most of us will never encounter ourselves and wouldn't even wish to. Sometimes they show us what it is to keep our humanity in the most difficult and seemingly hopeless of circumstances. None of us would want to have Etty Hillesum's experience in Nazi-occupied Holland: her gradual realization that the work she did for the Jewish Council was actually serving the Nazis and that neither she nor her family were likely to survive. Yet no one leaves her beautiful journal unchanged. Etty reflected, "Living and dying, sorrow and joy, the blisters on my feet and the jasmine behind the house, the persecution, the unspeakable horrors —it is all as one in me and I accept it all as one mighty whole and begin to grasp it better if only for myself, without being able to explain to anyone else how it all hangs together." More than any other diarist of that dark time, Etty Hillesum affirms the value of unconditional love.

And what of the shining courage and brilliant anger of Audre Lorde, who turned her own battle with breast cancer into a passionate invitation for all women to think differently about their lives? In her introduction to *The Cancer Journals*, she wrote,

> I do not wish my anger and pain and fear about cancer to fossilize into yet another silence, nor to rob me of whatever strength can lie at the core of this experience, openly acknowledged and examined. For other women of all ages, colors, and sexual identities who recognize that imposed silence about any area of our lives is a tool for separation and powerlessness, and for myself, I have tried to voice some of my feelings, and thoughts. . . . May these words underline the possibilities of self-healing and the richness of living for all women.

With her unsparing account of how breast cancer affected her personal life, Audre Lorde invites us to rethink our own priorities. What a gift this journal is to all women.

Etty Hillesum's diaries witness to an unquenchable flame of love in a time of horror and destruction. Audre Lorde's journal shatters the secrecy and shame surrounding women's experience of breast cancer. These and many other women's diaries provide a counter-history of radically personal perspectives on history and culture. While mainstream history has concentrated on the events that shape nations, women's diaries provide an intimate glimpse of everyday life. In Christa Wolf's retelling of the Trojan War, the seer Cassandra begs to be allowed to pass on her story of women's experience before she is killed, "so that alongside the river of heroic songs this tiny rivulet, too, may reach those faraway, perhaps happier people who will live in times to come." Even now the river of heroic songs still prevails. But the growing rivulet of women's diaries tells a different story.

A Sense of Belonging

We read journals, too, to feel less lonely. Entering another's inner life, we escape our isolation. Few diarists have managed to convey the difficulty of human relations as expressively as Emily Carr. It was December 28, 1940, a not uncommon time of year to feel low, when she reflected,

> Why do inexplicable sadnesses suddenly swell up inside one, aching sadness over nothing in particular? There is generally some self-condemnation at the bottom of the feeling, disappointment with yourself by yourself, or else a disappointment with someone else who makes you mad. (But in that case it is more mad than ache that ails you.) I am disappointed in everyone just now. I don't feel as if there was one solitary soul that I could open up to.

Writing in her journal at times like this was clearly a balm for Carr's loneliness. Reading her diary, our own may lessen. As we read women's journals, we find a sense of belonging. Noting similarities among various lives, voices, and stories, we participate in the community of journal writers and readers. We find this shared affinity in the published journals themselves. Many published diarists read other diaries. May Sarton, for one, copied long passages from Anne Truitt's *Daybook: The Journal of an Artist* into her own diary, engaging in a dialogue with Truitt. "There is much here I recognize," Sarton commented.

> When [Truitt] talks about David Smith's death, she says, "After his death the studio felt lonelier. I came to understand that David's essence for me was that while he was alive he was working. And, if he was working, I was not alone." I felt this kind of loss acutely when Virginia Woolf died and realized there was no one left whose opinion of my work mattered a hoot to me. . . . I did sense her as in some way "kin," as far as work went. I marked another page in Truitt.

Sixty years earlier, a week after Katherine Mansfield died in 1923, Virginia Woolf observed in her diary, "a depression which I could not rouse myself from all that day. When I began to write, it seemed to

me there was no point in writing. Katherine wont read it." Coinciden-
tally I read Sarton's *At Seventy* just after finishing *Daybook*. In the course
of reading that one paragraph in Sarton's journal, I'd made contact
with four other diarists: May Sarton, Anne Truitt, Virginia Woolf, and
Katherine Mansfield—all links in the communal chain.

Many published diarists themselves are avid readers of other wom-
en's journals. Not that they always admire what they read. Alice James,
for example, had nothing but scorn for George Eliot, whose journals
had, in fairness, been severely chopped by her second husband in the
interests of decorum. "But what a monument of ponderous dreariness
is the book!" Alice wrote in her own journal. "What a lifeless, dis-
eased, self-conscious being she must have been! Not one burst of joy,
not one ray of humour, not one living breath in one of her letters
or journals. . . . What a contrast to George Sand." But such scathing
response is rare! More often diarists find inspiration in what they read.
Maxine Kumin, for one, is "addicted to other people's journals."
Virginia Woolf read Fanny Burney and Dorothy Wordsworth, among
others. Katherine Mansfield read Marie Bashkirtseff. Anaïs Nin read
Mary Shelley and Virginia Woolf. Emily Carr read Marie Bashkirtseff.
May Sarton read Emily Carr. Gloria Bowles read Paula Modersohn-
Becker, and on it goes.

One Saturday night in July 1979, bell hooks, too, sat up late,
reading a biography of Käthe Kollwitz and writing in her diary. "I
have been thinking and talking again about the issue of why there are
not many committed women artists who achieve their full potential,"
she wrote. "One awareness that comes from my own life experiences
is that I seem to have a much harder time validating my creative work
than males I know . . . to really sustain creative work one must be
inwardly motivated." One lifetime listens to another; all links in that
invisible community.

Life Unfolding

The journal, unlike other kinds of personal writing, shows us life
unfolding. Autobiography gives us the writer's life from her current
perspective. Surveying her life from what Virginia Woolf called "the

little platform of present time on which I stand," she reinvents her past in the present. With the passing of time, memory has blurred the edges of scenes where too clear a focus would engender pain; like most of us, she wants to be loved and admired. The point of arrival is known in advance, and the past seems to have led inevitably to the present, as if it had to be "this way and no other." She irons out all the wrinkles in her life, converting the past's rough edges into a seamless now.

Reading Simone de Beauvoir's autobiographical account of her life with Jean-Paul Sartre, for example, I was left with many questions. She tells us they agreed in principle to have a nonmonogamous relationship. But how did she actually feel about this arrangement, week to week and year after year? How did she react to his numerous affairs? Did she keep a journal during those years, I wonder. If so, what did she write in it?

We read autobiography because of the coherent pattern it imposes on the events of the writer's life. Everything seems to have worked together to bring her to the present moment in time. Somehow, this cohesive retrospective narrative comforts us, given the mostly haphazard feeling of our own lives from one week to the next. The journal, in contrast, invites us on a journey. The diarist's life unfolds spontaneously before our eyes, with all of the loose ends and absurdities, paradoxes and mysteries that we experience in our own. We witness how she tries to make sense of its unexpected twists and detours, weaving a meaningful pattern from the many strands of her experience. The commonplace appears side by side with events of earth-shaking importance. On Saturday, April 15, 1939, Virginia Woolf wrote poignantly of "the severance that war seems to bring: everything becomes meaningless." The next sentence concludes the day's journal entry: "But I must order macaroni from London." This is how we live our lives: not as a series of distinguishable peaks and valleys, but as a fluid succession of moments, impressions, and experiences that interweave and that constitute the texture of our daily lives. And gradually, an inner coherence emerges, one not imposed after-the-fact through the rearview mirror of hindsight.

There is a German word that has haunted me for years: Unterwegs, or "on the way." All of our lives we are on the way. Imagine a woman wandering in the woods, uncertain about which path to take or whether she will find her way out. Eventually, after many wrong turns, she emerges into broad daylight. In telling her tale afterward, she remembers her feelings of confusion and anxiety, of being in the woods and wanting to see clear skies above. But now the story's ending is clearly etched. In retrospect, it seems inevitable that she would eventually find her way out. As she looks back on her experience, some moments strike her as turning points; others, literally, as false moves. In short, the story she tells after she has come safely through is different from what she experienced moment by moment in the woods. Had she kept a journal while she was lost, it would tell a different tale, reflecting her hope and despair as she explored many different paths, uncertain of the outcome.

Journal writing is writing in the woods. There is no secure vantage point from which to write our story. There is only the open road with its never-ending choice of paths. We are thickly, densely, in the midst. What reading—like writing journals—offers us is a series of rest stops, like comfort stations on a long trail. Here we can pause temporarily, rest our weary bodies and souls, and reflect on where we have come so far. We may replenish our energies and, if we are lucky, share our stories and a thermos of hot chocolate with other travelers. These are not small gifts.

Glimpses of the Artist's Life

The journals of writers and artists provide insights into the creative woman's role in society, and the inner and outer circumstances that make art possible. More often than not, they reveal a fierce conflict between the demands made on the artist and those made on the woman, a conflict unparalleled in the lives of our male counterparts. (Judy Chicago describes a conversation with an art critic, superficially supportive, who told her early in her career, " 'You know, Judy, you have to decide whether you're going to be a woman or an artist.' " Imagine a man seriously contemplating such a choice!)

Women's journals often offer glimpses of the social and cultural forces at play in the artist's life. Take, for example, Fanny Mendelssohn

Hensel (1805–1847). Though she was enormously gifted, her family thought it unseemly for Fanny to betray "the only calling of a young woman . . . the state of a housewife" by flaunting her musical gifts in public. Brother Felix was not averse to receiving credit for her work, however; some of her early songs appeared under his name. It was only when Fanny accompanied her husband, the artist Wilhelm Hensel, to Rome in 1839 that she found the appreciation and encouragement she so yearned for. Her diary of that time reflects her optimism: "Rome, Thursday, 23 April 1840. . . . A more improving audience would be hard to find. I also compose a great deal now, for nothing inspires me like praise, whilst censure discourages and depresses me." The following Sunday, she reflected, "It will cost us both a hard struggle to leave Rome. . . . I must not conceal from myself that the atmosphere of admiration and homage in which I have lived may have something to do with it . . . that this is very pleasant nobody can deny."

Nevertheless, Fanny felt duty-bound to return to Berlin, where, six years later, she finally saw her work published under her own name and, inspired, went on to compose a piano trio. Her journal of that time shows her at long last fulfilled in her musical vocation. In an undated entry written early in 1847, we read, "My inmost heart is at any rate full of thankfulness, and when in the morning after breakfasting with Wilhelm we each go to our own work, with a pleasant day to look back upon and another to look forward to, I am quite overcome with my own happiness." Fanny died shortly thereafter, at the age of forty-two, while conducting a choral rehearsal—only one month after the performance of her first major work. What determination it must have taken to persevere with her unladylike passion for music in the face of her family's disapproval. How many gifted women have had neither Fanny's supportive husband nor financial resources to enable them to create music, art, or literature?

Practical Realities

What of the harsh practical realities involved in following one's vocation as an artist while trying to be all things to all people? "How can

I do this thing? Serve my family or serve my work?" asked Sylvia Ashton-Warner in a moment of despair, in May of 1942. "I've got to reconcile the woman and the artist or the conflict between them will blow me asunder, scatter my pieces to the ends of the Pacific." Several years later, she wrote,

> The need for regular breaths of silence, the wetting of the lips, mouth and throat with the water of silence, is more desperate than before. What about my music, my thinking, my study and my attempt at writing, and the drawing which I loved? What hope of survival for that area within that is the real me? Denying all that, how can I remain sufficiently whole to become a worthwhile person? A worthwhile person must be *all there*.

For many women, as for Ashton-Warner, the journal has provided the one place where artist and woman can be reconciled. Sometimes the conflict has played itself out with tragic results. In the early part of this century, the young German Expressionist painter Paula Modersohn-Becker left her husband in order to ensure her own survival as an artist, after a decade of feeling torn between her art and the obligations of her married life. Several months later, Paula wrote in a letter to her mother,

> I couldn't stand it any longer, and I'll probably never be able to stand it again either. It was all too confining for me and not what—and always less of what—I needed. Now I am beginning a new life. Don't interfere, just let me be. It's so very beautiful. This last week I've been living as if in ecstasy. I feel I've accomplished something good.

In one of fate's cruel ironies, however, Paula's exultation was short-lived. Friends, no doubt well-meaning, urged her to allow Otto to join her in Paris, with the understanding that they would keep separate quarters. Paula's ambivalence is obvious in her diary but, succumbing to their pressure, she was reunited with her husband only months later. Soon after, she wrote to her mother, "I'm not very happy at the moment because with my moving, Otto's being here . . . I have completely stopped working." A year later, Paula Becker was dead. She died of an embolism, eighteen days after the birth of her daughter. In her short life span, Paula had created more than 1,400 works of art. What might she have accomplished if—instead of having been pressured to resume her conjugal duties—she had been allowed to freely obey the artistic calling she articulated so passionately in her diary?

Among those women who do manage to pursue an artistic calling, many combine it with familial obligations and paid work, living with a sense of perpetual shortage. There is never enough—of time, money, or belief in their own talent. Not surprisingly, this theme appears with particular intensity in the diaries of women with partners and children. In Silences, Tillie Olsen provides one example after another of women who, like herself, arose at dawn in order to write for an hour and keep their creative spirits alive, before turning to the practical demands of the day. Who can be surprised, then, to learn that many women writers and artists of the past two centuries neither married nor had children? Or, that if they did marry, they generally remained childless or had one child late in their reproductive lives? Asked by May Sarton about the cost of having a happy marriage, three children, and a distinguished career as a professor and novelist, Carolyn Heilbrun answered " 'The price is everything.' " What a story lurks behind those four words!

The romantic myth of the artist—happily suffering the temporary privations of the freezing garret, secure in the knowledge of future success—is shattered by Anne Truitt's description of the actual conditions in her studio. She recalls describing to an old friend "what I had never talked about before: the intense cold of the studio, the lack of water, the Easter basket of painty brushes and bowls toted back and forth from home for washing, the rats, the bleak isolation of my studio in a dead-end alley." Hardly conditions that foster creativity. "The financial roller coaster is, to speak plainly, a torture," she confided to her journal. Truitt's anxiety over finances was put to rest only after she accepted a teaching post that provided a measure of financial security for herself and her children. And what of Emily Carr, who, as we know from her journal, reluctantly made pottery for tourists, raised bobtail puppies, grew fruit, became a "landlady and janitor" and ran, most unhappily, a Ladies Boarding House, in order to eke out a livelihood? For fifteen years, she did not paint at all. Even May

Sarton observed that she didn't "start making a living out of writing until I was sixty-five." While there is no question that we have taken enormous steps toward economic and creative freedom in recent years, for all too many women a room of one's own and everything it symbolizes is still a dream rather than reality.

The Artistic Process

Reading artists' diaries affords us a fascinating insight into the artistic process itself. The artist's journal often reveals what inspired her to create a particular work of art, and how she dealt with periods of despair, success, and failure. In a series of journal entries in 1979, Gail Godwin described the evolution of her novel *Mother and Two Daughters*. In January, she received a letter from a friend, describing a family crisis following her father's death. Within a month, with her friend's blessing, Godwin had written a 48-page story based on that letter. The story continued to grow and, by December, there were 162 pages. The following May, half finished, it was 299 pages long. In December 1980, Godwin sent out her completed manuscript—all 767 pages of it. It all began with a friend's letter.

Again, Virginia Woolf's diary is a gold mine. In 1926, she noted, "The process of language is slow & deluding. One must stop to find a word; then, there is the form of the sentence, soliciting one to fill it." Several years later, she described with obvious relief "the exalted sense of being above time & death which comes from being again in a writing mood." Lest any of us think that published writers don't battle writer's block or the habit of procrastination, Antonia White laments, "I am writing in this notebook as an excuse for not getting down to my book . . . Every day I re-write what I have written—slower and slower with no idea whether the new version is better or worse." Katherine Mansfield had even harsher words for herself: "This is sheer sin, for I ought to be writing my book and instead I am pretending here." Self-doubt plays an all too central role in many writers' diaries. George Eliot, for example, confided to her diary, "As usual I am suffering much from doubt as to the worth of what I am doing, and fear lest I may not be able to complete it so as to make it a contribution to literature." Even after her first novel was favorably reviewed, Eliot confessed that "at present fear and trembling still predominate over hope."

The artist's diary offers other fascinations. Because her primary medium is nonverbal, the attempt to put into words what she wants to communicate through form, color, and image adds a whole new dimension to her work. Here is Emily Carr, camped out in the woods in order to sketch.

> Everything is green. . . . Everything is alive. The air is alive. The silence is full of sound. The green is full of colour. Light and dark chase each other. Here is a picture, a complete thought, and there another and there. . . . There are themes everywhere, something sublime, something ridiculous, or joyous, or calm, or mysterious. Tender youthfulness laughing at gnarled oldness. Moss and ferns, and leaves and twigs, light and air, depth and colour chattering, dancing a mad joy-dance, but only apparently tied up in stillness and silence. You must be still in order to hear and see.

This is the most engaging artist's journal I've read, perhaps because Emily Carr was both a visual artist and a writer, often discussing the relationship between word and image in her diary. In 1930, she wrote, "Trying to find equivalents for things in words helps me find equivalents in painting. That is the reason for this journal. Everything is all connected up. Different paths lead to the great 'it,' the thing we try to get at by hook and by crook." Throughout her long creative career, Carr was clear about what was most important to her as an artist. "Form is fine," she wrote, "and colour and design and subject matter but that which does not speak to the heart is worthless. It is the intensity of feeling you have about a thing that counts."

And here are excerpts from Frida Kahlo's journal in the mid-1940s, in which she explored the associations that various colors held for her.

> GREEN: warm and good light . . .
> YELLOW: madness, sickness, fear. Part of the sun and of joy.
> COBALT BLUE: electricity and purity. Love . . .
> NAVY BLUE: distance. Also tenderness can be of this blue.
> MAGENTA: Blood? Well, who knows!

The Artist's Workday

What about the intriguing glimpses we get of the artist's day: her
work habits and routines, personal inclinations and eccentricities?
Does she work first thing in the morning? How many hours each day?
Does she discipline herself to work, or is the work self-propelling?
What inspires her? I, for one, am interested in every detail of the
writer's day. I'm fascinated to discover that Virginia Woolf felt guilty
writing in her diary during the morning ("A disgraceful fact—I am
writing this at 10 in the morning in bed in the little room looking
into the garden"); that Burghild Nina Holzer writes at 10:30 every
morning in order to catch a particular slant of the sun on her writing
table; that when Anne Truitt's children were small, she often worked
in fifteen-minute segments between chauffeuring responsibilities.
Knowing this causes me to take all the more seriously her claim
that "the capacity to work feeds on itself and has its own course of
development."

Should anyone harbor the mistaken notion that the artist's life—if
she is single and without children—is one of inspired freedom and
creative "highs," May Sarton describes the need for daily structure and
disciplined work habits that every artist must work out for herself. "I
am in a limbo that needs to be patterned from within," she wrote in
November 1971. "People who have regular jobs can have no idea of
just this problem of ordering a day that has no pattern imposed on it
from without." Lacking external structure, the writer must create her
own work momentum and, for Sarton, at least, "If there is motivation
here, it is always self-ordering, self-exploratory, a perpetual keeping
gear in order for that never-ending journey."

Seeking Inspiration

And not least, reading women's journals provides inspiration for our
own writing, and for our lives. Don't we all open the diary of a writer
whose work we admire, hoping to find the key that will unlock our
own creative potential? Isn't there often the underlying hope that their
gift might rub off on us? Reading someone else's diary is a surefire

way to stimulate the creative juices. The intimate way in which it draws us into the diarist's thought process takes our own in new directions, while the reflective quality of the writing is an invitation to turn our own gaze inward, taking us to a deeper level of experience. "I know exactly how she feels!" we may say with excitement, or "No, I don't agree with that." Either way, we are energized. Jeannette S. Guildford found, "In recent years I have turned for nourishment to the enormous body of work written by women: journals, diaries, letters, biographies, autobiographies which provide constant encouragement and permission to be open and honest." For Guildford, it was particularly May Sarton's frank account of her frequent battles with depression that proved inspiring. Sometimes a single image or phrase can start a chain of associations that haunts us. For the journalist Anne Simpkinson, it was Marion Woodman's *Leaving My Father's House*, with its dense condensation of literally thousands of journal pages, that provoked her to write. She says,

> Stories feed our souls, particularly when told from a deep, inner source of truth. And ultimately this is why *Leaving My Father's House* succeeds. All four women have obviously done intensive work. Their images and metaphors shimmer and resonate in one's imagination. As a reader, I could literally feel images in my psyche being activated [and] more than once, while reading it, I got such a strong image in my mind's eye that I had to stop and jot down what I was envisioning before I could continue.

And finally, I want to close with this short passage from the journal of Barbara Godard that sums up so beautifully what we look for—and often find—in reading women's journals. She says,

> We seek to understand the writer's life so that we may enter into it. . . . Our drive to connect flows in the blood. To the text we bring our biological lives as women. Between the lines of the female text, unverbalized, we read the hidden text of our bodily experience. Blood line, life line, poetic line. . . . The word takes on flesh of woman and gives birth to us.

11

"Hearing One Another to Speech"

The Journal Workshop

Women are literally hearing one another to speech. But the speech is our speech. It may come on stumblingly or boldly. But it is authentically our own.

NELLE MORTON, *The Journey Is Home*

Female narratives will be found where women exchange stories, where they read and talk collectively of ambitions, and possibilities, and accomplishments.

CAROLYN G. HEILBRUN, *Writing a Woman's Life*

As a university student in Vancouver during the seventies, I dreamed of a circle of women with whom to explore this curious habit of journal writing. None existed at the time, so I continued to write on my own, but not without a nagging sense that something was missing. I was grateful for Doris Lessing's *The Golden Notebook*, read every published diary I could find, and compared notes with a friend who also kept a journal, though sporadically. Often I'd write in cafés, enjoying the sense of being alone in a group. From time to time I'd spot another lone diarist in a corner, writing absorbedly and sipping cappuccino.

The diarist's world has changed since that time. Even then, unbeknownst to me, Ira Progoff had already begun to conduct his Intensive Journal Workshops; Tristine Rainer was writing *The New Diary*; and Christina Baldwin, *One to One*. And interest in journal writing has continued to grow. In addition to classes in schools, colleges, and adult education programs, it is taught in nursing homes and retirement communities, hospitals and chronic care facilities, churches and prisons, wellness centers, and personal growth retreats. New courses and workshops continue to spring up.

Clearly, they are meeting a significant need, for longtime as well as new diarists. And yet, we might ask, aren't journal workshops, like published journals, paradoxical? After all, if you're writing in a room with ten, twenty, even a hundred other people and planning to share something with the group, how truthfully will you search your own heart and soul? How much will you censor yourself as you write?

A journal workshop can have many dimensions. To the extent that it offers a safe environment for exploring personal issues, it might resemble a support group or even group therapy. In providing an opportunity to experiment with your written voice and style, it has elements of a creative writing workshop. Where it looks at what it means to be a woman in male-dominated society, it's not unlike the consciousness-raising groups of the 1970s. And yet, a women's journal workshop is not identical with any of these. Its purpose is not to offer therapy, provide constructive criticism to the aspiring writer, or inspire political activism, feminist or otherwise, though all of these may occur. A good workshop makes possible a space for healing that releases blocked creativity—and conversely, for a creative process that makes us whole. The workshop leader's challenge is to facilitate an atmosphere of receptive openness in which each woman can be heard, without sacrificing the group's writing to its therapeutic role. Through the interplay of many women's lives, we see recurring themes and patterns and know that we are not alone on the journey.

Here is one diarist's account of her workshop experience. "I was given support and help from the other women in the workshop in accepting the nameless and scary places in my heart," Edie writes. "There was an incredible healing energy that occurred when women were reading their work aloud and a mutual shock of recognition would run through each woman listening. I discovered that all of us share common needs, experiences, and ideas."

If keeping a diary is such a personal affair, and there's no right or wrong way to do it, why do so many people participate in journal workshops, seminars, and classes? Some of the reasons workshop attenders have given include:

- To get me started writing.

- To discover how to use the diary more effectively in my life.

- To get fresh ideas and inspiration for my thinking and writing.

- To have a structured time during which I can reflect on my life.

- To experience the group energy and meet kindred spirits.

- To be nurtured and encouraged by the workshop leader and the others there.

- To give my creative side a chance to express itself.

- To get ideas about how journal writing might lead to other kinds of writing.

- To learn more about published journals, and get ideas for reading.

The workshop invites us to turn our focus inward. Who are we, and where are we going? What do we need and desire? What are our dreams telling us? What do we want to build on in our lives, and what must we change, before it makes us ill? Exploring these questions in the company of other women breaks the sense of isolation we may feel, grappling with them on our own. In the workshop setting we can address crucial life issues in an atmosphere of mutual support and shared endeavor. Along the way, we frequently discover that even our most quirky personal themes have echoes in other women's experiences.

Creating Time and Space

Journal writing may become an integral part of our daily routine, as habitual as morning coffee and afternoon tea. Or it can be a more occasional activity, squeezed in whenever possible amidst the necessities of our day-to-day lives. Some diarists have a fixed time and place in which to write. Anaïs Nin wrote in her bed each evening just before falling asleep, taking care that her husband did not see what she wrote (for reasons that have become clear since, in the unexpurgated version of her *Diary!*). Virginia Woolf consistently used the "comfortable bright hour after tea" to write in her journal, in order to relax her writing muscles. Since neither of them had children, they could enjoy a leisurely hour with their journals at times of the day when Woolf might otherwise have been occupied with an irritable child, and Nin, too exhausted from the day's activities, to write a single line.

But many women do not have the luxury of making a daily appointment with themselves to write. Some women find only a brief moment here and there; others, no time at all. For them, workshops have an important structural function. A regular weekly meeting with other diarists provides a psychic space uninvaded by the needs of family and friends, telephone calls, doorbells, or other interruptions. Indeed, when I began offering workshops, I discovered that some women, knowing their children were well taken care of by a husband or trusted friend, hadn't even left a telephone number, so great was the need for time for themselves. Judy, a full-time homemaker with two young children, said just that: "This is the only thing in my life right now that I'm doing just for myself and I don't *want* to know what's going on at home. Whatever happens, my husband will have to take care of it, and I'll find out soon enough!" Whether or not we have children or partners, most of us are trying to do too much too quickly, and getting "burned out" along the way. A workshop offers the chance to stop and catch our psychic breath, to be nourished, and to share the journey with kindred spirits on paths that cross our own.

Many of the women who come to my workshops say it is the one thing all week they do solely for themselves. Not only women with children, either. Lee is a thirty-two-year-old single woman whose mother died recently after a long and painful battle with cancer. She lives with her eighty-five-year-old semi-invalid father, pays the woman who cares for him during the day while she works, then comes home and cooks his dinner. Although she has three siblings, the unspoken agreement is that since she is the unmarried one, hers is the life that can be sacrificed. Wednesday evening has become her time. In the workshop Lee receives support and encouragement. Her journal has become her lifeline during this difficult time.

The very act of setting aside an entire day or a regular weekly evening affirms the journal's importance in our lives. This creates a positive momentum in which each writer's energy vitalizes the group and, in turn, is replenished by it. A sense of shared purpose evolves in the writing circle. The sound of pens and pencils moving across the paper, and the concentration on the women's faces generate a powerful focus that often amazes me. Conducting workshops in my home, I'm always struck by how the room itself changes. A neutral space only hours earlier, now it's charged with psychic energy. (At the end of a six-week session recently, Pam De Luca commented, "There is something about your living room. It would be interesting to know what the women felt about it. For example, what does the room feel like, leaving out all mention of decor? What does the air feel like? Does the energy of the room change and if so, how?") Each woman comes to the workshop with her own hopes and expectations, her own set of life circumstances, her unique questions about the journal's role in her life's journey. It's no wonder, then, that each group has its own special chemistry, a "flavor" all its own.

Diving in Deeply

The workshop provides an intensive introduction to the journal's rich possibilities. For the experienced writer, it can furnish renewed energy and a sense of the larger community to which she belongs. The very anticipation of an upcoming workshop will often stimulate writing in advance. An occasional workshop does not replace consistent journal writing over time, of course. We can't expect to sum up the gritty reality of a year's worth of living in a single entry on December 31, for example. What workshops do offer is intensive immersion into depths we don't usually reach in our daily writing-on-the-run. During a day of sustained writing, we may plunge far more deeply than we ever would in the same number of hours spread over weeks or months.

Workshop facilitators often begin with a meditation or guided visualization, or simply a few moments of silence during which attention is brought to the breath. This stillness allows us to disengage, gently, from our usual frenetic level of functioning, and enter into a slower, quieter, more receptive state of being. Each participant determines for herself the level at which she wants and needs to write that day. As the workshop progresses, she may be encouraged to move more deeply into her life. The circle of women writing privately together creates a *temenos*, or sacred space, in which anything is possible.

People engaged in a shared activity adapt to a common rhythm (for example, women living in close proximity to each other often adjust to a common menstrual cycle). Stephen Nachmanovitch describes the fascinating phenomenon of "entrainment," or "the synchronization of two or more rhythmic systems into a single pulse," claiming,

> For writers, art colonies or libraries are often good places to work, because even though the people around us are total strangers and are all doing their own private work, the silent rhythm of working together strengthens everyone's work energy. We feel a self-reinforcing entrainment of our concentration and commitment to *be* with our work.

The same is true of diarists writing in a workshop. Indeed, synchronicities often occur in the group. On more than one occasion, the similarities among various women's entries on a certain theme have been striking. Once, for example, seven out of eight women not only wrote on the same topic (chosen from three), but the same image appeared repeatedly—that of a tree under whose harboring branches they found shelter and comfort. In another workshop, everyone saw similar colors in the course of a guided visualization: red and gold. Was psychic energy being exchanged at some deep, nonverbal level? It would appear so.

Finding Community

Oftentimes, a woman may begin to keep a diary on an impulse, writing furtively on whatever happens to be around—scraps of paper, the backs of envelopes, sales slips, and napkins. She may not even be aware that she is joining a tradition dating back hundreds of years, that she is part of an ongoing body of diarists spanning centuries and continents. Entering a coffee shop in Manhattan with a friend not long ago, I saw that the young woman in the booth next to us was writing in a small bound book, lost in thought and oblivious to her surroundings. Immediately I had a sense of "Aha, she's one of us!" I've been noticing similar scenes for decades now, but each time it gives me a feeling of being a member of a vast underground community. Participating in a workshop makes this community visible. It helps overcome the sense of isolation we can feel as we write in our diaries year after year, and reveals the subculture of journal writers to which we belong.

By its very nature, the workshop encourages trust, intimacy, and self-disclosure. Where else in our lives do we come together in order to peel off roles and disguises and to see ourselves more authentically? In contrast to most group settings, where we hope to project an image of confidence, fluency, and knowledge, the journal workshop is one place where uncertainty and questioning are welcome. In such an environment, genuine friendship can take root and grow.

Workshops also provide an experience, rare even now, of women-in-community. The issue of feminine identity is always central. What does it mean to be a woman in a society where male is norm and the masculine pronoun claims to serve everyone? Where a woman has had little opportunity to speak openly about her experiences in sexist society, it can provide a powerful sense of solidarity and sisterhood. Just as women historically have not had a collective voice, many individual women have been silent most of their lives. Sharing is voluntary. Each woman is free to speak from the center of her life, and to witness her words being received by others, without judgment or correction. Here is an excerpt from Jarda Bailey's journal, written on the final evening of a six-week series, that manifests this feeling.

> I feel good. I'm in an environment that offers me such comfort and potential. This collective feeling of selfness has awesome results. I walk away feeling so totally alive in myself. Being here with other women greets my soul with joy and a sense of commonality that are lacking in so many of my other environments. . . . Here is a place where self is a shared experience, a sense of community.

The importance of women speaking and listening to one another cannot be overstated. "We empower one another by hearing the other to speech," Nelle Morton said. "Hearing to speech is political." Judith Duerk, a leader of women's retreats, echoes this, claiming, "We women must listen to ourselves and to each other as the individual voice of each of us is born. We must learn to . . . be present to one another." As Carolyn Heilbrun plainly states, "We must begin to tell the truth, in groups, to one another," for, "as long as women are isolated one from the other, not allowed to offer other women the most personal accounts of their lives, they will not be part of any narrative of their own." Stephanie Demetrakopoulos expresses it in slightly different terms in *Listening to Our Bodies: The Rebirth of Feminine Wisdom*. She says, "The more that a woman can bring the symbolism of other women to a conscious level, the more she can enhance her own life and all lives around her with her ability to live out many sides of herself." This, too, may begin in the workshop setting.

When I started the Women's Journal Workshop, I hoped and believed it could help women find their written voices, whether or not they wanted to be writers. What I didn't anticipate was that, even more radically, it would help them discover an *existential* voice. As the sole expert on her life, a woman will frequently speak out in the workshop with a level of confidence and conviction she didn't know she possessed. This experience of being heard in turn enables her to speak up in other situations. It affirms that personal experience is a valid and important form of knowledge, and that she has a right to be heard! The psychic energy and emotional support tangible in the group allow each woman to take an honest look at herself. Drawing courage from other women who share their life stories, she may be able to confront personal demons too daunting to take on in solitude. Knowing that the group can contain any anger or grief that surfaces through her writing leaves her less isolated and less fearful. I recall clearly one such occasion.

In the course of an all-day workshop, Terry found herself writing about an evening she had spent in a bar with her brother. During that time, he told her what he had seen and done in Vietnam. The horror of his experiences and her sorrow over what it had done to him had lain heavily on her heart ever since, but she hadn't written about it until that day. Eight women were there with her as she wept, remembering his pain and her own horror. On another occasion, one member of the group wrote on her questionnaire, "I knew I was in a deep funk, however the workshop exercises revealed an underlying reason, a reason I was aware of, but reluctant to face head on. When it kept coming up in the exercises I realized I could not ignore it. I must deal with my demons before I can move on." Another wrote, "It is reassuring to know there are others such as myself struggling along to write on a daily basis."

Interpersonal dynamics are indeed important. The group is not just so many discrete individuals, each "doing her own thing." As in any interactive, experiential group, each member is affected not only by the physical environment and the group's size, but by the other members of the group (especially when it's small), and by the workshop leader's personality and style. Something that Anne shares with the group may cause Connie to recall a similar experience she had long forgotten, which she then incorporates into her next piece of writing. There are also more subtle undercurrents among workshop participants. After one day-long workshop, one woman commented, "I found it especially interesting when unspoken thoughts and feelings were captured in a journal exercise by more than one person (for example, images of water). I felt like there was an energy or presence in the room linking us together."

Not least, the workshop offers the promise of good conversation. Many longtime diarists love to talk about their writing habits and, like Gail Godwin, have all too few opportunities to do so. "Sometimes I'll happen upon a diarist and we greet each other like lonely explorers," she says.

> Last spring I discovered a fellow diarist over lunch, and what a time we had discussing the intricacies of our venture-in-common, our avocation . . . specialty . . . compulsion? We confessed eccentricities (he has a pseudonymn for the self that gambles; I often reread old journals and make notes to my former selves in the margin). We examined our motives: why keep these records, year after year? What would happen if we stopped. Could we stop? We indulged in shop-talk: hardbound or softcover? lined or unlined? about how many pages a night? proportion of external events to internal? Did one write more on bad days than on good? . . . Ah, it was a good lunch we had.

I know exactly how she feels. That's the kind of talk I was longing for during those years of solitary writing in Vancouver. That's the kind of conversation a workshop community provides.

Gathering Inspiration, Expanding the Quest

That kind of talk leaves new energy in its wake. In the course of a good session, each woman's impulse to write is stimulated and multiplied by the many personalities, life experiences, and journal styles, combined with the workshop leader's guidance. Listening to other women's stories, we begin to see new life choices open to us, options we hadn't considered before. The workshop environment also helps each participant become conscious of her own self-limiting rules and expands her sense of the possibilities open to her. If she has always written in small lined notebooks, she may experiment with writing in an artist's sketch pad. Perhaps she writes only when she is upset or depressed; if so, she might remind herself to write the next time she is in a mellow mood. If she writes only on scraps of paper, let her go out and buy the most beautiful bound book she can find, put her name on the first page, and see how that feels.

Well-trained, obedient student that I was, I kept a journal for years before it occurred to me that I didn't have to write on the lines; that I didn't have to write complete, or even, God forbid, grammatically correct sentences; and that I didn't have to fill up one book before starting another. These are just a few of the rules I had subconsciously carried over from other spheres of my life. Over time, as I read every book on journals I could lay my hands on, it slowly dawned on me that there was no "correct" way to keep a journal. The rules I'd unwittingly created and adhered to over the years were simply irrelevant.

Our unconscious internalization of rules runs deep. One frequent workshop participant, a retired elementary school art teacher, quickly made two important discoveries. These, she claims, dramatically changed her writing. First, she realized that she didn't always have to be "happy, kind, and generous" in her journal. Second, she discovered that, when in a hurry, she could write down phrases and brief notes to be picked up and further developed at another time. Obvious? Perhaps. But radical, in terms of how these insights have expanded her writing. And also liberating. After all, how many of us actually live our lives with relentless goodwill or in complete sentences? Not all the journal writing rituals that we evolve over time are limiting, of course. Some diarists like to mark the entry into sacred time and space by turning the telephone off, lighting a candle, and putting on some special music. Others write only with a particular kind of pen or when sitting in a favorite spot. Any routine that starts to feel oppressive, however, will surely discourage you from writing and should probably be rethought or discarded altogether.

In the course of a workshop, journal writing is explored as a creative experiment in which anything goes. To encourage the loosening of constraints, I have incorporated some techniques from Gestalt therapy, an approach introduced by Fritz Perls in the 1960s. One useful Gestalt concept is precisely that of the "experiment": deliberately undertaking an exercise with no idea about how it will turn out. This can be a liberating process. It certainly helped to balance my own perfectionist streak during the early months and years of conducting workshops! Rather than use only exercises previously tried and tested, it enabled me to be creative and adventurous, to take risks in designing new workshops and, likewise, to encourage workshop participants to be bold in their choice of topics. Journal writing, like Gestalt therapy, can be serious business. But one thing a workshop should provide in our goal-driven era is the chance to play: to try something new without worrying about the outcome, to open ourselves to the unexpected with the hope that something magical will happen. And it often does.

The workshop affords an ideal setting in which the would-be writer can build confidence and explore her own writing voice without the need to turn out a "good product." It offers a sustained opportunity to write and to read aloud, if she wishes, without fear of criticism or rejection. Over the years, I've had many telephone conversations with women who say, "I want to write but I'm not sure I have anything to say. I thought this might be a good way to start." Absolutely. The freedom to experiment, with no pressure to perform, paradoxically may yield surprising results. Sometimes a journal entry may evolve into a publishable piece of writing. And sometimes it signals the beginning of a transformation in the diarist's life.

The Workshop Experience

Journal workshops differ in significant ways; size and duration, focus and aim may vary dramatically. But there are certain conditions common to most, perhaps all, of them. Foremost is that verbal participation is voluntary. Each diarist writes for herself alone (or himself— most workshops are coed), and simply may not be pressured to share or read anything that would leave her feeling exposed and vulnerable. (In the workshops I conduct, occasionally someone will come and go, barely having spoken a word. I tell everyone at the outset, "You're not here to meet anyone's needs except your own.") It's understood that what is disclosed during the workshop is confidential. We have the right to discuss our own intimate issues as freely as we like, but not those of another. There is also agreement that no one talks during a period of writing. In my workshops, early finishers may help themselves to coffee or tea or browse through the journal bookcase. Furthermore, problem solving is not required of anyone, including the facilitator. Generally, no advice or criticism is given; rather, the emphasis is squarely on self-awareness and listening. The innate wisdom of each diarist is respected as her only authority. A box of tissues is provided. Weeping may be part of the process but it usually doesn't call for emergency intervention.

If you are considering a workshop, remember that there can also be notable differences among them. Group size can range from five or six to a hundred-plus, and the degree of interaction among participants will vary greatly. In some groups, it is given equal importance with the writing itself; in others, it's negligible. In Ira Progoff's workshops, which range in size from a dozen to over a hundred, the emphasis is on "active privacy," and interaction among group members is discouraged.

In earlier chapters I've discussed some of the reasons why my own workshops have been directed to women. But there is one I haven't mentioned yet. It's widely recognized now that women and men have different styles of communication, both one on one, and in collective settings. In general terms, men speak in order to assert their individuality and establish a point of view; women, to receive affirmation and to create bonds with those around them. These are very different ends. In some circumstances, they are even at cross-purposes.

As Deborah Tannen has pointed out, conversation between women and men is essentially cross-cultural communication, requiring constant translation if misunderstanding is to be avoided. In a group, men are more likely to dominate; women, to take a backseat and listen. Yet ironically, our perceptions as members of this society are so skewed that women may be perceived as speaking "too much," even when video- and audiotapes show them talking less than half the time. This says something important about the amount of space women are granted and feel entitled to in our culture. To ignore this issue in a mixed workshop was inconceivable to me, yet to take it seriously would radically alter the group's focus. I did not want to use my energy monitoring the group to ensure that women were getting equal time. For many reasons, then, the decision to conduct workshops for women only was an obvious one.

The emphasis on creating a space in which women's written and spoken voices can emerge makes for a radically different approach from Ira Progoff's, for example. For Progoff, the individual is "he," and gender is not an issue. In his workshops, large groups of men and women silently write together, with minimal interaction or conversation. Even if they decide to read something aloud, "they do not expect that anyone in the group will necessarily be listening to them," because "each participant is engaged primarily in moving deeper into his own life." I appreciate the validity of this approach. But in place of "active privacy" and passive listening, I prefer active privacy and *active* listening. Many women today need an experience of being heard, especially in a group. For a woman who has rarely or never experienced this, a journal workshop may be the ideal setting. The feminist theologian Nelle Morton told a fascinating story about an event that changed her understanding of the relationship between speaking and listening. In a workshop she conducted in 1971, one woman who had remained silent throughout, on the last day began to speak, hesitantly and painfully. "Then she talked more and more," Morton recounts.

> Her story took on fantastic coherence. When she reached a point of the most excruciating pain, no one moved. No one interrupted her. No one rushed to comfort her. No one cut her experience short. We simply sat . . . in a powerful silence. The women clustered about the weeping one went with her to the deepest part of her life as if something so sacred was taking place they did not withdraw their presence or mar its visibility. Finally the woman . . . finished speaking. Tears flowed from her eyes in all directions. She spoke again: "You heard me. You heard me all the way. . . . I have a strange feeling you heard me before I started. You heard me to my own story. *You heard me to my own speech.*"

Morton found, in this experience, "a complete reversal of the going logic . . . a depth hearing that takes place before speaking—a hearing that is more than acute listening. A hearing that is a direct transitive verb that evokes speech—new speech that has never been spoken before." This is the sort of speech that may emerge in the course of the workshop. When this happens, a woman has been heard into her own voice.

I have wanted to offer a setting and experience that were holistic and harmonious, serene but stimulating—the kind of environment I had sought myself, in vain, fifteen years earlier. Since many sessions take place in my living room, the atmosphere is personal, informal, and intimate. Size fluctuates between six and fourteen. As nourishment for body and soul, I set out fresh flowers, play meditative music, and prepare a lunch with freshly baked cakes and muffins. Women are usually the caretakers of the hearth, and I wanted them to see a reflection of their own loving efforts. Even when the workshops are held in classrooms or seminar rooms, I arrange to have a tape player and a coffeepot available, and bring along a cake or muffins for the coffee break.

During the workshop itself, I offer general suggestions only. Keep writing. Mark places where you are aware of censoring yourself. Don't stop to correct spelling or grammar. Date all entries. It's not my business (nor any group member's) to "fix" anyone: to solve problems or resolve conflicts that surface. It is often tempting to jump in prematurely with ideas and answers, instead of giving the speaker the opportunity, as the woman above found, simply to tell her story and experience it being received. This is not to say that the workshop can't serve as a support group on those occasions. Several summers ago, four participants were in the midst of separations and divorces. In every instance, the men involved were fighting the proceedings and, in several cases, using particularly nasty tactics. One evening during the break I saw them clustered together, sharing and comparing experiences, clearly drawing strength and encouragement from one another's stories.

And of course, journal writing is itself inherently a source of comfort and support. Robin Garber-Kabalkin, whose mother had died without warning several weeks earlier, wrote,

> I came to journal writing a fractured person, holding within a frame
> of flesh and bone the shattered pieces of a grieving soul. The workshop
> exercises put me in touch with my inner self—the self I rarely reached
> to and only minimally acknowledged. Over time, the ability and desire
> to write in my journal—of colours, visions, dreams and even of night-
> mares—became the cushioning filler against which my broken parts
> could rest and eventually set. I was able to feel whole again—if only
> for isolated moments, and with increasing regularity. . . . What a re-

markable feeling—to know that even if I forget who I am, my journal will aways remember, speak for me, to me, tell me where I have been and where I have wanted to go.

No topic of discussion is taboo in the workshop, but if anyone is uncomfortable with something said or done, they are welcome to raise it in the group or tell me privately. If the dialogue strays too far into someone's personal issues, I will get a consensus on how the group feels about bringing it back to journal writing. There is usually quiet background music during periods of writing, but majority rules on this issue, too. At the beginning of a workshop, I often read or distribute short passages from published journals as a way of setting the mood and starting the flow of writing. Whether it's Emily Carr or Anaïs Nin, Etty Hillesum or May Sarton, this always draws an enthusiastic response and provides a catalyst for the session's writing. Although I prepare photocopied handouts of related materials, exercises, and reading lists, there are no assignments of any kind. A woman whose sole time to herself is a weekly workshop doesn't need one more thing to cram into her already overbusy life.

Over the years I have found, along with Burghild Nina Holzer, that the "rhythm of living, writing, and sharing with others, usually becomes a deeply comforting feeling, something many people never had in their lives before." At its best, this is what a workshop offers us.

12

A Voice of Her Own

To live fully, outwardly and inwardly, not to ignore external reality for the sake of
the inner life, or the reverse—that's quite a task.

ETTY HILLESUM, *An Interrupted Life*

The beloved journal grounds the ego in two directions, inner and outer reality.

MARION WOODMAN, *Addiction to Perfection*

March 13, 1995. Noon.

I am very blocked and don't understand why. Everything I can think of writing for
Chapter Twelve sounds like a stale cliché and I can't even bring myself to write it down.
I've raged and complained in my journal but I'm still blocked. I read Nachmanovitch's
passage about persevering gently and all I want to do is knock the computer over and walk
away. It's glorious outside and I am imprisoned, hostage to a deadline. I'd forgotten how
much I hate writing under pressure. I don't think I want closure. I want to keep writing
this book, but at my own pace, rewriting, reflecting, editing, carrying on. If I can't work
through this block (which has been around for a few days), I'll have to hand the
manuscript in without the final chapter and continue working on it, even after the
deadline.

I have loved working on this book so much and have experienced so few blocks that it's
a downer to have such a bad one near the end, just when I need an extra burst of energy to

carry me through. Goddess, where are you? Animus, I thought this is where I could count on you to keep me focused on my task and help me complete the book.

3:38 PM. This has been the worst day ever of my work on this book. Then, not more than an hour ago, the mail brought loving cards from Jarda and Kathie, and a "yes" from Marion Woodman. She will write a foreword. Steve said, "There's the goddess showing herself."

Women and the Journal Writing Journey

The journal writing journey is full of paradox. The most radical action we take to change our lives may be simply to express what ails us. As we focus on the inner realms, our outer lives are unmistakably altered. In Marion Milner's words, "Turning attention inwards makes the outer resurrected, reborn in vividness." Laying aside all thought of writing well, we may discover a natural flow and organic unity in what we write. The process is not separate from the product. Journeying, we are at home. Listening may precede speaking, and the body have knowledge the mind has no words for. Acknowledging our fragmentation, we become whole and, attending fully to our personal concerns, we go beyond them to the universal.

Personal, intimate, unique for each diarist, this is nevertheless a shared journey. In the workshops I've described, we see evidence of the community to which we belong. Reading other women's published diaries, we find proof of the healing and creative promise the journal holds out to all of us, and of a communion that exists beyond superficial shared affinities. Gail Godwin, for one, has found many sides of herself reflected in other women's diaries and believes that "In these unedited glimpses of the self in others, of others in the self, is another proof of our ongoing survival, another of the covenants eternity makes with the day-to-day."

But our journey is a shared endeavor in other respects as well. We are not separate from the world in which we live. If journal writing can change the way I regard myself and others, it has the potential to transform social relations. This is precisely what Anaïs Nin discovered. In the summer of 1956, she wrote in her journal, "I notice that whenever I clear up something for myself it quickly affects everyone around me, as if it were a psychic liberation which in turn affects others' conflicts. My change of mood affects shopkeepers, bus drivers, policemen, cleaners, messenger boys, besides those close to me. It is like the distribution of a positive current." Modern physics has intimated that the whole is fully embodied in each of its parts, that every individual contains the world. Any change in ourselves, any move toward greater self-awareness, authenticity, and openness, will affect those around us. Each step we take toward genuine creative expression sends ripples out into the world, and often, they may spread much further than we might imagine. The personal is universal.

Many diarists have celebrated the communal dimension of our journey. Virginia Woolf contrasted "the little separate lives which we live as individuals" with "the common life which is the real life." She believed that "behind the cotton wool is hidden a pattern; that we— I mean all human beings—are connected with this: that the whole world is a work of art; that we are parts of that work of art." May Sarton observed, "One must believe that private dilemmas are, if deeply examined, universal, and so, if expressed, have a human value beyond the private." And Anaïs Nin claimed, "The personal life, deeply lived, takes you beyond the personal . . . and reaches universality." She believed that "Any experience carried out deeply to its ultimate leads you beyond yourself into a larger relation to the experience of others."

As Christa Wolf ponders the significance of the Chernobyl nuclear disaster in *Accident: A Day's News*, she comes to the conclusion that the human species' only hope of survival is to acknowledge our own blind spots—both personal and cultural. "Why shouldn't there be a chance for an entire civilization if as many of its members as possible can dare to look their own truth in the eyes without fear?" she asks. This is just what the journal encourages us to do—look our own truth in the eyes without fear. Clearly this kind of vision is not only a radical personal act but a truly political one. The women's liberation slogan of the 1970s proclaimed, "The personal is political." Today, this is more true than ever. Deena Metzger recently wrote in her journal, "How we live our lives, act toward ourselves and others, treat the environment, regulate our inner lives, are crucial; the health of the soul, the body, the body politic and of the planet have become as one." So our personal journeys also have a transpersonal dimension. And Marion Woodman tells us that "It is at the place of wounding that we find ourselves connected to each other in love . . . open to loving other people, loving the planet, loving the cosmos."

How beautifully we see this embodied in Etty Hillesum's life and writing. During a time when hatred and cruelty were running rampant, she refused to cut herself off from anyone or to distance herself from even the ugliest, most painful experiences. A sense of passionate connection with everything in the world around her permeates her journal. On September 22, 1942, during a short reprieve from the Westerbork transit camp, Etty wrote,

> Surrounded by my writers and poets and the flowers on my desk I loved life. And there among the barracks, full of hunted and persecuted people, I found confirmation of my love of life. Life in those draughty barracks was no other than life in this protected, peaceful room. Not for one moment was I cut off from the life I was said to have left behind. *There was simply one great, meaningful whole* [my emphasis].

Etty's recurrent refrain was " 'Let me be the thinking heart of these barracks' " and we know that she was, from those who survived her. Her spirit inspired all those who knew her, and it still radiates today, from the pages of her journal. And finally, Nelle Morton, too, had something to say about the shared nature of our quest. In the last journal entry in her book, she reflected, "Maybe 'journey' is not so much a journey ahead, or a journey into space, but a journey into presence. The farthest place on earth is the journey into the presence of the nearest person to you." But before that can happen, *we must be present to ourselves.*

A Voice of Your Own

What does it mean, then, through journal writing to find a voice of our own? In the examples and quotes provided throughout this book, we find many variations on this theme. One that we did not consider in detail is that of our actual speaking voices. Many of us don't even know their authentic register; witness how many young women in their teens and early twenties seem to sound alike, regardless of size or body shape. How rare it is to hear a woman speak with a voice that resonates throughout her body. "Women, in particular, have lost their voices," Marion Woodman tells us, "both metaphorically and literally. The voice tends to come from the throat because we're afraid to breathe deeper. We're afraid to hit the pain." Our fear and anger are so great, Woodman tells us, that we may spend years recovering our authentic voices.

The importance of speaking from a voice that is securely grounded in the body has been a constant refrain in the work of many feminist writers, particularly in France. "Women must write through their bodies," claims Hélène Cixous, and Marguerite Duras tells us, "We must move on to the rhetoric of women, one that is anchored in the organism, in the body." Chantal Chawaf asks, "Isn't the final goal of writing to articulate the body?" She claims, "Language through writing has moved away from its original sources: the body and the earth," but now we need "languages that regenerate us, warm us, give birth to us." Indeed, Chawaf says, "the word must comfort the body." Woodman, too, wants to bring our speaking and writing back to their bodily origins, urging us to recover the mother tongue of the conscious body, whose "rhythms beat with the heart, with the emotions that circle and repeat and again repeat with totally new vibrations of feeling. Its vocabulary is simple; its knowing deep," she tells us. "It is heart language calling out to other hearts."

Finding a voice will mean different things for different women, and will echo differently for each of us at other times in our lives. Gloria Naylor found that just as journal writing provided her with an important mode of self-expression during her teenage years, so, too, it later helped her find her writing voice. She tells us that she has always kept journals, "to give voice to things I couldn't say with my mouth. I never spoke much when I was younger. I was very shy. So the diary my mother gave me helped me do that. I have often said that I consider my work an extension of this: trying to give form to the inarticulate inside of myself." Gloria's words speak for many of us, including one workshop participant, who said, "I'm forty years old and I feel as if I'm discovering my own voice for the first time in my journal. I don't think I ever knew what it was, before."

For one woman, finding her voice may mean breaking away from the collective values she grew up with, leaving a community that she has called home. She may begin to express herself honestly in her closest relationships, speak up for herself at the workplace, and exercise her voice in a public setting, perhaps for the first time in her life. This may well involve alienating family and friends and, in the process, she will almost certainly come up against her own inner demons. Again we find this conflict clearly expressed in Etty Hillesum's journal. She reflected, "Back into darkness, into your mother's womb, into the collective. Break free, find your own voice, vanquish the chaos within. I am pulled to and fro between these two poles." But, as Etty intuitively knew, we can't stay in the womb forever. We may feel safe in the comfortable anonymity of the collective, but we remain there only at high cost to ourselves. The individuation process is essential to realizing our mature identity. If we avoid it, we deprive ourselves of our authentic lives—and voices. This is the process we engage in, in our journals.

For another woman, finding her voice means getting past the voices of "the fathers" reverberating in her head, in order to speak from her innermost core. Patriarchal discourses surround us in all directions. Science and technology, religion and commerce, the media and the academy—each has its own specialized language signifying mastery of the field. None of them truly values concrete subjective experience, much less regards it as a source of knowledge. In the age of mass media, what gets sacrificed is precisely the individual human voice—with its faltering tempos and uneven pitch, its unglossy imperfections and stubborn inconsistencies. This is precisely why it is so precious: its uniqueness refuses to be programmed out. The human voice, speaking its truth in a painstaking, halting, and vulnerable language, free from jargon and unencumbered by the need to impress or persuade, is a rare phenomenon today. Our journals, yours and mine, may be one of its few remaining abodes!

To write a journal is to insist that your life is unique, different from mine and the next person's, that it does not conform to the flat, uniform images constructed by television, popular journalism, and political rhetoric. I suspect that as technology moves further in the direction of reducing us to a set of numbers stored in a giant computer database, our determination to assert our voices will grow. Even more of us will turn to journal writing as a priceless channel of self-expression. "We are living in a renaissance of personal writing," Christina Baldwin observes. "People are rebalancing the impersonalization endemic to modern society with an increase in personal introspection," and, as a result, "we are undergoing a shift in paradigms in which we are trying to develop new models for humanness and human responsibility." The new paradigm surely will not involve a new form of regimentation, not even a feminist one. Years ago I was reprimanded in a women's literature course for not using the rhetoric of oppression and liberation in my essay. But the opposite of abstract patriarchal discourse is not abstract feminist discourse. It is authentic, thoughtful, joyous, individual utterance—what Marion Woodman called "heart language," and Christa Wolf, "the living word." Hélène Cixous tells us,

> In women's speech, as in their writing, that element which never stops resonating, which, once we've been permeated by it, profoundly and imperceptibly touched by it, retains the power of moving us—that element is the song: first music from the first voice of love which is alive in every woman.

For many of us, this means becoming more aware of the voices we have internalized over the years, in order to speak our own truth, in our own words. Here again, the diary is our best ally. "We are not culturally accustomed to speaking," says Hélène Cixous. "That is why writing is good, letting the tongue try itself out—as one attempts a caress, taking the time a phrase or a thought needs to make oneself loved, to make oneself reverberate." Writing in our journals, we let the tongue try itself out. The voice that emerges in the process is no longer governed by the language of the collective. But neither does it define itself in simple opposition. Neither lost in the chorus nor simply singing solo, the new voice of woman rings out beyond this very dichotomy. Each note we sing is wholly, authentically our own —and just as much, we sing each other.

Another variation on the theme is that of the writer or artist attempting to find her creative voice. "Originality does not mean being unlike the past or unlike the present," Stephen Nachmanovitch tells us. "It means being the origin, acting out of your own center. Out of your spontaneous heart you may do something reminiscent of the very old, and it will be original because it will be yours." We don't have to alter our voice in order to distinguish it from the next person's, because "quality arises from, and is recognized by, resonance with inner truth." Instead of comparing our own contribution with those of others, we focus on its inner authenticity. And again, paradoxically, it is precisely when the writer most distinctively speaks with her own voice that she may go beyond her personal experience and speak for all of us.

Often it's a matter of integrating form and content so that her art is in harmony with her life's truth. "There's no doubt in my mind that I have found out how to begin (at 40) to say something in my own voice," Virginia Woolf wrote in her diary in 1922. At that time she had already published five novels and countless essays. Indeed, it is difficult to imagine there was ever a time when Virginia Woolf didn't have her own voice, so distinctive is it! Anne Truitt, too, found that after years of struggling and uncertainty, "At the age of forty, it became clear to me that I was doing work I respected within my own strictest standards." Paula Modersohn-Becker began to have intimations of her voice in her late twenties; perhaps she sensed that her time was limited. On December 1, 1902, she confided to her journal, "Strange, it's as if my voice had totally new sounds and my being a new register. I feel it growing greater within me and broader. God willing, I will become something." For Paula as well, her journal was the first sounding board for that emerging voice.

"A Diary Means Yes Indeed"

And now we arrive at the end of our journey together. Journal writing, with its capacity to inspire and comfort us, to illuminate and transform us is an affirmation of our lives, our selves, and our emerging voices. In joy and in sorrow the diary is a faithful friend on the journey of life. Indeed, as Burghild Nina Holzer suggests, "Perhaps only in a journal can one see how life and art intertwine and are really only one great journey."

Gertrude Stein said, in her inimitable way, "A diary means yes indeed." For Marion Woodman, too, the journal plays a critical role in this journey of self-affirmation. She tells us, "If you travel far enough, one day you will recognize yourself coming down the road to meet yourself. And you will say—YES." And finally, here is Luce Irigaray, celebrating what is already ours—the open world. "We have so much space to share," she exults.

> Our horizon will never stop expanding; we are always open. Stretching out, never ceasing to unfold ourselves, we have so many voices to invent in order to express all of us everywhere, even in our gaps, that all the time there is will not be enough. We can never complete the circuit, explore our periphery: we have so many dimensions. . . . The sky isn't up there: it's between us.

Our journey has no end; the path unfolds before us, as far as we can see. Our voices are still evolving.

Postlude

March 27, 1995.
And so I come to the last page of this book. I hope that in some way it too has the fugue-like, spiralic quality I envisioned when I began to write.

Journal entry, March 19, 1994.
What a perfect and beautiful way to end this volume of my journal. Here is what happened. Thinking about what I would do with my "Woman as Hero" class this Friday, it occurred to me to give them the talk I wrote a few years ago on Paula Modersohn-Becker and Adrienne Rich's beautiful poem about her. This time, I thought, I could balance it by including a woman writer or artist who *did* live to make art, and Käthe Kollwitz came to mind. Immediately I remembered that Muriel Rukeyser wrote a poem about Kollwitz. (That would provide the perfect opportunity to bring in poetry, since several women in the class have asked whether we would be looking at any poems in the course.) I looked the poem up in the *Norton Anthology of Women's Literature*, and what should hit me in the face but "My lifetime listens to yours," the line I have been looking for, calling and asking about for two years, because I want to quote it as the title of my chapter about reading journals. I could not believe my eyes. What a gift!

There's more. I went in to tell Steve. He was amazed and told me he too had a major breakthrough in his work this morning. Something he'd been working on for two years fell beautifully into place in a most definitive way. He'd refrained from coming in to tell me because he didn't want to interrupt my work. Then he commented on the fugue-like quality of the process. I said I had looked up "fugue" yesterday and told the class that Toni Morrison's *Beloved* had a fugue-like structure, and explained to them what that meant. We had discussed fugues and

counterpoint, and the interweaving of voices that don't stop. I returned
to my study to finish reading Rukeyser's poem and lo and behold, what
did I read, but " 'The process is after all like music / like the development of a piece of music. / The fugues come back and / again and
again / interweave.' "

So many levels of synchronicity, all interwoven. What is amazing is
that I was longing for some sign that this book is not just my fabrica-
tion, my willed intention painstakingly carried out. I considered asking
for a dream tonight, one that would give me an insight into my block
and the critical voices that give me such a hard time as I try to write.
The sign came swiftly. (I've also been wondering what to do with the
women's literature class, too, for the remaining weeks of the semester.
Now I know. Poems, journals, and a general discussion of women as
creators.) Many people would say this is just coincidence. I know it
isn't. It's simply too complex, too beautiful and multifaceted to be pure
chance. It all seems to be connected, part of a whole. This book, Steve's
book, our life together, the theme of women's creativity, my teaching,
the workshop and my love for the women in it. The fugue enacts itself
in our lives as well. What a sense I have right now of women's lives
interweaving and listening to each other. Every now and then—the
pattern emerges and things shimmer.

> "The process is after all like music,
> like the development of a piece of music.
> The fugues come back and
> > again and again
> interweave.
> A theme may seem to have been put
> aside,
> but it keeps returning—
> the same thing modulated,
> somewhat changed in form.
> Usually richer.
> And it is very good that this is so."

The theme that keeps returning—modulated, changed in form,
and richer—is the next turn of the spiral, the next step in our unfolding. And the next entry in our journals.

Appendix

Writing Topics to Accompany Chapters Four–Nine

Chapter Four

1. Write about the warmest, strongest, most vivid event of the past twenty-four hours. Where are you in your life right now? What are you feeling at this moment?

2. Open your journal and write down:
   I think . . .
   I feel . . .
   I want . . .
Without stopping to think about what you will say, write a paragraph or two starting with each one. When you have finished, go back and read what you just wrote. Are there any surprises? You can also do this as a rapid writing exercise, using: I was . . . / I am . . . / I will be. . . . / I am looking forward to . . . / I am tired of . . . / More than anything I want. . . .

3. By whom or by what are you led?

4. Write a dialogue between your feminine and masculine sides. Give each of them a name. How do they feel about each other? What are the defining qualities and capacities of each? What do they want to tell each other? What kind of relationship have they had in the past? What do they want from each other now?

5. If you had been able to choose your own name, what would it have been? What would your name be if you were a man?

6. Write about your inner journey. Embellish it with colors and sketches, if you like. What is it that prompts you to turn inward?

7. Following Marion Milner, make a list of your purposes, large and small. Is there a common thread that runs through them?

8. What do you desire? Make a list and include everything, large and small, no holds barred.

9. Describe a recent confrontation you had with another person. What does the immediate issue seem to be? What are you feeling as you write about it? How does your understanding of what really happened change as you dwell on it?

10. Where is your center? Where are you grounded? Write about what it means to be centered in yourself.

11. Where do you channel your greatest life energy?

12. Get acquainted with your inner critic. Give him or her a name. What does he/she look like? Write a dialogue between the critic and your conscious self. How do they talk to each other?

13. What inner voices are clamoring to be heard? Give them names. Where do they come from? What do they wish to tell you?

14. Write about your earliest memory. Why has it stayed with you? What is its meaning for you now?

15. What is your earliest memory of school, of rebellion, of friendship, of hatred, of accomplishment, of independence?

16. Make a list of memories important to your sense of identity. Include all of them. Then go back and reread them until one of them leaps out at you, and write about it in detail.

17. Take your list of memories and title them as you would chapters in a book. What patterns do you observe? What is the secret logic of your life?

18. What events in your life do you need to claim and possess in order to be "fierce with reality," in the words of Florida Scott-Maxwell?

19. Imagine a scenario that you want for your life in the future. It could be six months from now, a year, or longer. Take your time and allow yourself to savor the experience richly. Describe it in detail. Now imagine your life five years from now. Do the same thing. How would you like to be living five years from now?

20. What positive messages do you send your body? What negative messages? Where do they come from?

21. What are the roles you play? Complete the following sentences in as many ways as you can. Feel free to slip into metaphor! I am . . . / I am a . . . / I am the. . . . How do these roles relate to your central self?

22. Who are your inner figures? Write about your subpersonalities and give them voices.

23. What color is your life right now? What color do you want it to be?

Chapter Five

1. If you are in therapy, take some time after your next session to describe your feelings and thoughts about the work you did, and any emotion that you feel now. If your therapist isn't familiar with the healing dimension of journals, check out some books on the topic.

2. If you are doing battle with depression, let your journal be a loving, listening ear. Write something every day, even if it's only a paragraph or two. Make an effort to treat yourself with special kindness, as you would a friend who is suffering. Be gentle with yourself, buy a beautiful notebook and some special coffee or tea, put on your favorite music, or go out to a café to write.

3. Write a letter to your depression. Invent a dialogue between your depression and your Self.

4. The next time you are angry, sit down with your journal and pour it all out. Write quickly and resist the temptation to cross out mistakes. If you can't write about your anger, visualize the block that prevents you from writing and describe that or sketch it in your journal. What does it feel like? What does it look like? What color and texture does it possess? What would it take to get through it? To dissolve it? When you have finished, take several deep breaths and observe how you feel.

5. Dialogue with a physical symptom or ailment. It might be a headache or rash, an allergy, a feeling of nausea, or something else.

What does it want to teach you about restoring a healthy balance in your life?

6. Write a letter to your demons, whatever and whoever they are. This could be an addiction or a guilt complex, whatever you feel is robbing you of your life energy.

7. Describe an old resentment, an unhealed hurt. Write a letter in your journal forgiving someone who has hurt you, releasing that person and yourself.

8. What thoughts are you ashamed of? Following Marion Milner, allow your thoughts to "write themselves."

9. Write about envy in your life. Whom do you envy, and why? What is it that you don't have in your own life, and yearn for? Do you believe that if you had it, you would be truly happy?

10. Do Muriel Schiffman's exercise on tracking hidden emotions. What do you uncover?

11. Write about your inner child. What does she want to tell you? What does she need from you? Write a letter to her. If you have trouble hearing her voice, find a photo of yourself at a young age and listen to what it tells you. You may have to be patient while she builds up courage to speak.

12. Invent a dialogue with her. Write the adult's perspective with your dominant hand, and the inner child's voice with your nondominant hand. If your first language was not English, freewrite about her in that language. Write a dialogue between your inner child and your parents, grandparents, and so on. Describe her from someone else's perspective: your mother's, father's, a sibling's.

13. If you suspect she was traumatized, offer her extra love and attention. Keep a picture of her nearby and give her a journal of her own. Write about what you see on the photo. Sit down with a box of crayons and give her free rein. What does she draw?

14. What are the critical voices wreaking havoc with your self-esteem? Dialogue with them. Where do they come from? If you suffer from the impostor syndrome, write a letter to your inner impostor.

15. Describe yourself as if you were your own best friend.

16. Write an autobiography of your body. What are the defining events, moments, changes, and insights you have experienced? Write about your happiest bodily memories. Then write about some of the

sad ones. If there is a part of your body that you find problematic, dialogue with it, and find out what it wants and needs. Write about a time when you let go and honored your body's need to simply be. If you can't remember one, invent one. What is your unique beauty in the "Family of Woman"?

17. What does wholeness mean to you? What activities give you a sense of wholeness? Write about that feeling. Write about the broken places in your life.

18. Write an unsent letter to someone, living or dead, with whom you have unfinished business. Tell that person exactly what is in your heart, what you wish he or she knew.

Chapter Six

1. What "hidden gold" is there to be discovered in the unbidden fluctuations in your life?

2. Write about the continuities and the discontinuities of your life. Allow plenty of time. Write your life story as a story of changes. Now, write it as a story of continuity. What are the threads that unify your life? What is the underlying pattern?

3. Where are your roots? What is your cultural story? What is the role of ethnicity in your life?

4. Rapid writing exercise: What is changing in your life right now?
- What are you bidding farewell to?
- What are you welcoming into your life?
- What remains constant?

5. Tell the story of your losses. What losses have you experienced in the past year? In the past five years? Ten years? If you have never acknowledged or mourned these losses, do so in your journal. Write for short periods (five or ten minutes) if the task is overwhelming. What new beginnings have accompanied those losses?

6. What have you consciously loved and left in your lifetime? What have you gone on to?

7. What places hold special significance for you? Write about the meanings, literal and symbolic, that a particular place holds for you.

8. Describe the physical changes you observe in your body. Explore their meaning and symbolism for you. Dialogue with them.

9. What does growing older suggest to you? Write your own story of what it means to grow older.

10. Write yourself a postcard from anywhere in the world. Where are you, and what are you doing there?

11. You have just won a "hundred-thousand-dollars-a-year-for-life" sweepstakes. What changes do you make in your life?

12. Make a list of five ways in which you have changed in the last ten years. What changes would you like to make during the next decade?

13. Imagine your life as an adventure whose meaning will emerge only through writing. What story do you tell and what meanings do you discover?

14. When and where have you felt homesick? Where are you at home?

15. What caretaking roles have you played in your life? Which do you play now?

16. Write about your own "dark night of the soul." What were you forced to let go of? What was trying to enter your life at that time?

17. How has your relationship with your journal changed over time? What role did it play when you began? What does it mean to you now? How do you see it evolving in the future?

Chapter Seven

Writing suggestions are given in the chapter itself.

Chapter Eight

1. Following Emily Carr, write about what you want to express. What attracted you to this theme and "what is its core, the thing you are trying to express?"

2. Where, in your life, are you creative? What do you know

about your own creative process? When, where, and how do ideas come to you?

3. How could keeping a notebook open at your workplace enhance your creative process there?

4. If you don't already have one, buy yourself a small notebook to carry in your coat pocket or handbag. Take it with you, wherever you go. When the germ of an idea flickers across your mind, get it down, however sketchy.

5. Leave a pad of paper and pen on the table/desk/wherever you spend your waking hours. You never know when the glimmer of an idea or the solution to a problem will come to you.

6. Get a pen in a new color and use it for creative inspirations and ideas for special projects that come to you while you are writing in your journal.

7. Keep a separate notebook for a specific creative project, whether it is an essay or story you are writing, plans for a holiday, or an assignment at work.

8. The next time you have to write something public, brainstorm, outline, and write a rough draft in your journal. Promise yourself that if you don't like it, no one else will ever see it.

9. Look for the "diamonds in the dustheap" in your own journal. Where are they hidden?

10. Go through a past volume of your journal with an eye toward finding an idea for a story, essay, or poem. Underline or highlight likely passages that seem to have untapped life in them, that elicit some kind of emotional response. What do you feel strongly about in the pages of your diary?

11. Virginia Woolf referred to her diary as "a deep old desk and a capacious hold-all." How would you describe yours?

12. If you are involved in a creative project of some kind, let your journal be your companion along the way. Keep it on your desk, in your car, wherever you work, as a sounding board, a patient friend, a source of comfort and inspiration.

Chapter Nine

1. Taking stock at the beginning of the year:
• What did you accomplish last year? Make a list of everything you consider an accomplishment, large or small, whether it is finishing your college degree, painting your bathroom, or paying off your credit card debt. What are you most proud of or satisfied with? What regrets do you have about the past year?
• What "color" was last year?
• What is the link between last year and this year? What "color" would you like this year to be?
• Freewrite about five to ten goals for the new year. Choose one or two that feel urgent, and consider specific steps you could take in order to accomplish it. Describe a single day in which you take concrete steps toward accomplishing this goal.
• Project yourself exactly one year into the future. What do you most want to be able to say then, about the year just past? What specific things in your life would have to change for you to get from here to there?
• What do you sense you are supposed to do before your life is over?

2. Write a year-end entry summing up what the year has brought you. Following Antonia White's example, you could write a paragraph about the most exciting, upsetting, important things, and so on.

3. If the year just past was a rough one, start the new one with a new journal. Write about your hopes and goals for the new year.

4. Try writing at different times of the day, in different ways. What won't allow itself to be written at noon may form easily at 11 P.M.

5. The next time you travel, get yourself a small notebook in which to write about your trip. Unless you are particularly interested in them, don't record all the "facts" of your journey, but focus on Milner's "beads"—the glowing moments of significance during your trip.

6. Start a journal for your baby or young child. Not only will she/he find it fascinating in years to come, this will set a precedent for your child to start his or her own journal.

7. What do you like best about yourself, in rereading? What do you like least? What patterns do you observe in your journals over time? What silences do you keep in your journal? What secrets do you keep, even from yourself?

8. What do you want to have happen to your journals at the end of your life? What arrangements have you made, could you make, do you want to make?

Additional Exercises

1. If your life story was a book, what would it be titled? What would its chapter titles be?

2. Write about a friendship / an object / a color that is especially important to you right now.

3. Looking back over your interactions with other people last week, what sticks out as the most meaningful?

4. What is the essential core of friendship for you?

5. As you read other women's journals (Chapter Ten), with whom in particular do you have an affinity? Write about it.

6. What does "greatness" mean to you? Who is great, and why? What is heroism?

7. What do you believe in?

8. If you could change one thing about yourself, what would it be?

9. You have been given a day and an expense account as a gift. You can spend it entirely as you like, without restrictions. What will you do?

• With a week and a thousand dollars?

• With a year and a hundred thousand dollars? A million?

10. What would you most like to believe about yourself and your life's journey?

11. What are the sacred tasks that you perform daily?

12. When, where, and by whom are you truly seen as yourself?

13. Who are your mothers? Sisters? What are the safe places, the homes, and communities that you have loved?

14. What are the values you cherish even though they run counter

to societal values? Where do you bring them into expression in the patterns of your daily life?

15. If your tears could speak to you, what would they say?

16. What is the journey you are on? What other paths can you imagine yourself having taken?

17. What does "feminine voice" mean to you? Where in your life are you speaking with a feminine voice? Where do you hear it around you?

18. What does the word "family" mean to you? Who is your family? What kinds of things do you get from your family? What kinds of things do you give them?

19. What word or words best describe your relationship with the world?

20. What is the most important gift another woman ever gave you? What influence does that gift have in your life now? What is the best thing you ever gave another woman? What would you like to give other women?

21. What four or five relationships have had the greatest impact on your life? Draw a map of these relationships. Give them a place, a shape, a color, and so on.

22. What do you recall about yourself as an eight-year-old? What remains of her in you now? What other qualities and characteristics of hers would you like to reclaim now?

23. Write an elaborate lie about yourself. Believe it as you write and tell it with conviction and energy.

Guided Visualization
"Meeting Your Essential Self"

* If possible, have a friend read this to you slowly, or tape yourself reading it; then listen. Ellipses indicate a pause of five to ten seconds. Do not rush.

Make yourself comfortable. Stretch and shift your body until every part of you feels comfortable. . . . Close your eyes, sit back gently, and relax into your body. . . . Bring your attention to your breathing and take several long, slow, deep breaths. . . . Each time you exhale, feel cares and tension fall away as you sink more and more deeply into your inner self. . . .

Before your inner eye, imagine a long, clear, peaceful path. It may be along a river bed, or through a cool wood or sunny meadow. In the distance, the outline of a woman begins to come into view. You are walking leisurely toward each other, and you sense that you are about to encounter your future self, a self who has cleared all extraneous clutter and baggage from her life and retains only what is most essential, most precious and meaningful to her. . . .

As you stroll down the path, notice the sounds and sensations around you. . . . Perhaps there is a rustle of leaves in the air, the sound of waves, or the cry of birds in the distance. . . . Notice how the air feels on your skin, how the sun and wind feel on your face. . . . As your future self comes nearer, observe how she carries herself, and the expression on her face. . . . Notice the details of her clothing, the colors and textures she is wearing. . . .

As you meet each other on the path, she leads you in the direction of her home. . . . Walking down a side path together, you reach a dwelling that is your future home. What does it look like? . . . What are the surroundings like? . . . As you step up to the door and enter the house, notice how simply and harmoniously it is arranged. She has cleared away all clutter, leaving only objects of comfort and beauty. What do you see around you? . . . What has been cleared out of your life? . . . What colors and textures draw your attention? . . . You hear music softly from another room. What is it? . . . How do you feel in this environment? . . .

Exploring the house, you come to a large airy room, simply arranged, that reflects your tastes and interests, and current occupation. What does it contain? . . . What is your vocation? . . . What are you doing with your life? . . . How are your talents and energy being engaged? . . . How do you spend your days? . . . With whom? . . . What is the most significant part of each day? . . . Who are the most important people in your life? . . .

Spend a few moments in this special room that holds such meaning for you. . . . Feel the peace and serenity it emanates. . . . Before you leave, your future self hands you an envelope with a beautiful card containing an image and words of wisdom about what you must do to get here. What image does the card hold? . . . What message do you find written inside it? . . .

As you leave the house, carry this message with you, knowing it will help you make contact with your essential self, and your ideal life. Feel the joy of anticipation, knowing that you will return to this place before long. . . .

When you are ready . . . take your time . . . slowly return from the meditation . . . stretch . . . open your eyes . . . and describe this experience in your journal.

Rapid Writing Topics

- Write about a question that looms large in your mind at this time.
- Write about a person from whom you have learned a crucial lesson.
- Write about emptiness.
- I want to write about . . .
- I don't want to write about . . .
- The best thing about my life right now is . . .
- The worst thing about my life right now is . . .
- My worst fear is . . .
- My biggest secret is . . .

Endnotes

Chapter One
The Diary Habit

Page 15: Susan Crean, in Libby Scheier et al., eds., *Language in Her Eye: Writing and Gender*, p. 90.

Page 17: Toi Derricotte, in Patricia Bell-Scott, ed., *Life Notes: Personal Writings by Contemporary Black Women*, p. 79.

Page 17: Le Anne Schreiber, *Midstream*, p. 10.

Page 18: Etty Hillesum, *An Interrupted Life: Diaries, 1941–43*, p. 41.

Page 19: Portions of the diaries of Carolina Maria de Jesus and Virginia Woolf are published in Mary Jane Moffat and Charlotte Painter, eds., *Revelations: Diaries of Women*.

Page 20: More recently, questions of deliberate distortion have created considerable controversy over Nin's published diaries. But love her or hate her, there is no disputing the dynamic effect she had, and continues to have, on women's journal writing.

Page 20: Christina Baldwin, *One to One: Self-Understanding Through Journal Writing*, and Tristine Rainer, *The New Diary: How to Use a Journal for Self-Guidance and Expanded Creativity*. Since then, a number of other books on journal writing have appeared, but *The New Diary* remains a favorite of mine, along with two more recent volumes: Baldwin's *Life's Companion: Journal Writing as a Spiritual Quest* and Deena Metzger's *Writing for Your Life: A Guide and Companion to the Inner Worlds*. The latter is more broadly focused but offers rich inspiration for journal writers. Interestingly, Metzger was also a close friend of Anaïs Nin's.

Page 21:   May Sarton, *Journal of a Solitude*. Another excellent anthology, Lyn Lifshin's *Ariadne's Thread: A Collection of Contemporary Women's Journals*, sadly, is no longer in print. But in 1994, an exciting new anthology appeared: *Life Notes: Personal Writings by Contemporary Black Women*, the first of its kind, according to Patricia Bell-Scott, its editor. This collection includes many diary selections from fifty contributors.

Page 22:   Virginia Woolf, *The Diary of Virginia Woolf, Volume One, 1915–1919*, p. 95.

Page 23:   Nicole Brossard, "Interview: 'Before I became a feminist, I suppose I was an angel, a poet, a revolutionary,' " in Janice Williamson, ed., *Sounding Differences: Conversations with Seventeen Canadian Women Writers*, p. 65.

Page 26:   Marlene A. Schiwy, "Language and Silence: 'Sprachlosigkeit' in the Work of Christa Wolf."

Chapter Two
An Hour of Her Own

Page 32:   Muriel Rukeyser, "Käthe Kollwitz," in Sandra M. Gilbert and Susan Gubar, eds., *The Norton Anthology of Literature by Women*, p. 1783.

Page 32:   Carl G. Jung, *Women in Europe*, cited in Esther Harding, *The Way of All Women*, p. v.

Page 33:   Marion Woodman, *The Pregnant Virgin: A Process of Psychological Transformation*, p. 53. Elsewhere, Woodman describes Sophia as "an emerging archetypal pattern, not yet fully in consciousness, that is bringing to our Western culture a new understanding of the relationship between spirit and matter." Woodman, *Addiction to Perfection: The Still Unravished Bride*, p. 74.

Page 33: Maureen Murdock, *The Heroine's Journey: Woman's Quest for Wholeness*, p. 11.

Page 34: Kim Chernin, *Reinventing Eve: Modern Woman in Search of Herself*, p. xviii.

Page 35: Carolyn G. Heilbrun, *Writing a Woman's Life*, p. 117.

Page 35: Kim Chernin, *Reinventing Eve*, p. 11. Recent books in which journal writing plays a crucial role in women's quest for self-discovery include Marion Woodman's *Leaving My Father's House: The Journey to Conscious Femininity*; Maureen Murdock's *The Heroine's Journey*; Judith Duerk's *Circle of Stones: Woman's Journey to Herself*; and Naomi Ruth Lowinsky's *The Motherline: Every Woman's Journey to Find Her Female Roots*. There are many more.

Page 35: Anaïs Nin, *The Journals of Anaïs Nin: Volume Two, 1934–1939*, p. 262.

Page 35: I first came across the concept of "being heard into one's own speech" in Nelle Morton's *The Journey Is Home*.

Page 36: Robin Garber-Kabalkin, personal journal. This and all subsequent quotes from personal journals are used with permission and henceforth will be acknowledged by use of the diarist's name in the text.

Page 37: Marion Milner (pseudonym, Joanna Field), *A Life of One's Own*, p. 39.

Page 38: Emily Hancock, *The Girl Within*.

Page 38:   Lyn Mikel Brown and Carol Gilligan, Meeting at the Crossroads.
             This is also the time during which girls begin to fail at math
             and science and generally do better in same-sex schools than
             boys do, because they aren't worried about coming across as
             too "brainy." The boys, on the other hand, don't do as well
             in single-sex as in coed schools.

Page 40:   Anaïs Nin, in Laurel Holliday, ed., Heart Songs: The Intimate Diaries
             of Young Girls, p. 17.

Page 41:   Kate Danson, in Marion Woodman et al., Leaving My Father's
             House: A Journey to Conscious Femininity, pp. 39, 43.

Page 41:   Cinthia Gannett, Gender and the Journal: Diaries and Academic Dis-
             course, p. 179.

Page 41:   Hélène Cixous, in Elaine Marks and Isabelle de Courtivron,
             eds., New French Feminisms: An Anthology, p. 251.

Page 42:   Carol Gilligan, In a Different Voice: Psychological Theory and Women's
             Development, pp. 173–74.

Page 42:   Maureen Murdock, The Heroine's Journey, p. 10.

Page 42:   Kate Danson, in Marion Woodman et al., Leaving My Father's
             House, p. 105.

Page 43:   Marion Woodman, The Pregnant Virgin, pp. 8, 9.

Page 44:   Linda Schierse Leonard, On the Way to the Wedding: Transforming
             the Love Relationship, p. 7.

Page 44:   Emily Hancock, The Girl Within, p. 232.

Page 44:   Naomi Ruth Lowinsky, The Motherline: Every Woman's Journey to
             Find Her Female Roots, p. 22.

Page 44:   Kim Chernin, Reinventing Eve, p. 16.

Page 45:   Edward F. Edinger, cited in Beverly Moon, ed., An Encyclopedia
             of Archetypal Symbolism, p. 216. Monica Sjöö and Barbara Mor
             state, "The spiral involution of energy into matter is the
             primary movement of the universe, into created beings; the
             spiral evolution of matter into energy is the creative move-
             ment of these beings, consciously evolving back to their
             source. . . . The Spiral is the symbolic key to immortality—
             or eternal process—and is identified with the moon." The
             Great Cosmic Mother: Rediscovering the Religion of the Earth, p. 63.

Page 45:   Naomi Ruth Lowinsky, The Motherline, p. 23.

Page 45:   Nelle Morton, The Journey Is Home, p. xx.

Page 45:   Marion Woodman, Addiction to Perfection, p. 8.

Page 46:   Marion Woodman, Addiction to Perfection, p. 84.

Page 47:   Anaïs Nin, The Journals of Anaïs Nin: Volume Two, 1934–1939,
             p. 187.

Page 48:   Patricia Bell-Scott, ed., "Black Women Writing Lives: An In-
             troduction," Life Notes, p. 22.

                              Chapter Three
                              Getting Started

Page 50:   Anaïs Nin, A Woman Speaks: The Lectures, Seminars, and Interviews of
             Anaïs Nin, p. 163.

Page 51:   Yvonne Blue, in Penelope Franklin, ed., Private Pages, p. 67.

Page 52:   Sylvia Plath, in Lyn Lifshin, ed., Ariadne's Thread: A Collection of
             Contemporary Women's Journals, p. 89.

Page 52:   Mary MacLane, in Margo Culley, ed., *A Day at a Time: The Diary Literature of American Women from 1764 to the Present*, p. 188.

Page 53:   Etty Hillesum, *An Interrupted Life*, p. 1.

Page 53:   Emily Carr, *Hundreds and Thousands*, p. 20.

Page 53:   *Hopes and Dreams: The Diary of Henriette Dessaulles 1874–1881*, p. 15.

Page 53:   Edith Wharton, cited in Judy Simons, *Diaries and Journals of Literary Women from Fanny Burney to Virginia Woolf*, p. 146.

Page 54:   Elizabeth Barrett Browning, cited in Judy Simons, *Diaries and Journals of Literary Women*, pp. 87, 88.

Page 55:   Anne Frank, *The Diary of a Young Girl*, pp. 104–5.

Page 55:   Cosima Wagner, cited in Carol Neuls-Bates, ed., *Women in Music: An Anthology of Source Readings from the Middle Ages to the Present*, p. 178.

Page 55:   Antonia White, *Diaries, 1926–1957*, p. 57.

Page 55:   Susan Kinnicutt, in Lyn Lifshin, ed., *Ariadne's Thread*, pp. 106–7.

Page 56:   Anaïs Nin, *The Journals of Anaïs Nin: Volume Two, 1934–1939*, p. 218.

Page 58:   Judith Thurman, *Isak Dinesen: The Life of a Storyteller*, p. 99.

Page 59:   Patricia Hampl, in Lyn Lifshin, ed., *Ariadne's Thread*, p. 320.

Page 61:   Luise Rinser, *Prison Journal*, p. 13.

Page 62:   Gail Godwin, in Lyn Lifshin, ed., *Ariadne's Thread*, pp. 12, 13.

Page 63: Lou Nelson, in Frances Rooney, ed., *Our Lives: Lesbian Personal Writings*, p. 180.

Page 63: Virginia Woolf, *The Diary of Virginia Woolf, Volume Five, 1936–1941*, p. 205.

Page 63: Kaethe Kollwitz, *The Diary and Letters of Kaethe Kollwitz*, p. 111.

Page 64: Diane Kendig, in Lyn Lifshin, ed., *Ariadne's Thread*, p. 193.

Page 66: You might want to look at one of Christina Baldwin's books, Deena Metzger's *Writing for Your Life*, or Kimberly Snow's *Word Play/Word Power*, for example. Special topic writing books include June Gould's *The Writer in All of Us: Improving Your Writing Through Childhood Memories*; Lesléa Newman's *SomeBody to Love: A Guide to Loving the Body You Have*; and Gabriele Rico's *Pain and Possibility: Writing Your Way Through Personal Crisis*.

Page 69: My summary of writing techniques is not intended to be exhaustive. For additional description and examples, see Tristine Rainer's *The New Diary*; Christina Baldwin's *One to One*; Kay Leigh Hagan's *Internal Affairs*; Kathleen Adams's *Journal to the Self*; and George Simons's *Keeping Your Personal Journal*.

Page 76: Anne Frank, *The Diary of a Young Girl*, p. 3.

Page 76: Fanny Burney, quoted in Sandra M. Gilbert and Susan Gubar, eds., *The Norton Anthology of Literature by Women*, p. 127.

Page 76: George Sand, *The Intimate Journal*, p. 50.

Page 81: Antonia White, *Diaries, 1926–1957*, pp. 32, 33.

Page 82: Dorothy V. Claire, in Frances Rooney, ed., *Our Lives*, p. 51.

Page 84: Gabriele Rico, *Pain and Possibility*, p. 16.

Chapter Four
Writing Below the Surface

Page 89:   Emily Carr, *Hundreds and Thousands*, p. 67.

Page 89:   Marion Milner, *A Life of One's Own*, p. 69.

Page 89:   Anaïs Nin, *The Journals of Anaïs Nin: Volume Five, 1947–1955*, p. 41.

Page 91:   Etty Hillesum, *An Interrupted Life*, pp. 162, 81.

Page 95:   Marion Milner, *A Life of One's Own*, pp. 44, 71.

Page 95:   Burghild Nina Holzer, *A Walk Between Heaven and Earth: A Personal Journal on Writing and the Creative Process*, p. 5.

Page 95:   Sylvia Ashton-Warner, *Myself*, p. 156.

Page 96:   Etty Hillesum, *An Interrupted Life*, p. 75.

Page 96:   Gloria Steinem, *Revolution from Within: A Book of Self-Esteem*, p. 267.

Page 96:   Mary Catherine Bateson, *Composing a Life*, p. 41.

Page 99:   Stephen Nachmanovitch, *Free Play: Improvisation in Life and Art*, pp. 133, 36, 47.

Page 100:   Marion Milner, *A Life of One's Own*, p. 60.

Page 101:   Oliver Sacks, *The Man Who Mistook His Wife for a Hat*, p. 28.

Page 101:   Florida Scott-Maxwell, *The Measure of My Days*, p. 42.

Page 102:   Rainer Maria Rilke, quoted in Sam Keen and Anne Valley-Fox, *Your Mythic Journey*, p. 74.

Page 103:   Marion Milner, A Life of One's Own, p. 89.

Page 104:   Steven M. Rosen, Science, Paradox, and the Moebius Principle: The
            Evolution of a "Transcultural" Approach to Wholeness, pp. 117–18,
            125.

Page 106:   Eugene Gendlin, Focusing.

Page 106:   Kim Chernin, The Hungry Self: Women, Eating and Identity, p. 42.
            Mary Catherine Bateson makes a similar point, in Composing a
            Life: "Women with a deep desire to be like their mothers are
            often faced with the choice between accepting a beloved
            image that carries connotations of inferiority and depen-
            dency or rejecting it and thereby losing an important sense
            of closeness," p. 39.

Page 108:   Judith Duerk, Circle of Stones, p. 44.

Page 108:   Marion Woodman, Addiction to Perfection, p. 13.

Page 109:   Anaïs Nin, The Diary of Anaïs Nin: Volume Three, 1939–1944,
            p. 166.

Page 109:   Anaïs Nin, quoted in Mary Jane Moffat and Charlotte Painter,
            eds., Revelations, p. 6.

Page 109:   Anaïs Nin, The Diary of Anaïs Nin: Volume Four, 1944–1947,
            p. 105.

Page 109:   Ruth Benedict, in Mary Jane Moffat and Charlotte Painter,
            eds., Revelations, p. 150.

Page 110:   R. H. Douglas, in Patricia Bell-Scott, ed., Life Notes, p. 249.

Page 110:   Marion Woodman, Addiction to Perfection, p. 99.

Page 111:   Marion Milner, A Life of One's Own, p. 97.

Page 111:   Sylvia Ashton-Warner, *Myself*, p. 158.

Page 111:   Anaïs Nin, *The Diary of Anaïs Nin: Volume One, 1931–1934*, p. 286.

Page 112:   Carl G. Jung, cited in Naomi Ruth Lowinsky, *The Motherline*, p. 51.

Chapter Five
Healing Dimensions of the Journal

Page 113:   Anonymous diarist, in Patricia Bell-Scott, ed., *Life Notes*, p. 19.

Page 113:   Carole Bovoso, in Penelope Franklin, ed., *Private Pages*, p. 378.

Page 114:   Alice Miller, *The Drama of the Gifted Child: The Search for the True Self*, p. 7.

Page 114:   The etymology of "therapy" comes from Eric Partridge's *Origins: A Short Etymological Dictionary of Modern English*, p. 711.

Page 114:   Kim Chernin, *Reinventing Eve*, pp. 15, 16, 29.

Page 115:   Carl G. Jung, quoted in May Sarton, *Journal of a Solitude*, p. 110.

Page 115:   Marion Woodman, *Addiction to Perfection*, p. 23.

Page 115:   *Prevention Magazine*, January 1992, p. 131.

Page 115:   Lydia Temoskok and Henry Dreher, *The Type C Connection: The Mind-Body Link to Cancer and Your Health*, pp. 132, 330–31.

Page 115:   Dean Ornish, *Dr. Dean Ornish's Program for Reversing Heart Disease*, pp. 90–91.

Page 116:   Cinthia Gannett, *Gender and the Journal: Diaries and Academic Discourse*, pp. 204–5.

Page 116:   Chris Watson, quoted in Toni Ann Laidlaw and Cheryl Malmo, eds., *Healing Voices: Feminist Approaches to Therapy with Women*, p. 187.

Page 117:   Marion Woodman, *Addiction to Perfection*, p. 104.

Page 120:   Marion Woodman et al., *Leaving My Father's House*, p. 351.

Page 120:   Stephen Nachmanovitch, *Free Play*, p. 185.

Page 120:   Quo Vadis Gex-Breaux, in Patricia Bell-Scott, ed., *Life Notes*, p. 348.

Page 121:   Muriel Schiffman, *Self-Therapy: Techniques for Personal Growth*, p. 35.

Page 121:   Alice Koller, *An Unknown Woman*, pp. 33, 215.

Page 122:   Bibi Wien, in Lyn Lifshin, ed., *Ariadne's Thread*, p. 63.

Page 122:   May Sarton, *After the Stroke: A Journal*, p. 15.

Page 122:   May Sarton, *Recovering: A Journal*, p. 49.

Page 122:   Carroll Parrott Blue, in Patricia Bell-Scott, ed., *Life Notes*, pp. 175–76.

Page 123:   Melina Brown, in Patricia Bell-Scott, ed., *Life Notes*, p. 355.

Page 123:   Horace B. English and Ava Champney English, *A Comprehensive Dictionary of Psychological and Psychoanalytical Terms* (New York: David McKay, 1958), p. 77.

Page 123:   Lydia Temoskok and Henry Dreher, *The Type C Connection*, p. 275.

Page 123:   Sylvia Plath, *The Journals of Sylvia Plath*, p. 255.

Page 124:   Emily Carr, Hundreds and Thousands, p. 322.

Page 124:   Anne Frank, The Diary of a Young Girl, pp. 114, 117.

Page 124:   Shamara Shantu Riley, in Patricia Bell-Scott, ed., Life Notes, p. 92.

Page 125:   Audre Lorde, The Cancer Journals, pp. 10, 18, 13, 53.

Page 126:   Carolyn G. Heilbrun, Writing a Woman's Life, p. 15.

Page 126:   Harriet Lerner, The Dance of Anger: A Woman's Guide to Changing the Patterns of Intimate Relationships, p. 3.

Page 127:   Alice Miller, The Drama of the Gifted Child, p. 7.

Page 127:   Janet O. Dallett, When the Spirits Come Back, pp. 49, 50, 53, 54.

Page 128:   Adrienne Rich, Of Woman Born: Motherhood as Experience and Institution, pp. 25, 21, 22.

Page 128:   Audre Lorde, The Cancer Journals, p. 15.

Page 129:   Muriel Schiffman, Gestalt Self-Therapy, p. 133.

Page 129:   Muriel Schiffman, Self-Therapy, pp. 34, 35.

Page 130:   Anaïs Nin, A Woman Speaks, pp. 17–18.

Page 131:   Alice Miller, The Drama of the Gifted Child, pp. 24, 25.

Page 131:   Naida D. Hyde, "Voices from the Silence: Use of Imagery with Incest Survivors," in Toni Ann Laidlaw et al., eds., Healing Voices, p. 177–78.

Page 131:   Rebecca (pseudonym), cited in "Ending the Cycle of Vio-
            lence: Overcoming Guilt in Incest Survivors," in Toni Ann
            Laidlaw et al., ed *Healing Voices*, pp. 286–87.

Page 132:   Jane (pseudonym), cited in Marion Woodman, *Addiction to
            Perfection*, p. 109.

Page 132:   Kate Danson, cited in Marion Woodman et al., *Leaving My
            Father's House*, p. 79.

Page 133:   Christa Wolf, *A Model Childhood*, pp. 7, 406.

Page 133:   Stephen Nachmanovitch, *Free Play*, p. 47.

Page 133:   Emily Hancock, *The Girl Within*, p. 224.

Page 135:   Mary Catherine Bateson, *Composing a Life*, pp. 39–40. Bateson
            adds, "Often, American men learn to project their disap-
            pointments outward [while] women tend to internalize their
            losses. When a proposal is turned down or a job not offered,
            women tend to say, I wasn't worthy. Men more often contend
            that the process was crooked." p. 206.

Page 136:   Marion Woodman, *Conscious Femininity*, p. 133.

Page 136:   Deena Metzger, *Tree & The Woman Who Slept with Men to Take the
            War Out of Them*, p. 34.

Page 136:   Peggy Orenstein, *School Girls: Young Women, Self-Esteem, and the
            Confidence Gap*, p. xxvii.

Page 138:   Marion Woodman, *Conscious Femininity*, p. 113.

Page 139:   Michele Murray, in Lyn Lifshin, ed., *Ariadne's Thread*, pp. 98,
            99.

Page 139:   Gloria Steinem, *Outrageous Acts and Everyday Rebellions*, p. 166.

Page 140:   Audre Lorde, *The Cancer Journals*, pp. 11, 53.

Page 140:   Deena Metzger, *Tree*, pp. 35, 70, 68.

Page 141:   Audre Lorde, *The Cancer Journals*, p. 39.

Page 141:   Adrienne Rich, *Of Woman Born*, pp. 285–86.

Page 142:   Elly Danica, in Janice Williamson, ed., *Sounding Differences*, pp. 80–81.

Page 142:   Stephanie Demetrakopoulos, *Listening to Our Bodies: The Rebirth of Feminine Wisdom*, p. 170.

Page 142:   Judith Duerk, *Circle of Stones*, p. 56.

Chapter Six
Reinventing the Self

Page 143:   Etty Hillesum, *An Interrupted Life*, p. 113.

Page 143:   Mary Catherine Bateson, *Composing a Life*, p. 223.

Page 143:   Eva Hoffman, *Lost in Translation: A Life in a New Language*, p. 274.

Page 145:   Mary Catherine Bateson, *Composing a Life*, pp. 9, 10.

Page 146:   Mary Catherine Bateson, *Composing a Life*, p. 41.

Page 146:   Anaïs Nin, *The Diary of Anaïs Nin: Volume Four, 1944–1947*, p. 127.

Page 146:   Rainer Maria Rilke, "Duino Elegies," cited in Linda Leonard, *The Wounded Woman*, p. 139.

Page 147:   Wilma Shore, "Pages from a Widow's Journal," *Women's Studies Quarterly* 17, nos. 3–4 (1989): 61, 63.

Page 147:   Mary Shelley, "From Mary Shelley's Journal," in Joan Goulianos, ed., *By a Woman Writt*, pp. 166, 180.

Page 148:   Elizabeth Cox, *Thanksgiving: An AIDS Journal*, pp. 223–24.

Page 148:   Rebecca Rice, *A Time to Mourn: One Woman's Journey Through Widowhood*, pp. 105, 106.

Page 149:   May Sarton, *At Seventy: A Journal*, pp. 212–13.

Page 149:   Nancy Esther James, in Lyn Lifshin, ed., *Ariadne's Thread*, pp. 223, 227.

Page 149:   Le Anne Schreiber, *Midstream*, pp. 10, 11.

Page 150:   Emily Carr, *Hundreds and Thousands*, pp. 253, 258, 259.

Page 150:   Anne Morrow Lindbergh, *Locked Rooms and Open Doors: Diaries and Letters, 1933–1935*, p. 229.

Page 153:   Marlene Nourbese Philip, in Janice Williamson, ed., *Sounding Differences*, p. 241.

Page 154:   Eva Hoffman, *Lost in Translation*, p. 278.

Page 155:   Anaïs Nin, *A Woman Speaks*, p. 157.

Page 155:   Gwendolyn Bennett, cited in Lenore Hoffman, "The Diaries of Gwendolyn Bennett," *Women's Studies Quarterly* 17, nos. 3–4 (1989): 67.

Page 156:   Paula Modersohn-Becker, *The Letters and Journals of Paula Modersohn-Becker*, J. Diane Radycki, trans., Metuchen, N. J.: The Scarecrow Press, 1980, p. 109.

Page 156:   Paula Modersohn-Becker, *The Letters and Journals*, (German origi-
             nal edited by Günter Busch and Liselotte von Reinken), Ar-
             thur S. Wensinger and Carole Clew Hoey, eds. and trans.,
             Evanston: Northwestern University Press, 1990, p. 158.

Page 156:   *The Letters and Journals of Paula Modersohn-Becker*, ed. J. Diane Ra-
             dycki, pp. 280, 286.

Page 157:   Eva Hoffman, *Lost in Translation*, pp. 151, 120–21, 269, 273,
             275–76.

Page 158:   L. L. Zeiger, "Colonial Days," in Lyn Lifshin, ed., *Ariadne's
             Thread*, pp. 197–98, 203, 204.

Page 159:   Antonia White, *Diaries, 1926–1957*, p. 38.

Page 160:   Germaine Greer, *The Change: Women, Aging and the Menopause*,
             p. 378.

Page 161:   Melissa Gayle West, *If Only I Were a Better Mother*, pp. 49–50.

Page 162:   Anne Truitt, *Daybook: The Journal of an Artist*, pp. 184, 209–10.

Page 163:   Kaethe Kollwitz, *The Diary and Letters of Kaethe Kollwitz*, pp. 53, 94.

Page 164:   Elaine Marcus Starkman, *Learning to Sit in the Silence: A Journal of
             Caretaking*, pp. 11, 21–22, 87, 147, 156.

Page 165:   Mary Catherine Bateson, *Peripheral Visions: Learning Along the Way*,
             pp. 82–83.

Page 166:   May Sarton, *Endgame: A Journal of the Seventy-ninth Year*, pp. 128,
             130, 10.

Page 166:   Elaine Shelly, in Patricia Bell-Scott, ed., *Life Notes*, pp. 282,
             290–91.

Page 167:   Alice James, *The Diary of Alice James*, pp. 25, 229–30.

Page 169:   Mary Hamilton, in Marion Woodman et al., *Leaving My Father's House*, pp. 128–32, 135, 164.

Page 169:   Gabriele Rico, *Pain and Possibility*, pp. 143–45.

Page 170:   Hannah Hinchman, *A Life in Hand: Creating the Illuminated Journal*, pp. 13–14.

Page 171:   Joyce Mary Horner, in Margo Culley, ed., *A Day at a Time*, p. 302.

Page 171:   Etty Hillesum, *An Interrupted Life*, pp. 180–81. More recently, Diane Carlson Evans, a nurse in Vietnam, said she stopped writing in her journal because the horror she witnessed was such that no one would believe what she wrote anyway. Cited in Terrie Claflin, "Monumental Achievement," *MS* 4, no. 3 (December 1993): 86.

Page 171:   Martha Martin, in Mary Jane Moffat and Charlotte Painter, eds., *Revelations*, p. 301.

Page 172:   Sylvia Plath, *The Journals of Sylvia Plath*, pp. 280, 293.

Page 172:   Linda Schierse Leonard, *Witness to the Fire: Creativity and the Veil of Addiction*, p. 130.

Page 172:   Jean Rhys, cited in Linda Schierse Leonard, *Witness to the Fire*, p. 135.

Page 172:   Anaïs Nin, *The Journals of Anaïs Nin: Volume Two, 1934–1939*, p. 215.

Page 173:   Anaïs Nin, *A Woman Speaks*, p. 149.

Page 173:   Nelle Morton, *The Journey Is Home*, p. 201.

Page 173:   Gail Godwin, "A Diarist on Diarists," in Joyce Carol Oates, ed., *First Person Singular: Writers on Their Craft*, pp. 27, 28.

Chapter Seven
Dreams and Other Exceptional Experiences

Page 175:   Marie Cardinal, *The Words to Say It*, p. 170.

Page 176:   Anaïs Nin, *The Diary of Anaïs Nin: Volume Three, 1939–1944*, p. 300.

Page 176:   Christa Wolf, *Cassandra: A Novel and Four Essays*, p. 113.

Page 177:   Carl G. Jung, "Psychology and Literature," in *Modern Man in Search of a Soul*, p. 166.

Page 177:   Montague Ullman, "Dreams as Exceptional Human Experiences," *American Society of Psychical Research Newsletter* 18, no. 4:5.

Page 177:   Christa Wolf, *The Author's Dimension: Selected Essays*, pp. 83–84.

Page 178:   Carl G. Jung, *Memories, Dreams, Reflections*, p. 413.

Page 178:   Janet Dallett, *When the Spirits Come Back*, p. 20.

Page 179:   Marion Woodman, *The Pregnant Virgin*, pp. 167–68.

Page 179:   Amy Tan, in Naomi Epel, ed., *Writers Dreaming*, p. 282.

Page 179:   Joy Kogawa, in Janice Williamson, ed., *Sounding Differences*, pp. 155–56.

Page 180:   Sheila Moon, *Dreams of a Woman: An Analyst's Inner Journey*, pp. 108–9.

Page 182:   Bharati Mukherjee, in Naomi Epel, ed., *Writers Dreaming*, p. 161.

Page 183:   Antonia White, Diaries, 1926–1957, pp. 254–55.

Page 185:   Mary Elsie Robertson, in Lyn Lifshin, ed., Ariadne's Thread, p. 125.

Page 185:   Marion Woodman, The Ravaged Bridegroom: Masculinity in Women, p. 28.

Page 186:   Marion Woodman et al., Leaving My Father's House, p. 124.

Page 188:   Amy Tan, in Naomi Epel, ed., Writers Dreaming, p. 288.

Page 188:   Marion Woodman, Conscious Femininity, p. 135.

Page 189:   Burghild Nina Holzer, A Walk Between Heaven and Earth, p. 19.

Page 190:   Karen Signell, Wisdom of the Heart: Working with Women's Dreams, pp. 7, 8.

Page 192:   Montague Ullman, "Access to Dreams," in Benjamin B. Wolman and Montague Ullman, eds., Handbook of States of Consciousness, pp. 552, 526.

Page 193:   Karen Signell, Wisdom of the Heart, pp. 8–9.

Page 200:   Rhea White, "Personal Experiences and the Legitimation of Parapsychology: Feed Ye the Sheep." See also Rhea's journal, Exceptional Human Experience, 414 Rockledge Road, New Bern, NC, 28562.

Page 201:   Burghild Nina Holzer, A Walk Between Heaven and Earth, pp. viii, 62.

Page 201:   Loran Hurnscot, in Mary Jane Moffat and Charlotte Painter, eds., Revelations, p. 346.

Page 202:   Rebecca Cox Jackson, in Margo Culley, ed., *A Day at a Time*,
            p. 95.

Page 202:   Carl G. Jung, *Memories, Dreams, Reflections*, p. 217.

Page 202:   Montague Ullman, "Dreams as Exceptional Human Experi-
            ences," p. 5.

Chapter Eight
"This Drama of the Process": Journal Writing and Creativity

Page 203:   Ethel Schwabacher, *Hungry for Light: The Journal of Ethel
            Schwabacher*, p. 219.

Page 203:   Virginia Woolf, *The Diary of Virginia Woolf, Volume Four*, 1931–
            1935, p. 286.

Page 203:   Emily Carr, *Hundreds and Thousands*, p. 215.

Page 204:   Gabriele Rico, *Pain and Possibility*, pp. 24, 25.

Page 204:   May Sarton, *At Seventy*, p. 106.

Page 204:   Carl G. Jung, "Psychology and Literature," in *Modern Man in
            Search of a Soul*, p. 170.

Page 205:   Etty Hillesum, *An Interrupted Life*, p. 107.

Page 205:   Stephen Nachmanovitch, *Free Play*, pp. 27, 18, 70.

Page 206:   Sue Grafton, in Naomi Epel, ed., *Writers Dreaming*, p. 62.

Page 206:   Virginia Woolf, *The Diary of Virginia Woolf, Volume Five*, 1936–
            1941, pp. 244–45.

Page 206:   Virginia Woolf, *The Diary of Virginia Woolf, Volume Three*, 1925–
            1930, p. 231.

Page 206: Katherine Mansfield, cited in Judy Simons, *Diaries and Journals of Literary Women*, p. 152.

Page 206: Anaïs Nin, *A Woman Speaks*, p. 172.

Page 207: Sylvia Ashton-Warner, *Teacher*, pp. 210–11.

Page 207: Gail Godwin, "A Diarist on Diarists," in Joyce Carol Oates, ed., *First Person Singular*, p. 26.

Page 208: "Preface," Virginia Woolf, *A Writer's Diary*, p. 9.

Page 208: Anaïs Nin, *The Journals of Anaïs Nin: Volume Two, 1934–1939*, p. 118.

Page 208: Anaïs Nin, *A Woman Speaks*, p. 170.

Page 208: Antonia White, *Diaries, 1926–1957*, p. 168.

Page 208: Katherine Mansfield, cited in Judy Simons, *Diaries and Journals of Literary Women*, p. 164.

Page 208: Paula Modersohn-Becker, *The Letters and Journals of Paula Modersohn-Becker*, J. Diane Radycki, ed., p. 232.

Page 209: "Clara Schumann," in Carol Neuls-Bates, ed., *Women in Music: An Anthology of Source Readings from the Middle Ages to the Present*, pp. 154, 104–5, 107–8.

Page 209: Virginia Woolf, *The Diary of Virginia Woolf, Volume One, 1915–1919*, p. 234.

Page 210: Virginia Woolf, *The Diary of Virginia Woolf, Volume One, 1915–1919*, p. 266.

Page 210: Judith Minty, in Lyn Lifshin, ed., *Ariadne's Thread*, p. 118.

Page 211:   Tristine Rainer, The New Diary, p. 291.

Page 211:   Marie Cardinal, The Words to Say It, pp. 157, 165.

Page 212:   Smaro Kamboureli, in Janice Williamson, ed., Sounding Differ-
            ences, p. 139.

Page 212:   Gail Scott, in Janice Williamson, ed., Sounding Differences,
            p. 257.

Page 213:   Christa Wolf, The Reader and the Writer: Essays, Sketches, Memories,
            p. 72.

Page 213:   Erica Jong, in Bill Strickland, ed., On Being a Writer, p. 63.

Page 214:   Linda Pastan, in Lyn Lifshin, ed., Ariadne's Thread, p. 313.

Page 214:   Yvonne Moore Hardenbrook, in Sondra Zeidenstein, ed.,
            A Wider Giving: Women Writing After a Long Silence, p. 295.

Page 214:   Alix Kates Shulman, in Lyn Lifshin, ed., Ariadne's Thread, p. 55.

Page 214:   Sara Ruddick, in Carol Ascher et al., eds., Between Women:
            Biographers, Novelists, Critics, Teachers and Artists Write About Their Work
            on Women, p. 142.

Page 215:   Fanny Burney, in Judy Simons, Diaries and Journals of Literary
            Women, pp. 29, 30.

Page 215:   Dorothy Wordsworth, Journal of Dorothy Wordsworth, p. 109.

Page 215:   Hayden Herrera, Frida: A Biography of Frida Kahlo, pp. 264, 266.

Page 216:   Virginia Woolf, The Diary of Virginia Woolf, Volume One, 1915–
            1919, p. 266.

Page 216:   Katherine Mansfield, in Judy Simons, *Diaries and Journals of Literary Women*, p. 167.

Page 216:   Deborah E. McDowell, in Patricia Bell-Scott, ed., *Life Notes*, p. 54.

Page 216:   Patricia Hampl, in Lyn Lifshin, ed., *Ariadne's Thread*, p. 320.

Page 217:   Natalie Goldberg, *Writing Down the Bones*, p. 13.

Page 217:   Anaïs Nin, *The Diary of Anaïs Nin: Volume Three, 1939–1944*, p. 173.

Page 218:   Stephen Nachmanovitch, *Free Play*, pp. 141, 148.

Page 218:   Gloria Naylor, in Naomi Epel, ed., *Writers Dreaming*, p. 177.

Page 218:   Barbara Pym, *A Very Private Eye: An Autobiography in Diaries and Letters*, p. 167.

Page 218:   Antonia White, *Diaries, 1926–1957*, pp. 58, 132.

Page 220:   Anaïs Nin, *The Diary of Anaïs Nin: Volume Four, 1944–1947*, pp. 38, 39.

Page 220:   Anne Truitt, *Daybook*, p. 68.

Page 220:   bell hooks, in Patricia Bell-Scott, ed., *Life Notes*, p. 153.

Page 221:   Emily Carr, *Hundreds and Thousands*, pp. 72, 176.

Page 221:   Sylvia Ashton-Warner, *Myself*, p. 158.

Page 221:   Katherine Mansfield, in Judy Simons, *Diaries and Journals of Literary Women*, p. 167.

Page 222:   Emily Carr, *Hundreds and Thousands*, pp. 31, 32, 261.

Page 222:   Kaethe Kollwitz, *The Diary and Letters of Kaethe Kollwitz*, pp. 69, 82.

Page 222:   Etty Hillesum, *An Interrupted Life*, p. 125.

Page 222:   Sylvia Ashton-Warner, *Myself*, pp. 130–31.

Page 223:   Virginia Woolf, *The Diary of Virginia Woolf, Volume Two*, 1920–1924, pp. 317, 263, 272.

Page 223:   Etty Hillesum, *An Interrupted Life*, p. 209.

Page 224:   Emily Carr, *Growing Pains: An Autobiography*, pp. 264–65.

Page 224:   Georgia O'Keeffe, cited in Hannah Hinchman, *A Life in Hand*, p. 58.

Page 224:   Anne Truitt, *Daybook*, p. 82.

Page 224:   Emily Carr, *Hundreds and Thousands*, p. 260.

Page 225:   Virginia Woolf, *The Diary of Virginia Woolf, Volume One*, 1915–1919, p. 214.

Page 225:   Antonia White, *Diaries, 1926–1957*, p. 245.

Page 225:   May Sarton, *Journal of a Solitude*, pp. 53, 65.

Page 226:   Cinthia Gannett, *Gender and the Journal*, p. 147.

Page 226:   Marie Bashkirtseff, in Mary Jane Moffat and Charlotte Painter, eds., *Revelations*, p. 52.

Page 226:   Sylvia Ashton-Warner, *Myself*, p. 115.

Chapter Nine
Writing for Your Life: Further Suggestions for the Journey

Page 227:   Florida Scott-Maxwell, The Measure of My Days, p. 42.

Page 228:   Barbara Godard, "Becoming My Hero, Becoming Myself: Notes Towards a Feminist Theory of Reading," in Libby Scheier et al., eds., Language in Her Eye, p. 120.

Page 229:   Burghild Nina Holzer, A Walk Between Heaven and Earth, p. x.

Page 229:   Ethel Schwabacher, Hungry for Light, pp. 160, 215, 238, 162.

Page 230:   Deena Metzger, Tree, p. 35.

Page 230:   Antonia White, Diaries, 1926–1957, p. 7.

Page 230:   Kate Tomibe, in Penelope Franklin, ed., Private Pages, pp. 120–21.

Page 230:   Elaine Marcus Starkman, Learning to Sit in the Silence, pp. 2–3.

Page 232:   Christina Baldwin, Life's Companion: Journal Writing as a Spiritual Quest, p. 7.

Page 232:   Barbara Marie Brewster, Journey to Wholeness, p. 87.

Page 232:   Eleanor Smith, in Patricia Bell-Scott, ed., Life Notes, pp. 401–402.

Page 233:   Anaïs Nin, The Diary of Anaïs Nin: Volume Three, 1939–1944, pp. 3, 4.

Page 233:   Anaïs Nin, The Journals of Anaïs Nin: Volume Six, 1955–1966, p. 27.

Page 234: Gloria Bowles, "Going Back Through My Journals: The Unsettled Self, 1961–1986," *National Women's Studies Association Journal* 6, no. 2 (1994):274–75.

Page 235: Michelle Herman, in Lyn Lifshin, ed., *Ariadne's Thread*, pp. 238–40.

Page 235: Flora Tristan, *Flora Tristan, Utopian Feminist: Her Travel Diaries and Personal Crusade*, p. 130.

Page 235: Eslanda Goode Robeson, in Margo Culley, ed., *A Day at a Time*, p. 227.

Page 236: Marion Milner, *Eternity's Sunrise: A Way of Keeping a Diary*, p. 1.

Page 238: Dawn B. Bennett-Alexander, in Patricia Bell-Scott, ed., *Life Notes*, pp. 233–34.

Page 238: Ethel Robertson, in Penelope Franklin, ed., *Private Pages*, p. 413.

Page 239: Lydia Chukovskaya, *The Akhmatova Journals: Volume 1, 1938–1941*, pp. 5–7.

Page 239: Etty Hillesum, *An Interrupted Life*, p. 227.

Page 239: Virginia Woolf, *The Diary of Virginia Woolf, Volume One, 1915–1919*, p. 266.

Page 241: George Eliot, in Mary Jane Moffat and Charlotte Painter, eds., *Revelations*, pp. 222–23.

Page 241: Virginia Woolf, *The Diary of Virginia Woolf, Volume Four, 1931–1935*, p. 134.

Page 241: Antonia White, *Diaries, 1926–1957*, pp. 258, 270.

Page 241: Virginia Woolf, *The Diary of Virginia Woolf, Volume Two*, 1920– 1924, p. 324.

Page 241: Kaethe Kollwitz, *The Diary and Letters of Kaethe Kollwitz*, p. 111.

Page 242: Gloria Bowles, "Going Back Through My Journals," p. 256.

Page 242: Virginia Woolf, *The Diary of Virginia Woolf, Volume Four*, 1931– 1935, p. 167.

Page 242: Antonia White, *Diaries*, 1926–1957, p. 149.

Page 243: Tristine Rainer, *The New Diary*, pp. 271–73.

Page 243: Virginia Woolf, *The Diary of Virginia Woolf, Volume Two*, 1920– 1924, p. 62.

Page 243: Gail Godwin, "A Diarist on Diarists," in Joyce Carol Oates, ed., *First Person Singular*, p. 29.

Page 244: Gloria Bowles, "Going Back Through My Journals," pp. 257, 260, 269.

Page 244: Burghild Nina Holzer, *A Walk Between Heaven and Earth*, pp. viii, ix.

Page 245: Anne Morrow Lindbergh, *Locked Rooms and Open Doors*, p. 279.

Page 245: Gloria Bowles, "Going Back Through My Journals," p. 256.

Page 246: Barbara Marie Brewster, *Journey to Wholeness*, p. 69.

Page 246: Marion Milner, *A Life of One's Own*, p. 30.

Page 247: Harriet Blodgett, *Centuries of Female Days: Englishwomen's Private Diaries*, pp. 58–61.

Page 247: Lou Nelson, in Frances Rooney, ed., *Our Lives*, p. 180.

Page 248: Gail Godwin, in Lyn Lifshin, ed., *Ariadne's Thread*, p. 75.

Page 248: Frances Rooney, ed., *Our Lives*, p. 202.

Page 249: Brigitte Reimann, *Die geliebte, die verfluchte Hoffnung: Tagebücher und Briefe, 1947–1972*, pp. 65–66. My translation.

Page 249: Emily Carr, *Hundreds and Thousands*, p. 20.

Page 249: Virginia Woolf, *The Diary of Virginia Woolf*, Volume Four, 1931–1935, p. 24.

Page 250: Virginia Woolf, *The Diary of Virginia Woolf*, Volume Three, 1925–1930, p. 67.

Page 250: Virginia Woolf, *The Diary of Virginia Woolf*, Volume Three, 1925–1930, p. 125.

Chapter Ten
"My Lifetime Listens to Yours": The Pleasure of Reading Journals

Page 255: Carolyn G. Heilbrun, *Writing a Woman's Life*, p. 37.

Page 255: Muriel Rukeyser, "Käthe Kollwitz," in Sandra M. Gilbert and Susan Gubar, eds., *The Norton Anthology of Literature by Women*, p. 1783.

Page 257: Amelia Stewart Knight, in Margo Culley, ed., *A Day at a Time*, p. 119.

Page 258: Marie Bashkirtseff, in Mary Jane Moffat and Charlotte Painter, eds., *Revelations*, pp. 47–48.

Page 259: Yvonne Blue, in Penelope Franklin, ed., *Private Pages*, p. 69.

Page 259:   Gloria Bowles, "Going Back Through My Journals," pp. 264,
            266–67.

Page 259:   Toi Derricotte, in Patricia Bell-Scott, ed., Life Notes, p. 79.

Page 260:   May Sarton, Encore: A Journal of the Eightieth Year, pp. 330–31.

Page 260:   Deborah Norris Logan, in Penelope Franklin, ed., Private Pages,
            pp. 467, 472.

Page 260:   Virginia Woolf, The Diary of Virginia Woolf, Volume Five, 1936–
            1941, p. 107.

Page 260:   Beatrice Webb, cited in Harriet Blodgett, Centuries of Female Days,
            p. 76.

Page 261:   Margo Culley, ed., "Introduction," A Day at a Time, p. 16.

Page 261:   Anne Morrow Lindbergh, Locked Rooms and Open Doors, pp. xxii,
            xxiv, xxv.

Page 261:   Anne Truitt, Daybook, p. 4.

Page 262:   Emily Carr, Hundreds and Thousands, p. x.

Page 262:   Virginia Woolf, A Writer's Diary, p. 7.

Page 262:   Maxie Wander, Leben wär' eine prima Alternative: Tagebuchaufzeich-
            nungen und Briefe, p. 6. My translation.

Page 263:   Ted Hughes, "Foreword," in Sylvia Plath, The Journals of Sylvia
            Plath, p. xv.

Page 263:   Mary Lynn Broe, "Plathologies: The Blood Jet Is Bucks, Not
            Poetry," Belles Lettres 10, no. 1 (1994):61–62.

Page 263:   Hayden Herrera, Frida, p. 263.

Page 263: J. G. Gaarlandt, "Introduction," in Etty Hillesum, An Interrupted Life, p. xvii.

Page 265: Mary Catherine Bateson, Composing a Life, p. 5.

Page 265: Barbara Godard, "Becoming My Hero, Becoming Myself," in Libby Scheier et al., eds., Language in Her Eye, pp. 115–16.

Page 266: Käthe Kollwitz, Die Tagebücher, p. 176. My translation.

Page 267: Emily Carr, Hundreds and Thousands, pp. 47, 50.

Page 268: bell hooks, in Patricia Bell-Scott, ed., Life Notes, pp. 153–54.

Page 268: Deborah Norris Logan, in Penelope Franklin, ed., Private Pages, p. 461.

Page 268: May Sarton, The House by the Sea: A Journal, p. 128.

Page 269: Florida Scott-Maxwell, The Measure of My Days, pp. 7, 8.

Page 269: Joyce Mary Horner, in Margo Culley, ed., A Day at a Time, pp. 293–303.

Page 269: Emily Carr, Hundreds and Thousands, p. 306.

Page 269: Etty Hillesum, An Interrupted Life, p. 161.

Page 270: Audre Lorde, The Cancer Journals, pp. 9–10.

Page 270: Christa Wolf, Cassandra, p. 81.

Page 271: Emily Carr, Hundreds and Thousands, pp. 328–29.

Page 271: May Sarton, At Seventy, pp. 49, 50.

Page 272:   Virginia Woolf, The Diary of Virginia Woolf, Volume Two, 1920–1924, p. 226.

Page 272:   Alice James, The Diary of Alice James, pp. 41, 42.

Page 272:   Maxine Kumin, cited in Lyn Lifshin, ed., Ariadne's Thread, p. 15.

Page 272:   bell hooks, in Patricia Bell-Scott, ed., Life Notes, pp. 156, 157.

Page 273:   Virginia Woolf, Moments of Being, p. 98.

Page 273:   Virginia Woolf, The Diary of Virginia Woolf, Volume Five, 1936–1941, p. 215.

Page 274:   Judy Chicago, Through the Flower: My Struggle as a Woman Artist, p. 37.

Page 275:   "Fanny Mendelssohn Hensel," in Carol Neuls-Bates, ed., Women in Music, pp. 146, 149–52.

Page 276:   Sylvia Ashton-Warner, Myself, pp. 88, 117, 184.

Page 276:   Paula Modersohn-Becker, The Letters and Journals of Paula Modersohn-Becker, pp. 286, 297.

Page 277:   May Sarton, Journal of a Solitude, p. 140.

Page 277:   Anne Truitt, Daybook, pp. 155–56.

Page 278:   May Sarton, Endgame, p. 195.

Page 278:   Gail Godwin, in Lyn Lifshin, ed., Ariadne's Thread, pp. 83–85.

Page 278:   Virginia Woolf, The Diary of Virginia Woolf, Volume Three, 1925–1930, p. 102.

Page 278:   Virginia Woolf, *The Diary of Virginia Woolf, Volume Four, 1931–1935*, p. 245.

Page 278:   Antonia White, *Diaries, 1926–1957*, p. 293.

Page 278:   Katherine Mansfield, cited in Harriet Blodgett, *Centuries of Female Days*, p. 206.

Page 279:   George Eliot, cited in Harriet Blodgett, *Centuries of Female Days*, p. 211.

Page 279:   George Eliot, in Mary Jane Moffat and Charlotte Painter, eds., *Revelations*, p. 223.

Page 279:   Emily Carr, *Hundreds and Thousands*, p. 193.

Page 279:   Emily Carr, *Hundreds and Thousands*, pp. 22, 148–49.

Page 279:   Hayden Herrera, *Frida*, p. 284.

Page 280:   Virginia Woolf, *The Diary of Virginia Woolf, Volume Three, 1925–1930*, p. 40.

Page 280:   Burghild Nina Holzer, *A Walk Between Heaven and Earth*, p. 29.

Page 280:   Anne Truitt, *Daybook*, p. 126.

Page 280:   May Sarton, *Journal of a Solitude*, p. 53.

Page 281:   Jeannette S. Guildford, in Sondra Zeidenstein, ed., *A Wider Giving*, pp. 320–21.

Page 281:   Anne A. Simpkinson, in Marion Woodman, *Conscious Femininity*, p. 131.

Page 281:   Barbara Godard, "Becoming My Hero, Becoming Myself," in Libby Scheier et al., eds., *Language in Her Eye*, p. 116.

Chapter Eleven
"Hearing One Another to Speech": The Journal Workshop

Page 282:   Nelle Morton, The Journey Is Home, p. 55.

Page 282:   Carolyn G. Heilbrun, Writing a Woman's Life, p. 46.

Page 287:   Stephen Nachmanovitch, Free Play, pp. 99, 100.

Page 289:   Nelle Morton, The Journey Is Home, pp. 128, 210.

Page 289:   Judith Duerk, Circle of Stones, p. 65.

Page 289:   Carolyn G. Heilbrun, Writing a Woman's Life, pp. 45, 46.

Page 289:   Stephanie Demetrakopoulos, Listening to Our Bodies, p. 172.

Page 291:   Gail Godwin, "A Diarist on Diarists," in Joyce Carol Oates, ed., First Person Singular, p. 25.

Page 295:   Ira Progoff, At a Journal Workshop, pp. 49, 50.

Page 295:   Nelle Morton, The Journey Is Home, p. 205.

Page 297:   Burghild Nina Holzer, A Walk Between Heaven and Earth, p. 63.

Chapter Twelve
A Voice of Her Own

Page 298:   Etty Hillesum, An Interrupted Life, p. 24.

Page 298:   Marion Woodman, Addiction to Perfection, p. 111.

Page 299:   Marion Milner, Eternity's Sunrise, p. 110.

Page 299:   Gail Godwin, "A Diarist on Diarists," Joyce Carol Oates ed., First Person Singular, p. 29.

Page 300:   Anaïs Nin, *The Journals of Anaïs Nin: Volume Six, 1955–1966*, pp. 59, 60.

Page 300:   Virginia Woolf, *A Room of One's Own*, p. 113.

Page 300:   Virginia Woolf, *Moments of Being*, p. 84.

Page 300:   May Sarton, *Journal of a Solitude*, p. 60.

Page 300:   Anaïs Nin, *A Woman Speaks*, pp. 162–63.

Page 300:   Anaïs Nin, *The Diary of Anaïs Nin: Volume Three, 1939–1944*, p. 299.

Page 300:   Christa Wolf, *Accident: A Day's News*, p. 94.

Page 301:   Deena Metzger, *Tree*, p. x.

Page 301:   Marion Woodman, *Conscious Femininity*, p. 109.

Page 301:   Etty Hillesum, *An Interrupted Life*, pp. 219, 236.

Page 301:   Nelle Morton, *The Journey Is Home*, p. 227.

Page 302:   Marion Woodman, *Conscious Femininity*, p. 137.

Page 302:   Hélène Cixous, in Elaine Marks and Isabelle de Courtivron eds., *New French Feminisms*, p. 256.

Page 302:   Marguerite Duras, in Elaine Marks and Isabelle de Courtivron eds., *New French Feminisms*, p. 238.

Page 302:   Chatal Chawaf, in Elaine Marks and Isabelle de Courtivron, eds., *New French Feminisms*, p. 177.

Page 302:   Marion Woodman et al., *Leaving My Father's House*, p. 124.

Page 303:   Gloria Naylor, in Naomi Epel, ed., *Writers Dreaming*, p. 177.

Page 303:   Etty Hillesum, *An Interrupted Life*, p. 57.

Page 304:   Christina Baldwin, *Life's Companion*, pp. 11, 13.

Page 304:   Hélène Cixous, in Elaine Marks and Isabelle de Courtivron, eds., *New French Feminisms*, p. 251.

Page 304:   Hélène Cixous, "Sorties," pp. 92, 93.

Page 305:   Stephen Nachmanovitch, *Free Play*, pp. 179–80.

Page 305:   Virginia Woolf, *The Diary of Virginia Woolf, Volume Two*, 1920–1924, p. 186.

Page 305:   Anne Truitt, *Daybook*, p. 23.

Page 305:   Paula Modersohn-Becker, *The Letters and Journals of Paula Modersohn-Becker*, p. 216.

Page 306:   Burghild Nina Holzer, *A Walk Between Heaven and Earth*, p. 35.

Page 306:   Gertrude Stein, cited in Mary Jane Moffat and Charlotte Painter, eds., *Revelations*, p. 18.

Page 306:   Marion Woodman, cited in Maureen Murdock, *The Heroine's Journey*, p. 12.

Page 306:   Luce Irigaray, *This Sex Which Is Not One*, p. 213.

Postlude

Page 308:   Muriel Rukeyser, "Käthe Kollwitz," p. 1784.

Bibliography

Adams, Kathleen. *Journal to the Self: 22 Paths to Personal Growth.* New York: Warner, 1990.

Ascher, Carol; Louise DeSalvo; and Sara Ruddick, eds. *Between Women: Biographers, Novelists, Critics, Teachers and Artists Write About Their Work on Women.* New York: Routledge, 1993.

Ashton-Warner, Sylvia. *Myself.* New York: Bantam, 1968.

———. *Teacher.* New York: Simon & Schuster, 1963.

Baldwin, Christina. *Life's Companion: Journal Writing as a Spiritual Quest.* New York: Bantam, 1991.

———. *One to One: Self-Understanding Through Journal Writing.* New York: M. Evans, 1977.

Bateson, Mary Catherine. *Composing a Life.* New York: Plume, 1989.

———. *Peripheral Visions: Learning Along the Way.* New York: HarperCollins, 1994.

Begos, Jane DuPree, ed. *A Women's Diaries Miscellany.* Weston, Conn.: Magic Circle Press, 1989.

Belenky, Mary Field, et al. *Women's Ways of Knowing: The Development of Self, Voice, and Mind.* New York: Basic Books, 1986.

Bell-Scott, Patricia, ed. *Life Notes: Personal Writings by Contemporary Black Women.* New York: Norton, 1994.

Blodgett, Harriet. *Centuries of Female Days: Englishwomen's Private Diaries.* New Brunswick, N.J.: Rutgers University Press, 1988.

Bowles, Gloria. "Going Back Through My Journals: The Unsettled Self, 1961–1986," *NWSA (National Women's Studies Association) Journal* 6, no. 2 (Summer 1994): 255–75.

Brewster, Barbara Marie. *Journey to Wholeness.* Portland, Ore.: Four Winds Publishing, 1992.

Broe, Mary Lynn. "Plathologies: The Blood Jet Is Bucks, Not Poetry," *Belles Lettres* 10, no. 1 (1994):48–62.

Brown, Lyn Mikel, and Carol Gilligan. *Meeting at the Crossroads.* New York: Ballantine, 1992.

Burrow, Trigant. *The Social Basis of Consciousness.* New York: Harcourt, Brace, 1927.

Cardinal, Marie. *The Words to Say It*, trans. Pat Goodheart. London: Picador, 1983.

Carr, Emily. *Growing Pains: An Autobiography*. Toronto: Clarke Irwin, 1971.

————. *Hundreds and Thousands: The Journals of an Artist*. Toronto: Clarke Irwin, 1966.

Chernin, Kim. *The Hungry Self: Women, Eating and Identity*. London: Virago, 1985.

————. *Reinventing Eve: Modern Woman in Search of Herself*. New York: Harper & Row, 1987.

Chicago, Judy. *Through the Flower: My Struggle as a Woman Artist*. London: The Women's Press, 1982.

Chukovskaya, Lydia. *The Akhmatova Journals: Volume 1, 1938–1941*, trans. Milena Michalski and Sylva Rubashova. New York: Farrar, Straus and Giroux, 1994.

Claflin, Terrie. "Monumental Achievement," *MS* 4, no. 3 (1993).

Cox, Elizabeth. *Thanksgiving: An AIDS Journal*. New York: Harper & Row, 1990.

Culley, Margo, ed. *A Day at a Time: The Diary Literature of American Women from 1764 to the Present*. New York: Feminist Press, 1985.

Dallett, Janet O. *When the Spirits Come Back*. Toronto: Inner City Books, 1988.

Demetrakopoulos, Stephanie. *Listening to Our Bodies: The Rebirth of Feminine Wisdom*. Boston: Beacon, 1983.

Dessaulles, Henriette. *Hopes and Dreams: The Diary of Henriette Dessaulles, 1874–1881*, trans. Liedewy Hawke. Willowdale, Ontario: Hounslow Press, 1986.

Duerk, Judith. *Circle of Stones: Woman's Journey to Herself*. San Diego: LuraMedia, 1989.

Eberhardt, Isabelle. *The Passionate Nomad: The Diary of Isabelle Eberhardt*, ed. Rana Kabbani, trans. Nina de Voogd. London: Virago, 1987.

English, Horace B., and Ava Champney English. *A Comprehensive Dictionary of Psychological and Psychoanalytical Terms*. New York: David McKay, 1958.

Epel, Naomi, ed. *Writers Dreaming*. New York: Carol Southern Books, 1993.

Fitzhugh, Louise. *Harriet the Spy*. New York: Harper Trophy, 1964.

Frank, Anne. *The Diary of a Young Girl*. New York: Pocket Books, 1953.

Franklin, Penelope, ed. *Private Pages: Diaries of American Women, 1830s-1970s*. New York: Ballantine, 1986.

Gannett, Cinthia. *Gender and the Journal: Diaries and Academic Discourse*. Albany, N.Y.: State University of New York Press, 1992.

Gendlin, Eugene. *Focusing*. New York: Bantam, 1978.

Gilbert, Sandra M., and Susan Gubar, eds. *The Norton Anthology of Literature by Women*. New York: Norton, 1985.

Gilligan, Carol. *In a Different Voice: Psychological Theory and Women's Development*. Cambridge, Mass.: Harvard University Press, 1982.

Gillikin, Jo, ed. *Women's Nontraditional Literature*. Special issue of *Women's Studies Quarterly* 17, nos. 3–4 (1989).

Goldberg, Natalie. *Writing Down the Bones*. Boston: Shambhala, 1986.

Gould, June. *The Writer in All of Us: Improving Your Writing Through Childhood Memories*. New York: Penguin, 1991.

Goulianis, Joan, ed. *By a Woman Writt: Literature from Six Centuries by and About Women*. New York: Penguin, 1973.

Greer, Germaine. *The Change: Women, Aging and the Menopause*. New York: Fawcett Columbine, 1991.

Hagan, Kay Leigh. *Internal Affairs: A Journalkeeping Workbook for Self-Intimacy*. New York: Harper & Row, 1990.

Hancock, Emily. *The Girl Within*. New York: Ballantine, 1989.

Harding, Esther. *The Way of All Women*. New York: Harper & Row, 1970.

Heilbrun, Carolyn G. *Writing a Woman's Life*. New York: Ballantine, 1988.

Herrera, Hayden. *Frida: A Biography of Frida Kahlo*. New York: Harper & Row, 1983.

Hillesum, Etty, *An Interrupted Life: The Diaries, 1941–43*, trans. Arnold J. Pomerans. New York: Washington Square Press, 1985.

Hinchman, Hannah. *A Life in Hand: Creating the Illuminated Journal*. Salt Lake City: Peregrine Smith Books, 1991.

Hoffman, Eva. *Lost in Translation: A Life in a New Language*. New York: Viking Penguin, 1989.

Hogan, Rebecca. "Engendered Autobiographies: The Diary as a Feminine Form," *Prose Studies* 14, no. 2 (1991):95–107.

Holliday, Laurel. *Heart Songs: The Intimate Diaries of Young Girls*. Guerneville, Calif.: Bluestocking Books, 1978.

Holzer, Burghild Nina. *A Walk Between Heaven and Earth: A Personal Journal on Writing and the Creative Process*. New York: Bell Tower, 1994.

Huntington, Lee Pennock. *Hill Song: A Country Journal*. Woodstock, Vt.: The Country-man Press, 1985.

Irigaray, Luce. "When Our Lips Speak Together," in *This Sex Which Is Not One*, trans. Catherine Porter. Ithaca, N.Y.: Cornell University Press, 1985.

James, Alice. *The Diary of Alice James*, ed. Leon Edel. New York: Penguin, 1982.

Jung, Carl G. *Memories, Dreams, Reflections*. London: Fontana, 1983.

———. "Psychology and Literature," in *Modern Man in Search of a Soul*, trans. W. F. Dell and Cary S. Baynes. New York: Harcourt Brace Company, 1933.

Keen, Sam, and Anne Valley-Fox. *Your Mythic Journey: Finding Meaning in Your Life Through Storytelling and Writing*. Los Angeles: Tarcher, 1989.

Koller, Alice. *An Unknown Woman: A Journey to Self-Discovery*. New York: Bantam, 1981.

Kollwitz, Kaethe. *The Diary and Letters of Kaethe Kollwitz*, ed. Hans Kollwitz, trans. Richard and Clara Winston. Evanston, Ill.: Northwestern University Press, 1988.

Kollowitz, Käthe. *Die Tagebücher*, ed. Jutta Bohnke-Kollwitz. Berlin: Siedler Verlag, 1988.

Laidlaw, Toni Ann, and Cheryl Malmo and Associates. *Healing Voices: Feminist Approaches to Therapy with Women*. San Francisco: Jossey-Bass Publishers, 1990.

Leonard, Linda Schierse. *On the Way to the Wedding: Transforming the Love Relationship*. Boston: Shambhala, 1986.

———. *Witness to the Fire: Creativity and the Veil of Addiction*. Boston: Shambhala, 1990.

———. *The Wounded Woman: Healing the Father-Daughter Relationship*. Boston: Shambhala, 1985.

Lerner, Harriet. *The Dance of Anger: A Woman's Guide to Changing the Patterns of Intimate Relationships*. New York: Harper & Row, 1985.

Lifshin, Lyn, ed. *Ariadne's Thread: A Collection of Contemporary Women's Journals*. New York: Harper & Row, 1982.

Lindbergh, Anne Morrow. *Bring Me a Unicorn: Diaries and Letters, 1922–1928*. New York: Harcourt Brace, 1993.

————. *Hour of Gold, Hour of Lead: Diaries and Letters, 1929–1932*. New York: Harcourt Brace, 1993.

————. *The Flower and the Nettle: Diaries and Letters, 1936–1939*. New York: Harcourt Brace, 1994.

————. *Locked Rooms and Open Doors: Diaries and Letters, 1933–1935*. New York: Harcourt Brace, 1993.

Lorde, Audre. *The Cancer Journals*. San Francisco: Spinsters/aunt lute, 1980.

Lowinsky, Naomi Ruth. *The Motherline: Every Woman's Journey to Find Her Female Roots*. New York: Tarcher/Perigee, 1992.

Malina, Judith. *The Diaries, 1947–1957*. New York: Grove, 1984.

Mallon, Thomas. *A Book of One's Own: People and Their Diaries*. New York: Ticknor & Fields, 1984.

Marks, Elaine, and Isabelle de Courtivron, eds. *New French Feminisms: An Anthology*. Brighton, Sussex: Harvester Press, 1981.

Metzger, Deena. *Tree & The Woman Who Slept with Men to Take the War Out of Them*. Oakland, Calif.: Wingbow Press, 1992.

————. *Writing for Your Life: A Guide and Companion to the Inner Worlds*. New York: HarperCollins, 1992.

Miller, Alice. *The Drama of the Gifted Child: The Search for the True Self*. New York: Basic Books, 1994.

Milner, Marion. *Eternity's Sunrise: A Way of Keeping a Diary*. London: Virago, 1987.

Milner, Marion (pseudonym, Joanna Field). *A Life of One's Own*. Los Angeles: Tarcher, 1981.

Modersohn-Becker, Paula. *The Letters and Journals of Paula Modersohn-Becker*, trans. J. Diane Radycki. Metuchen, N.J.: Scarecrow Press, 1980.

————. *The Letters and Journals*, ed. and trans. Arthur S. Wensinger and Carole Clew Hoey. Evanston, Ill.: Northwestern University Press, 1990.

Moffat, Mary Jane, and Charlotte Painter, eds. *Revelations: Diaries of Women*. New York: Vintage Books, 1975.

Moon, Beverly, ed. *An Encyclopedia of Archetypal Symbolism*. Boston: Shambhala, 1991.

Moon, Sheila. *Dreams of a Woman: An Analyst's Inner Journey*. Boston: Sigo Press, 1983.

Morton, Nelle. *The Journey Is Home*. Boston: Beacon Press, 1985.

Murdock, Maureen. *The Heroine's Journey*. Boston: Shambhala, 1990.

Nachmanovitch, Stephen. *Free Play: Improvisation in Life and Art*. Los Angeles: Tarcher, 1990.

Neuls-Bates, Carol, ed. *Women in Music: An Anthology of Source Readings from the Middle Ages to the Present*. New York: Harper Torchbooks, 1982.

Newman, Lesléa. *SomeBody to Love: A Guide to Loving the Body You Have*. Chicago: Third Side Press, 1991.

Nin, Anaïs. *The Diary of Anaïs Nin: Volume One, 1931–1934*, ed. Gunther Stuhlmann. New York: Harcourt Brace Jovanovich, 1966.

———. *The Journals of Anaïs Nin: Volume Two, 1934–1939*, ed. Gunther Stuhlmann. London: Quartet Books, 1967.

———. *The Diary of Anaïs Nin: Volume Three, 1939–1944*, ed. Gunther Stuhlmann. New York: Harcourt Brace Jovanovich, 1969.

———. *The Diary of Anaïs Nin: Volume Four, 1944–1947*, ed. Gunther Stuhlmann. New York: Harcourt Brace Jovanovich, 1971.

———. *The Journals of Anaïs Nin: Volume Five, 1947–1955*, ed. Gunther Stuhlmann. London: Quartet Books, 1976.

———. *The Journals of Anaïs Nin: Volume Six, 1955–1966*, ed. Gunther Stuhlmann. London: Quartet Books, 1979.

———. *The Diary: Volume Seven, 1966–1974*, ed. Gunther Stuhlmann. New York: Harcourt Brace Jovanovich, 1980.

———. *In Favor of the Sensitive Man and Other Essays*. New York: Harcourt Brace Jovanovich, 1976.

———. *A Woman Speaks: The Lectures, Seminars, and Interviews of Anaïs Nin*, ed. Evelyn J. Hinz. Chicago: Swallow Press, 1975.

Oates, Joyce Carol, ed. *First Person Singular: Writers on Their Craft*. Princeton: Ontario Review Press, 1983.

Olsen, Tillie, *Silences*. New York: Dell, 1965.

Orenstein, Peggy. *School Girls: Young Women, Self-Esteem, and the Confidence Gap*. New York: Anchor, 1994.

Ornish, Dean. *Dr. Dean Ornish's Program for Reversing Heart Disease*. New York: Random House, 1990.

Partridge, Eric. *Origins: A Short Etymological Dictionary of Modern English*. New York: Macmillan, 1958.

Plath, Sylvia. *The Journals of Sylvia Plath*, ed. Ted Hughes and Frances McCullough. New York: Ballantine, 1982.

Progoff, Ira. *At a Journal Workshop*. New York: Dialogue House, 1975.

Pym, Barbara. *A Very Private Eye: An Autobiography in Diaries and Letters*, ed. Hazel Holt and Hilary Pym. New York: Dutton, 1984.

Rainer, Tristine. *The New Diary: How to Use a Journal for Self-Guidance and Expanded Creativity*. Los Angeles: Tarcher, 1978.

Reimann, Brigitte. *Die geliebte, die verfluchte Hoffnung: Tagebücher und Briefe, 1947–1972*, ed. Elisabeth Elten-Krause and Walter Lewerenz. Darmstadt und Neuwied: Luchterhand, 1986.

Rice, Rebecca. *A Time to Mourn: One Woman's Journey Through Widowhood*. New York: New American Library, 1990.

Rich, Adrienne. *Of Woman Born: Motherhood as Experience and Institution*. New York: Norton, 1986.

Rico, Gabriele. *Pain and Possibility: Writing Your Way Through Personal Crisis.* Los Angeles: Tarcher, 1991.

Rinser, Luise. *Prison Journal,* trans. Michael Hulse. London: Macmillan, 1987.

Rooney, Frances, ed. *Our Lives: Lesbian Personal Writings.* Toronto: Second Story Press, 1991.

Rosen, Steven M. *Science, Paradox, and the Moebius Principle: The Evolution of a "Transcultural" Approach to Wholeness.* Albany, N.Y.: State University of New York Press, 1994.

Sacks, Oliver. *The Man Who Mistook His Wife for a Hat.* London: Picador, 1985.

Sand, George. *The Intimate Journal,* ed. and trans. Marie Jenney Howe. Chicago: Academy Chicago, 1929.

Sarton, May. *After the Stroke: A Journal.* New York: Norton, 1988.

———. *At Seventy: A Journal.* New York: Norton, 1984.

———. *Encore: A Journal of the Eightieth Year.* New York: Norton, 1993.

———. *Endgame: A Journal of the Seventy-ninth Year.* New York: Norton, 1992.

———. *The House by the Sea: A Journal.* New York: Norton, 1977.

———. *Journal of a Solitude.* New York: Norton, 1974.

———. *Plant Dreaming Deep.* New York: Norton, 1968.

———. *Recovering: A Journal.* New York: Norton, 1980.

Scheier, Libby; Sarah Sheard; and Eleanor Wachtel, eds. *Language in Her Eye: Views on Writing and Gender by Canadian Women Writing in English.* Toronto: Coach House Press, 1990.

Scherer, Migael. *Still Loved by the Sun: A Rape Survivor's Journal.* New York: Plume, 1992.

Schiffman, Muriel. *Gestalt Self-Therapy: Further Techniques for Personal Growth.* Berkeley: Wingbow Press, 1971.

———. *Self-Therapy: Techniques for Personal Growth.* Berkeley, Wingbow Press, 1967.

Schiwy, Marlene A. "Language and Silence: 'Sprachlosigkeit' in the Work of Christa Wolf." Doctoral thesis, University of London, 1988.

———. "Taking Things Personally: Women, Journal Writing, and Self-Creation," *NWSA (National Women's Studies Association) Journal* 6, no. 2 (1994): 234–54.

Schiwy, Marlene A., and Steven M. Rosen. "Spinning the Web of Life: Feminism, Ecology, and Christa Wolf," *The Trumpeter* 7, no. 1 (1990):16–26.

Schreiber, Le Anne. *Midstream.* New York: Viking, 1990.

Scott-Maxwell, Florida. *The Measure of My Days.* New York: Penguin, 1979.

Schwabacher, Ethel. *Hungry for Light: The Journal of Ethel Schwabacher,* ed. Brenda S. Webster and Judith Emlyn Johnson. Bloomington: Indiana University Press, 1993.

Senesh, Hannah. *Her Life & Diary,* trans. Marta Kohn. New York: Schocken Books, 1973.

Signell, Karen. *Wisdom of the Heart: Working with Women's Dreams.* New York: Bantam, 1990.

Simons, George. *Keeping Your Personal Journal.* New York: Ballantine, 1978.

Simons, Judy. *Diaries and Journals of Literary Women from Fanny Burney to Virginia Woolf.* Iowa City: University of Iowa Press, 1990.

Sjöö, Monica, and Barbara Mor. *The Great Cosmic Mother: Rediscovering the Religion of the Earth.* San Francisco: Harper & Row, 1987.

Solly, Richard, and Roseann Lloyd. *Journey Notes: Writing for Recovery and Spiritual Growth.* New York: Ballantine, 1989.

Starkman, Elaine Marcus. *Learning to Sit in the Silence: A Journal of Caretaking.* Watsonville, Calif.: Papier-Mâché Press, 1993.

Steinem, Gloria. *Outrageous Acts and Everyday Rebellions.* London: Fontana, 1983.

——. *Revolution from Within: A Book of Self-Esteem.* Boston: Little, Brown, 1991.

Sternburg, Janet, ed. *The Writer on Her Work.* New York: Norton, 1980.

——. *The Writer on Her Work. Volume 2: New Essays in New Territory.* New York: Norton, 1991.

Stocker, Midge, ed. *Cancer as a Women's Issue: Scratching the Surface.* Chicago: Third Side Press, 1991.

Strickland, Bill, ed. *On Being a Writer.* Cincinnati: Writer's Digest Books, 1989.

Temoskok, Lydia, and Henry Dreher. *The Type C Connection: The Mind-Body Link to Cancer and Your Health.* New York: Plume, 1992.

Thurman, Judith. *Isak Dinesen: The Life of a Storyteller.* New York: St. Martin's Press, 1982.

Tristan, Flora. *Flora Tristan, Utopian Feminist: Her Travel Diaries and Personal Crusade,* ed. and trans. Doris and Paul Beik. Bloomington: Indiana University Press, 1993.

Truitt, Anne. *Daybook: The Journal of an Artist.* New York: Penguin, 1982.

Ullman, Montague. "Access to Dreams," in *Handbook of States of Consciousness,* ed. Benjamin B. Wolman and Montague Ullman. New York: Van Nostrand Reinhold, 1986.

——. "Dreams as Exceptional Human Experiences," *ASPR Newsletter* (The American Society of Psychical Research), 18, no. 4:1–6.

Wander, Maxie. *Leben wär' eine prima Alternative: Tagebuchaufzeichnungen und Briefe.* Darmstadt und Neuwied: Luchterhand, 1980.

West, Melissa Gayle. *If Only I Were a Better Mother.* Walpole, N.H.: Stillpoint, 1992.

White, Antonia. *Diaries, 1926–1957,* ed. Susan Chitty. New York: Viking Penguin, 1982.

White, Rhea, "Personal Experiences and the Legitimation of Parapsychology: Feed Ye the Sheep," paper given at a symposium on the Unusual Experience of Parapsychologists, at the 36th annual convention of the Parapsychological Association, Toronto, August 15–19, 1993.

Williamson, Janice, ed. *Sounding Differences: Conversations with Seventeen Canadian Women Writers.* Toronto: University of Toronto Press, 1993.

Wolf, Christa. *Accident: A Day's News,* trans. Heike Schwarzbauer and Rick Takvorian. New York: Farrar, Straus and Giroux, 1989.

——. *The Author's Dimension: Selected Essays,* ed. Alexander Stephan, trans. Jan van Heurck. New York: Farrar, Straus and Giroux, 1993.

——. *Cassandra: A Novel and Four Essays,* trans. Jan van Heurck. New York: Farrar, Straus and Giroux, 1984.

——. *A Model Childhood,* trans. Ursule Molinaro and Hedwig Rappolt. New York: Farrar, Straus and Giroux, 1980.

————. *The Reader and the Writer: Essays, Sketches, Memories*, trans. Joan Becker. New York: International Publishers, 1977.

Woodman, Marion. *Addiction to Perfection: The Still Unravished Bride*. Toronto: Inner City Books, 1982.

————. *Conscious Femininity: Interviews with Marion Woodman*. Toronto: Inner City Books, 1993.

————. *The Pregnant Virgin: A Process of Psychological Transformation*. Toronto: Inner City Books, 1985.

————. *The Ravaged Bridegroom: Masculinity in Women*. Toronto: Inner City Books, 1990.

Woodman, Marion; Kate Danson; Mary Hamilton; and Rita Greer Allen. *Leaving My Father's House: A Journey to Conscious Femininity*. Boston: Shambhala, 1992.

Woolf, Virginia. *The Diary of Virginia Woolf, Volume One, 1915–1919*, ed. Anne Olivier Bell. New York: Harcourt Brace, 1977.

————. *The Diary of Virginia Woolf, Volume Two, 1920–1924*, ed. Anne Olivier Bell. New York: Harcourt Brace, 1978.

————. *The Diary of Virginia Woolf, Volume Three, 1925–1930*, ed. Anne Olivier Bell. New York: Harcourt Brace, 1980.

————. *The Diary of Virginia Woolf, Volume Four, 1931–1935*, ed. Anne Olivier Bell. New York: Harcourt Brace, 1982.

————. *The Diary of Virginia Woolf, Volume Five, 1936–1941*, ed. Anne Olivier Bell. New York: Harcourt Brace, 1984.

————. *Moments of Being*, ed. Jeanne Schulkind. St. Albans: Triad/Panther Books, 1978.

————. *A Room of One's Own*. New York, Harcourt Brace, 1989.

————. *A Writer's Diary*, ed. Leonard Woolf. St. Albans: Triad/Panther Books, 1978.

Wordsworth, Dorothy. *Journals of Dorothy Wordsworth*, ed. Mary Moorman. Oxford: Oxford University Press, 1983.

Zeidenstein, Sondra, ed. *A Wider Giving: Women Writing After a Long Silence*. Goshen, Conn.: Chicory Blue Press, 1988.

Zinker, Joseph. *Creative Process in Gestalt Therapy*. New York: Vintage Press, 1977.

Index

⌒

Tannen, Deborah: 294
techniques and styles:
  in journal writing, 68–86
Temoskok, Lydia, and Henry Dreher:
    115, 123
therapy: 114
  etymology of, 114
  journal writing as, 114–17, 122–
    123
  role of journal writing in, 116–
    120
  self-, 120–22, 168–70, 201
time: lack of, in women's lives, 46–
    48
Tomibe, Kate: diary of, 230
topics for journal writing: 309–20
travel-diaries: 47, 92, 227, 233–36
Tristan, Flora: diary of, 235
Truitt, Anne: diary of, 162, 203,
    277, 280
  on keeping a journal, 260
  on making art, 220, 224, 305
  May Sarton on, 271

Ullman, Montague:
  on dreams, 177, 202
  on dream-sharing groups, 192
unconscious, the: 82, 90, 113, 117,
    122, 175, 177, 182, 183,
    184, 186, 188, 189, 204
unsent letters, in the journal: 73–
    76, 131, 133

virtual reality: 176
visual journal keeping: 84–86
A Voice of Her Own:
  influences on, and sources of,
    21–22, 24, 25, 27
  organization of, 30–31
  perspective of, 23–24

voice:
  See feminine voice, finding a voice

Wagner, Cosima: diary of, 55
Wander, Fred: 261
Wander, Maxie: diary of, 262, 264
Watson, Chris: diary of, 116
Webb, Beatrice: diary of, 260
Webster, Brenda S.: 229
West, Melissa Gayle: diary of, 161
Western thought:
  dualism in 104, 138
  See also under dualism, masculine
    values, patriarchal language
    and rhetoric
Wharton, Edith: diary of, 53
White, Antonia: diary of, 81, 159,
    208
  on dreams, 183
  on journal writing, 55, 218–19,
    278
  multiple journals of, 230
  reaction to criticism, of, 225
  on rereading, 242
  taking stock, in her journal, 241
White, Rhea: 199–200
wholeness:
  of body and soul, 141–42
  creativity and, 204, 283
  etymology of, 113
  journal writing and, 92, 141,
    201, 300
  Jung on, 111–12
  mandala as symbol of, 85
  of mind and matter, 104
  of past and present, 100, 131
  psychic, 22, 113, 131, 202, 283,
    299
  in the universe, 200–2
    Emily Carr on, 279

About the Author

Marlene Schiwy, Ph.D., is the founder of The Women's Journal Workshop and is on the English and Women's Studies faculties at the College of Staten Island, City University of New York. She has also trained in Gestalt therapy. Born in British Columbia, Marlene lived in Vancouver before earning her doctorate in London, England. Since then, she has taught courses and workshops in journal writing in the United States, Canada, and England, and was a Canada Council Award recipient in 1995.

Letters and inquiries concerning workshops may be sent to the author c/o Department of English, College of Staten Island, 2800 Victory Boulevard, Staten Island, New York, 10314.

14 x $\frac{11}{17}$ 18 x ^{3}/02

15 x $\frac{5}{98}$